Hans Urs von Balthasar and Protestantism

Hans Urs von Balthasar and Protestantism

The Ecumenical Implications of his Theological Style

Rodney Howsare

T&T CLARK INTERNATIONAL
A Continuum imprint
LONDON • NEW YORK

Published by T&T Clark International
A Continuum imprint
The Tower Building, 11 York Road, London SE1 7NX
15 East 26th Street, Suite 1703, New York, NY 10010

www.tandtclark.com

British Library Cataloguing-in-Publication Data
A catalogue record for this book is available from the British Library

Typeset by Fakenham Photosetting Limited, Fakenham, Norfolk
Printed on acid-free paper in Great Britain by MPG Books Ltd, Cornwall.

ISBN 0 567 03019 9 (hardback)
0 567 03020 2 (paperback)

Contents

Preface and Acknowledgements

When I entered Marquette in 1992, I was a decidedly evangelical (in the American usage of that word) Protestant who had come to love Thomas Aquinas under the tutelage of Arvin Vos at Western Kentucky University. While at Marquette I became more deeply aware of other great lights of the Catholic past: Irenaeus, Augustine, Anselm, and Pascal, to name only a few. Unfortunately, when it came to more contemporary Catholic thinkers, I was reminded of much of the Liberal Protestantism that had already become stale to so many of my friends and me. Indeed, it seemed that while the leading theologians in Protestantism (George Lindbeck, Robert Jenson, Colin Gunton, Stanley Hauerwas, and others) were running fast from their Liberal past, numerous Catholic theologians were out to prove just how modern they were (especially with regard to the relatively recently allowed use of the historical-critical study of scripture). Then, in a seminar in Systematic Theology with Brad Hinze, I was introduced to the works of Hans Urs von Balthasar. Not only did I find a theologian in Balthasar who I thought would be immediately amicable to my Protestant friends – in spite of his dogged attachment to what one of them referred to as his 'two-fisted' Catholicism – I found one who could not have been less interested in kowtowing to the Enlightenment! It is not that Balthasar was pre-critical; he was already, and long before his time in Catholic circles at least, post-critical. One is reminded of the vastly overused phrase of my students: 'Been there, done that.'

The encounter I had with Balthasar in this excellent seminar led to an independent study with Brad wherein we must have read fifteen of Balthasar's books (little did I know that this was only the tip of the, almost literal, iceberg). But Brad was the first to admit that he was no expert in

Balthasar, and, so, when Fr Raymond Gawronski arrived at Marquette a year later, I quickly began to pursue the possibility of doing my doctoral work on the formidable Swiss theologian. (Gawronski, a polyglot, found Balthasar's German 'easy'!) This present work is the fruit of what began with Brad all those semesters ago and what was taken up quite ably by Fr Ray. This work is deeply personal insofar as Balthasar's unique approach to theology showed me a way, not only out of the impasse between the Protestantism of my youth and my present Catholic faith, but also out of the more recent 'liberal/conservative' divide that haunts both Protestant and Catholic theology. In other words, my first encounter with Balthasar was with Balthasar the ecumenist. This book is part of the result of that encounter.

I wish, then, first of all to thank Brad Hinze for introducing me to Balthasar and Fr Gawronski for being my guide through the great forest of Balthasar's works (and becoming a dear friend and inspiration in the process). I wish also to thank several other people who have especially – either knowingly or unknowingly – contributed to my understanding of Balthasar: David Schindler, Cyril O'Regan, Adrian Walker, Ed Oakes, Aidan Nichols, Francesca Murphy and Larry Chapp. Larry especially deserves a word of thanks for tolerating more conversations about Balthasar than he has probably had time for. He has become a great friend during my years at DeSales University, and my number one sounding-board. I also wish to thank my long-time friend Tony DiStefano of Phoenix for the numerous, long, arduous discussions which have contributed so significantly to my theology (and life). It should go without saying that none of these folk are in any way responsible for the many shortcomings of the present work.

Thanks also go to Stratford Caldecott for encouraging me to submit this study to T&T Clark, and then to Fiona Murphy, Philip Law and all the others at T&T Clark and Continuum who have helped to make this book a reality.

Finally I wish to thank some family members who are responsible in an eminent way for anything that I have accomplished, and in no way responsible for my numerous flaws. My mother and father were and remain my biggest supporters, even when I was that odd Junior High kid from the Southern Alleghenies (Pa.) who read 'strange books'. My two sisters, Linda and Gloria, have also been extremely supportive and encouraging over the years, as have my in-laws (Grace, Michael, Kim, Kris and Kevin). But most of all I wish to thank my wife, Kelly, who is the most authentic reflection of the beauty of Christ that I have ever met.

Abbreviations

Works by Hans Urs von Balthasar:

ET (I–IV)	*Explorations in Theology*, vols I–IV
GL (I–VII)	*The Glory of the Lord: A Theological Aesthetics*, vols I–VII
KB	*The Theology of Karl Barth*
KL	*Kosmische Liturgie*
MCW	*The Moment of Christian Witness*
MP	*Mysterium Paschale*
MW	*My Work in Retrospect*
OP	*The Office of Peter and the Structure of the Church*
TD (I–V)	*Theo-Drama: Theological Dramatic Theory*, vols I–V
TL (I–III)	*Theologik*, vols I–III
VBR	*The von Balthasar Reader*

Works by other authors:

CD	*Church Dogmatics* (Karl Barth)
HD	*Heidelberg Disputation* (Martin Luther)
LW	*Luther's Works*
WA	*D. Martin Luthers Werke. Kritische Gesamtausabe* (Weimar Ausgabe)

Introduction

The modern period is marked at its very origins by a debate in the Medieval universities between the radical Aristotelians and the radical Augustinians. This very theological debate, the importance of which has been too often underestimated by secular historians, has had a far-reaching influence on the so-called 'passage to modernity'.[1] The Aristotelians argued that because human reason has access to universals it has access to being, and that because it has access to being it has direct access to God. The Augustinians, rightly appalled by the hubris of their opponents, insisted that the surest place to find out about God was not through philosophical speculation but through God's self-revelation in scripture. In some way or other all of the remaining turning-points in the transition to modernity would be marked by this cataclysmic debate: the Reformation of the sixteenth century would be no exception. Martin Luther's fiercest criticism of the Scholastic theology of his day concerned its naive confidence in the ability of 'unaided' human reason to reach God. Of course this is not to downplay Luther's soteriological concerns, but in Luther's early disputations 'whore reason' was just as much an affront to the grace of God as was 'works righteousness'. Luther's attacks notwithstanding, the Catholic Church has typically been somewhat more defensive of the basic soundness of human reason, and of reason's ability to know about God on the basis of God's manifestation in creation. That this confidence remains somewhat of a point of contention for Protestants right down to our own century is born out by Karl Barth's famous statement that the analogy of being is the invention of the Antichrist. In what follows I would like to present Hans Urs von Balthasar's attempt to forge a Catholic theology which, while not denying the natural knowability of God, is sensitive to the legitimate concern of Luther and Barth to safeguard the freedom of God to reveal himself on his own terms.

A key argument in this presentation will be, in fact, that Balthasar's theology is intended to be ecumenical to its very core. In this study I will focus on two aspects of this ecumenism: First, I will show that Balthasar's style of theology – his 'theological aesthetics' – is intended to safeguard the uniqueness and newness of God's manifestation to the world in Jesus Christ, without thereby denying that this revelation really does fulfill humanity's immortal longings. Secondly, and more implicitly, I will refer to Balthasar's ecumenism as it mediates between the revelocentric and correlational trends in modern theology. This latter aspect is nicely articulated by David Tracy in his foreword to Jean-Luc Marion's, *God Without Being*:

> Christian theology today is marked by a great divide. The traditional historical divides within Christianity – Protestant, Catholic, Orthodox – remain intact but have become far less significant than they have been historically. Rather, a peculiarly modern conflict now crosses all the major Christian theological traditions, whether Catholic, Protestant or Orthodox. Since Schleiermacher and Hegel, Christian theology has been in intense internal conflict over its proper response to modernity (and more recently, as in Marion, to postmodernity). There are many ways to describe this pervasive modern theological conflict. For present purposes, we may name it a conflict between two basic theological strategies on the proper Christian response to modernity … One classic modern strategy wants to correlate the claims of reason and the disclosures of revelation. The other strategy believes that reason functions best in theology by developing rigorous concepts and categories to clarify theology's sole foundation in revelation. On this second view, since revelation alone is theology's foundation, any attempt at correlation is at best a category mistake – at worst, an attempt to domesticate the reality of God by means of reason and being.[2]

Although this latter divide no longer breaks down along Catholic and Protestant lines – as witness the Barth–Tillich or Balthasar–Rahner differences – it certainly finds its original high water mark in Luther's fierce rejection of Scholastic theology in his early disputations. What this means for the present study is that the two divides, the basic Catholic and Protestant one and the more recent revelocentric and correlational one, are interrelated, and that Balthasar's attempt to engage the former has far-reaching implications for the latter. That Balthasar is conscious of this fact becomes obvious in his study of Karl Barth, as will become clear in Chapter 4 below. Unfortunately, the official ecumenical dialogues have often glossed over these foundational differences in their interest in specific doctrinal differences. In what follows I would like to draw attention to the ecumenical implications of the theology of Hans Urs von Balthasar and, in the process, hope to correct a number of misconceptions concerning his work as a whole. First, I will argue that, even if Balthasar was often impatient with the hasty and sometimes compromising ecumenism of his later years, he had an urgent sense of the importance of unity among the Christian churches. This is evident in the fact that his 'theological aesthetics' was intended as a fully Catholic theological approach which, nevertheless, reflected the legitimate concerns of the spirit of the Reformation. In short, Balthasar was not, as many have supposed, a narrowly Catholic theologian. Secondly, I will argue against the tendency among some contemporary theologians to treat Balthasar as simply the 'Catholic Barth'. That is to say, while many readers of Balthasar have drawn attention to his critique of Rahner's 'foundationalism', insufficient attention has been paid to his equally penetrating critique of the pure actualism of Luther and Barth.

What I hope to show, in fact, is that Balthasar fits neither into the classic correlational approach, which begins with generally accepted truths of reason in order to build in-roads to the specific truths of Christianity, nor into the (early) Barthian dialectic approach, which refuses to see in the natural philosophical and religious quest of humanity an analogical relation to the historical revelation of God. Balthasar's is neither the way of foundationalism – the truths of revelation built upon the foundation of being/nature – nor the way of *sola fide* – the truths of revelation crashing the idols of human culture – but represents a 'third way' of love alone. In light of this third way it is possible to say that Balthasar is both revelocentric and correlational: revelocentric in that only love can measure love, only the free self-gift of the other provides access to the depths of that other; correlational in that even in the world of nature (creation), love (gift) precedes knowledge (being). Or, as Balthasar puts it, we awaken to being first of all in the smile of our mothers.

By examining the two aspects of Balthasar's ecumenism just noted, I hope to dispel any simplistic notion that Balthasar's theology is narrowly orthodox, and therefore not genuinely open to dialogue – whether with other Christian groups or with the modern world. I am not interested, then, primarily in contesting mainstream Balthasar scholarship – although I will at times point out the neglect of Balthasar's ecumenical concerns even among students of Balthasar – but in correcting certain misconceptions of Balthasar's work in the mainstream academic theological community. In spite of the fact that Balthasar has been engaged in serious theological work for nearly as long as Karl Rahner, there has only relatively recently arisen a serious interest in his work in America, especially among Catholics, and Balthasar's influence is only now approaching that of Rahner's. There are a number of possible reasons for this. First, Balthasar has produced a veritable mountain of writings. The bibliography of his works alone is nearly 200 pages![3] Secondly, his major trilogy – *Herrlichkeit*, *Theodramatik* and *Theologik* – has only recently, and still not entirely, become available in English.[4] In the third place, even those works available in English are not typical theological treatises; Balthasar's style is not that of the typical systematic theologian. His doctorate is in German letters, and his theology is often hidden in the midst of studies of other philosophical, literary or theological figures. Finally, as far as non-theological factors go, Balthasar is an extremely difficult thinker to fit into neat categories, or into the 'models' approach of so much American theology. All of these reasons combined have helped to make a general appreciation of Balthasar's work slow in coming; but there are other, theological reasons which have contributed to this phenomenon.

The earliest view of Balthasar – and here we are speaking primarily of American Catholics, as Europeans and Anglicans[5] in particular have been largely appreciative of Balthasar's work for quite some time – which arose in the USA came primarily from the viewpoint of *Concilium* that Balthasar was part of a 'conservative' backlash against the innovations of Vatican II. In fact, a rare article on Balthasar's theology appeared in one of the *Concilium* monograph series dedicated to the phenomenon of 'neo-conservatism'![6] As recently as 1994, in an introduction to Karl Rahner's, *Spirit in the World*, Francis Fiorenza has the following to say about Balthasar's critique of Rahner:

> These considerations [Fiorenza has been speaking of Rahner's differences from Kantian Idealism] illustrate the degree of misunderstanding contained in the criticism raised against Rahner by Hans Urs von Balthasar, who in the general context of his *conservative* evaluations and *negative criticism of contemporary tendencies within the Church attacks not only current aspects of biblical, liturgical, and ecumenical movements*, but also the attempts of Karl Rahner and Johannes Metz to develop a positive relationship to modern philosophy and the secularization of society and its institutions.[7]

I must confess to an inability to find the word 'conservative' in any way clarifying in this context. As I hope to show in Chapter 5, Balthasar's critiques of Rahner and of certain 'contemporary tendencies with the Church' are a mixture of conservative – insofar as they wish to salvage that which is valuable in the tradition but is being rejected with insufficient reason – and progressive – insofar as they wish to leave behind certain trends in Catholic theology such as the two-tiered approach to nature and grace or the *de Deo Uno–de Deo Trino* approach to the doctrine of God.

Again, I am not denying that Balthasar is often on the side of the theological tradition against various modern tendencies toward reductionism; I am merely pointing out that the simple epithet 'conservative' is not adequate to describe the subtlety and complexity of Balthasar's theological position. There are numerous ways, in fact, in which Karl Rahner is more 'conservative' than Balthasar: for instance, in his desire to work within a neo-Scholastic framework rather than move beyond it. This simply shows the poverty of the political terms 'conservative' and 'liberal' when applied to serious theology. If Balthasar was able to perform a 'thicker retrieval'[8] of the tradition than many of his contemporaries, it is because of a sensitivity (ahead of its time in many ways) to the 'postmodern' critique of the Enlightenment stemming from Kierkegaard, Nietzsche, Husserl, Heidegger, Marcel, Buber and others. As I will argue, Balthasar's criticism of Rahner stems more from his ecumenical desire to do justice to Luther's and Barth's critiques of Catholic rationalism and Nietzsche's and Heidegger's critiques of onto-theology than it does from an alleged conservatism.

A more nuanced view of Balthasar's place within contemporary Catholicism has emerged in light of the so-called linguistic turn in modern theology, and the concomitant critique of foundationalism implied therein. Indeed, the current flourishing of narrative approaches to theology has forced many to reevaluate, in a more positive light, Balthasar's critique of Joseph Maréchal's and Karl Rahner's tendency toward foundationalism.[9] Unfortunately, with this more nuanced view comes a more nuanced misunderstanding of Balthasar's work, which, briefly, places Balthasar squarely on the narrative-revelocentric side of the modern theological divide. As John Kevern has stated it:

> In the conversation over theological methodology that has found expression in the distinctive Chicago and Yale 'School' positions, the figure of Roman Catholic Theologian Hans Urs von Balthasar looms increasingly large. Both sides seem to be in agreement that Balthasar is a 'Yalie' – which is to say, Balthasar represents that option in modern theology which wants to theologize starting from revelation.[10]

While it is true that Balthasar insists that theology proceed from a 'theological a priori', this need not mean that Balthasar denies the need for appropriate correlations with philosophical thought, a point which Kevern, too, goes on to make. Correlation, yes, but a correlation that is not undertaken apart from certain necessarily *theological* presuppositions. A philosophy which provides for a point of contact between the revelation of God and the religious search of human beings will always, already be colored in a positive or negative way by its decision for or against the God who is love. This means that one cannot simply pick and choose indiscriminately between an indeterminate number of philosophical viewpoints, as if one will suit theology as well as the next.

What I hope to make clear, in short, is that Balthasar's theology is neither a conservative reaction against the *aggiornamento* of Vatican II, nor a simple revelocentric rejection of Karl Rahner's attempt to build a bridge between the Catholic and Enlightenment views of the world, but that his theology is an ecumenical attempt to mediate between the sometime Protestant rejection of analogy on the one hand and the sometime Catholic tendency towards a univocal understanding of the relationship between God and Being. Accordingly, it would not be too much of a stretch to speak of Balthasar as presenting a revelocentric–correlational theology, and, indeed, that he intends his theological aesthetics to be just that. This theology, I will argue, is of interest to the Protestant and Catholic divide (and therefore to the Yale/Chicago divide), because it presents a way of doing theology from its object, without thereby rendering this theology irrelevant to humanity's religio-philosophical quest. It is to the details of how I will present this that I will now turn.

In Chapter 1 I will present an overview of Balthasar's general understanding of ecumenical dialogue, first, in terms of the more fundamental question of the relationship between dialogue and truth and, second, in terms of his theology of dialogue. If Balthasar was somewhat suspicious of the official ecumenism of his later years, this should not be taken to mean that he did not continue to have a passionate interest in the dialogue between the various churches, nor that he waned in his desire to present a Catholic theology which reflected the legitimate concerns of the Reformation critique. In Chapters 2 and 3 I will examine, respectively, Balthasar's actual engagement with two central representatives of Protestant theology, Martin Luther and Karl Barth. The Luther chapter will take on a slightly different form from the Barth chapter, however, in that I will have to provide the basic understanding of Luther which Balthasar presupposes in his various treatments of Luther's theology. I am not interested, however, in presenting an introduction to Luther's theology on its own terms, but only insofar as it is relevant to Balthasar's particular theological evaluation and incorporation of Luther's position. As I hope to make clear, Balthasar wishes to preserve Luther's sensitivity to the utter newness and strangeness of the God revealed in the cross of Jesus Christ, without thereby abolishing the connection between the God of folly and the God of glory: God's glory is revealed (and necessarily also veiled) precisely in the folly of the cross.

In the chapter on Barth, on the other hand, the background for Balthasar's engagement has been provided by Balthasar himself in his book-length study of Barth's theology. Before offering a close reading of this study, however, I will present an overview of the problem of the analogy of being, especially as this has taken shape in the twentieth century in the writings of Étienne Gilson and Henri de Lubac. Barth's theology was attractive to Balthasar for a number of reasons, but primarily for its bold attempt to examine everything in the light of the re-creation of all things in Jesus Christ. Here Balthasar has found a Protestant attempt to carry out de Lubac's critique of the modern nature/grace dualism. If

Balthasar is critical of Barth, it is insofar as Barth is unwilling to apply the full implications of this fresh theological insight to his theological enterprise as a whole.

After this overview of Balthasar's engagement with Protestantism – in the persons of Luther and Barth – the reader will have to be prepared for a significant shift, for in Chapter 4 I will present Balthasar's critique of two styles of Catholic theology which are partially blind to the legitimate concerns of the Reformation: the cosmological and the anthropological. The first of these is found, at least in tendencies, in the theology of the Church Fathers and in their attempt to bring the revelation of God into dialogue with the classical philosophical understanding of Being. While Balthasar is appreciative of the 'adolescent' confidence of the early Church that Christianity will win out in its engagement with the competing ancient worldviews, he castigates the Fathers for a sometimes overhasty correlation of the Triune God of the Bible with Plotinus' One.

A similarly bold enterprise is found in the modern anthropological turn in theology, which attempts to relate the subject's immediate experience of transcendence, and the theological implications thereof, with the turn to the subject of modern philosophy. Again, Balthasar agrees with this endeavor insofar as theology must make use of the language of every age in order to proclaim its message, but he is critical of any tendency towards subjectivism and individualism which downplays the role of the self-gift of the other. This anthropological turn began in Protestantism largely with the work of Friedrich Schleiermacher, but appeared in Catholicism with the Modernist controversy. What Balthasar is primarily interested in, however, is the more orthodox attempt to appropriate this turn in the work of Joseph Maréchal and Karl Rahner. As we will show, nowhere does Balthasar simply reject this attempt, nor is he deaf to its legitimate concern to engage the philosophy of the Enlightenment. Nor is Balthasar's critique of the Enlightenment that of a 'reactionary'; rather, Balthasar's misgivings derive from the critique of subjectivism found in the personalist philosophy of the early part of the twentieth century. In the first volume of *Theo-Drama* Balthasar speaks of this revolution in Modern thought accordingly:

> It is not insignificant that, in 1918, the year that Simmel died, and in the following year, one of the strangest phenomena of 'acausal contemporaneity' in the history of the intellect took place. This was the simultaneous emergence of the 'dialogue principle' in thinkers who could not be farther apart. Altogether there were four of them: three were isolated individuals, namely, the solitary primary school teacher Ferdinand Ebner in Wiener Neustadt; Martin Buber in Frankfurt, who acknowledged the influence of Ebner on the third and last part of his *I and Thou* but who arrived as [*sic*] his central insight from much earlier reflections of his own; and Gabriel Marcel in France, who had edited his *Journal métaphysique* since 1914 and

> who in 1918, precisely, came to almost identical formulations. Finally there was the circle associated with Franz Rosenzweig. He had been a pupil of Hermann Cohen and had read, in manuscript, the latter's last work, *Religion der Vernunft aus den Quellen des Judentums* (1917–1918), where he found that 'it is the "thou", the discovery of the "thou", that brings to me the awareness of my "I"'.[11]

It could be argued that because Catholic theology was so slow to come to terms with the Enlightenment, it has been equally late in appropriating this bourgeoning 'postmodern' critique. It may just turn out that in many ways Balthasar's theology is actually more 'modern' – as in more aware of the current intellectual setting – than many of his modern detractors. This is in fact borne out by the recent interest in Balthasar's theology from the post-critical theologians. In any case, in Chapter 4 of this study we will attempt to demonstrate that Balthasar's critique of Rahner must be kept together with his dialogue with the Reformation. This means, first, that his critique is first of all ecumenical in its intentions,[12] and, second, that it is not a wholesale rejection. This latter point can be seen in those places where Balthasar attempts to distance himself from the approach of Luther and Barth in order to do justice to Rahner's more correlational concerns.

In the final chapter, then, I will simply sketch the implications of Balthasar's theological aesthetics for a series of unresolved tensions in contemporary theology: the relationship between nature and grace, between divine and human freedom, between the Trinity and the cross, and between philosophy and theology. With regard to each of these tensions, it would seem that modern theology has reached an impasse. Part of the problem is that much theology continues to labor under a series of outdated misconstruals of the issues at hand. For instance, at the beginning of modernity, disciples of a radical form of Aristotelianism raised the question concerning how far unaided reason could go towards knowing God. Luther's response to this question was an equally radical appeal to the God of revelation. In the twentieth century, under the guidance of such thinkers as Maurice Blondel, Joseph Maréchal and their disciples we are beginning to see that this question was misframed in the first place. What, for instance, is 'unaided' reason? But this breakthrough in the field of Fundamental Theology has yet to be plumbed for its ecumenical resources. I hope that this study will contribute to such a task.

1

Balthasar and Dialogue

I. The Problem of Dialogue

In a characteristically pointed response to the authors of *The Myth of God Incarnate*, Herbert McCabe has the following to say about Christianity as a world religion:

> One of the concerns of these authors is that the incarnation seems provincial in that it makes Christianity something utterly different from all other world religions. Now quite apart from the presence of grace and therefore of incarnation in the followers of other religions, it is really time we stopped and criticized this phrase. There is no significant world religion except Christianity. Every other religion, however many its adherents, has shown itself incapable of breaking free from a particular culture or even a particular people. Atheistic humanism is worldwide but not a religion. Indeed the paradoxical concept of a religion (something tied to history and tradition and particularity) which is nonetheless worldwide, transcending cultures and histories, is itself a peculiarly Christian and 'incarnational' notion. The Greek term for a world religion is Catholicism.[1]

McCabe's barbs concerning the false ecumenism of 'these authors' is a fitting way to begin our discussion of Balthasar's ecumenism. While more and more theologians are willing to acknowledge Balthasar's gifts as a dogmatic or doctrinal theologian, it is still rather common to suggest that one must look elsewhere for a theologian who is genuinely open to dialogue with outsiders. It has become relatively standard, accordingly, to think of Balthasar in terms of the narrative school of theology which, while offering helpful insights into the nature of Christianity and Christian revelation, has not been as helpful in assisting Christians in their dialogue with non-Christians. It has been suggested, for instance, that, while Balthasar's strength lies in his ability to provide a specific Christian language for interpreting revelation, one needs the methodology of someone like Bernard Lonergan in order to construct a 'general' language, one better suited for dialogue with outsiders.[2] Perhaps it would assuage some such fears if it were stated at the outset that this is a book about Balthasar's dialogue with *Protestantism*, and not explicitly about his dialogue with the world. But I would like to suggest that Balthasar is valuable precisely in his ability to formulate a genuinely dialogical theology without having to forfeit hard, theological content in the process. For Balthasar, in short, it is not necessary to choose between the relevance of the 'Chicago' school and the revelocentrism of the 'Yale' school. Furthermore, Balthasar's approach was not chosen out of ignorance of other more modern approaches, but intentionally, as an alternative to these widespread approaches. As Balthasar puts it:

> These days there seems to be inside the Catholic Church ... a trend toward short-circuiting the search for unity with a kind of supremacy that seeks to find unity more in the direction of a 'synthetic science of religion' than through an authentic competition of catholicities. This trend has relied not so much on an immediate importation of the sociological method as on the application in the realm of theology of the Kantian philosophical concepts of the 'transcendental' and 'categorial' (which are supposed to express the basic constitution of the human spirit). Such a basic starting-point can still emphasize, after the fact and to its heart's content, that the transcendence of the spirit can be realized only by turning back to a historical categorial. But it still cannot justify the incomparable nature of *this* definite categorial that is foundational for Christian catholicity.[3]

The purpose of this chapter, then, is to make a preliminary case for Balthasar as ecumenical theologian before actually looking at his dialogue with two chief figures in the history of Protestantism, Martin Luther and Karl Barth. The reader should be well aware that Balthasar had serious misgivings with certain forms of ecumenism which mark so much modern theology,[4] but the point here is that such misgivings were not based on a rejection of the importance of dialogue per se, but concerned the manner in which such dialogue was undertaken. What Balthasar was rejecting is what Adrian Walker has called the 'liberal' model of dialogue, based as it is on the so-called fact/value distinction.[5] Although those theologians who make use of Kant's 'transcendental/categorial' distinction do not necessarily subscribe to this liberal model of dialogue, they unwittingly support the modern prejudice against religious particulars by building inter-religious bridges upon the subjective experience of transcendence which is, it is maintained, common to all religions. Notice that unity is founded in such approaches not *on* religious particulars, but precisely on what lies *behind* such particulars. It will hopefully become clear in what follows why Balthasar wishes to provide an alternative to such a starting-point. It is crucial to remember, accordingly, that Balthasar does not devise a theological method which underestimates the importance of dialogue – and which is therefore narrowly Catholic˙but one which offers an alternative to the prevailing liberal model. I will begin this chapter, then, with a rather formal discussion of Balthasar's theological aesthetics and the particular approach to dialogue that this method entails. This will involve an examination of what might be called Balthasar's *philosophy* of dialogue. This will provide the necessary backdrop to Balthasar's discussion of dialogue between Christians. This latter theme will then be addressed in terms of Balthasar's understanding of doctrine and ecclesiology in order to highlight what we will call his *theology* of dialogue. The purpose of this chapter is by no means to give a full exposition of each of these aspects of Balthasar's thought, but simply to treat each of these matters in terms of what they imply about Balthasar's approach to dialogue.

II. Theological Aesthetics and Dialogue

If we argue the importance of the beautiful, if we argue, that is, that that which is universal can only come to us in the particular, and if, furthermore, we argue, with Balthasar, that *theologically* speaking, God also comes to us in that which is particular, then can genuine dialogue really play a central role in our theology? In a provocative and important essay, published for the first time in 1974 in *Skizzen zur Theologie*,[6] Balthasar raises the question of ecumenical dialogue in the context of 'the claim to Catholicity'. According to Balthasar's aesthetic understanding, the thing which makes Christianity distinctive is its claim that the universal is offered to humanity in the concrete form of a particular historical person: Jesus Christ is the *concrete universal.* The incarnation remains, then, the point of departure for everything which Balthasar says about theological aesthetics. As expressed in the Christmas preface,

> In the wonder of the incarnation
> your eternal Word has brought to the eyes of faith
> a new and radiant vision of your glory.
> In him we see our God made visible
> and so are caught up in the love of the God we cannot see.

Furthermore, as a Catholic, Balthasar believes that Christ entrusted this fullness to yet another concrete, historical existent: the Church. With the Second Vatican Council, Balthasar embraces the notion that *the* Church *subsists in* the Roman Catholic Church. To be Catholic is to believe that the fullness of the true, the good, and the beautiful has been entrusted to the heart of the Church, as a gift from her bridegroom, who is this fullness in his very person. This is in direct contrast to the Enlightenment notion – and modern prejudice – that the universal truths of reason cannot be derived from the accidental truths of history, and Balthasar knows full well the scandal which such a strong claim presents to the modern reader. The question which remains, then, is this: does not an approach which takes as its starting-point such a strong claim to universal validity preclude the very possibility of an openness to dialogue with alternative worldviews? Can such a starting-point still be considered legitimate in a pluralistic age? Would it not be more prudent to begin with those aspects of the Christian faith which it shares with other worldviews, and then treat the historical particularities at a later stage?

If Balthasar insists, in short, on beginning with the very aspect of Christianity that sets it apart from all other religious and philosophical approaches, does he not short-circuit the quest for mutual understanding and dialogue from the outset? It is in response to such questions that Balthasar formulates his theological aesthetics, and it is in response to such questions that he seeks to demonstrate that his approach, far from short-circuiting the quest for unity, is the best suited for such a quest.

> Unless we are much mistaken the standpoint which we have chosen should be more classical than the classicism which has grown sterile but also more modern than many superficial modernisms in Church and theology and more ecumenical than many hastily conceived attempts to bridge the gap between confessions which claim that title.[7]

Balthasar's 'aesthetic' approach will have consequences, then, not only for the Catholic who is in dialogue with the non-Catholic, but also for the Christian who wishes to enter into a dialogue with the modern world. Before looking at the latter, it will be helpful to take a brief look at the former because in Balthasar's thought the two are intimately related.

In 'The Claim to Catholicity', Balthasar contrasts his own aesthetic approach with that of Maréchal and his disciples. While I will deal with these differences at length in Chapter 4, I mention them now in order better to explain the distinctiveness of Balthasar's approach to dialogue. The transcendental approach begins with the subject and the subject's openness to transcendence. The 'method of immanence', as Balthasar calls it, is directed at the problem of secularization which has arisen as a result of the radical rupture in modernity between nature and grace. When Nietzsche, for instance, proclaimed 'God is dead,' he was referring to the fact that people tend to organize the prosaic world as if God does not exist or at least as if God makes no difference. Even if large numbers of people still claim to believe in God, such belief seems to have little impact on their ordinary lives. In order to illustrate the fundamental flaw in modern secularism and help construct a genuine dialogue with modernity, the transcendental method pointed to the fact that all individual acts of human knowing open up, beyond themselves, to that which transcends any individual object. The old Thomistic insight that when one knows anything one implicitly knows God, was made central to this approach. Without rejecting this approach, Balthasar intended his theological aesthetics as a necessary complement to it.

Indeed, Balthasar wanted to 'introduce a new complementary method that is different from the Kantian method, one that will expose the insufficiency of the initial starting-point'.[8] It is precisely the latter of these alternatives which Balthasar intends his theological aesthetics to provide. But notice that he says 'complementary' as well as 'different'. Balthasar was concerned that such a method, left to its own, would only play into modernity's tendency towards dualism, individualism and alienation. It is not that Balthasar rejects the basic notion that in every act of knowing one implicitly knows God, his concern had more to do with the prudence of the epistemological starting-point. Here Balthasar is following Przywara, who wanted to *reintegrate* epistemology and metaphysics (ontology).

> There is first the starting-point of a 'metaphysics [as an inquiry into the "inherent ground and meaning" of Being]' that primarily has to do 'with a reflection on the act of knowing, that is with a *metanoetics* of knowing as knowing'. Then there is a second starting-point of a metaphysics 'whose intention is immediately directed to the object of knowing, that is, of a *metaontics* of Being as Being.[9]

As Balthasar goes on to explain,

> So both point beyond themselves to a mutual but inconclusive interpenetration. The critically necessary starting-point of metaphysics in the metanoetic shows not only that the consciousness of the 'I' is indissolubly bound up with that of things and fellow egos but also that it can express itself only in ontic categories, even at its most formal.[10]

And this is so because,

> the existence of an alien but always personal freedom intersects the two concepts of 'transcendental' and 'categorial'. It can neither be captured by reflection nor arranged in a rubric that assumes its direct availability.[11]

Balthasar's concerns regarding the method of immanence, here, seem to be twofold. First, if the Church is going to engage the modern world, it must be able to bring something to the table that modernity does already think it has. Since Vatican II it has become quite clear that the problem with modernity is not so much an aggressive atheism which needs to be convinced of transcendence, but rather its notion of religious belief as purely private, having nothing whatsoever to do with 'public' truth. Balthasar wonders whether the 'Kantian' starting-point is sufficient to overcome the sense of alienation which the modern subject must feel, both from the cosmos as a whole and from other subjects. As Balthasar puts it in *Theo-Logic*:

> Modern rationalism, attempting to narrow the range of truth to a supposedly isolable core of pure theory, has exiled the good and the beautiful from the domain of the rationally verifiable, relegating them to arbitrary subjectivity or to a world of private belief and personal taste. As a result, the picture of being, the unified view of the world, is torn to shreds, *so that any real conversation about truth becomes impossible.* Discourse remains at the level of the generically accessible, hence ultimately trivial, while the deepest questions of truth, which need decision and taste even to be seen, are *buried under the silence of a false modesty*. If truth lacks decision, then decision, the personal decision that determines one's view of the world, lacks truth.[12]

It is not that Balthasar finds Maréchal's disciples guilty of this sort of reductionism, it is simply that he wonders whether the subjectivist starting-point is sufficient to overcome the sense of alienation that the modern self feels vis-à-vis the outside world. Secondly, Balthasar seems especially concerned about modernity's understanding of knowledge as a sort of *power* that the subject wields over the external world. This concept of knowledge has led to innumerable problems, the increasing rape of the environment being just one of them. Such a conception began, not in the industrial age, however, but with Descartes and his reduction of the world external to the level of a machine. Truth, in such a view, can no longer be something that inheres in all that is; it is now something that is a property of the spiritual subject. Kant, for instance, along with almost all modern philosophy, rejects the notion common to classical and medieval philosophy that 'all that is, is true', when he states that truth pertains to 'certain logical requirements and conditions inherent in any *perception* of things'.[13]

It is not, then, that Balthasar simply rejects either modernity or the method of immanence or the need for the Church to enter a genuine dialogue with the modern world; it is rather that Balthasar sees modernity as being caught in the awkward situation of embracing certain truths – the dignity and rights of the individual, for instance – for which it no longer has any metaphysical basis. If Christianity is to be of some assistance at this point – and Balthasar is constantly insisting that Christianity will have to be the guardian of metaphysics in the modern world – it is not enough to point out the subject's openness to transcendence and therefore implicit relationship with God, it is also necessary to speak once again in terms of the classic transcendental properties of being: the true, the good and the beautiful. And it is in the context of these sorts of considerations that Balthasar develops his understanding of *Gestalt*.

A. Balthasar's Use of Gestalt

Gestalt is the German word which Balthasar uses to convey the idea put forth by the Greek *eidos* and the Latin *forma*.

> Here, where it is always the totality of being that presents itself in various degrees of clarity in the individual things that exist, the concept of *form* [*Gestalt*] is appropriate ... This concept, taken over from Plato and Aristotle (as *eidos* and *morphe*), stood in the midpoint of medieval ontology (as *species* and *forma*) and likewise in the midpoint of the teaching about nature in Herder (against Kant!) and Goethe ... [14]

The precise use of 'form' in Balthasar's writings, however, cannot simply be traced to its usage in Greek metaphysics. This is so because neither Plato nor Aristotle were able to do full justice to the inextricable unity of the form and the matter which manifests it. Both were still too much under the influence of Parmenides and the notion that the material world represents a fall from the world of spirit.[15]

If Plato, especially, although not totally, devalued the material as a realm fallen from that of the ideal, spiritual realm, modern 'metaphysics', since Descartes, has tended to treat the material as *mere* matter, in need of a spiritual subject who can invest it with meaning. In the concept of *Gestalt*, then, Balthasar wishes to highlight the simultaneity of form and matter, and here he is quick to acknowledge his debt to Herder and Goethe.[16] What is crucial for Balthasar in this understanding of form is the notion that that which makes an object comprehensible to a subject has as much to do with the light shining forth from the object itself as it does with the constitution of the subject. This is not to eliminate the role of the subject, however, it is only to reclaim its role as primarily one of 'perception'. The German here is *Wahr-nehmung*, and conveys the sense of 'seeing truly'. In order to perceive the form which shines forth from the visible object, we must have the right eyes, eyes that are capable of grasping the whole. The modern scientific view has become so accustomed to beginning with the parts and understanding the whole in this light that it has lost its vision for wholeness. Here Balthasar again echoes Gadamer in his concern that modernity has fallen into the trap of understanding all forms of knowing in terms of the exact sciences. 'For this reason psychology (in the contemporary sense of the term) has taken the place of philosophy.'[17] Against this scientific reduction Balthasar insists that we must attempt to regain our ability to see, that we 'must possess a spiritual eye capable of perceiving (*wahrnehmen*) the forms of existence with awe'.[18]

B. Truth and Dialogue

These cursory statements concerning Balthasar's understanding of form will provide a helpful backdrop to Balthasar's understanding of the relationship between dialogue and truth. If dialogue has a goal, it is, of course, unity; but it must be unity in the truth. Genuine dialogue cannot occur any time there is an impoverished notion of truth. Two extremes in particular render dialogue either superfluous or trivial. Naive realism – the first extreme – reduces the subject to a recorder of the external world of objects, while reducing said objects to that which appears. Such a realism can be found, for instance, in certain scientistic notions of truth, wherein what can be empirically measured is thought to be the extent of truth. One cannot help but detect, however, that Balthasar is not merely criticizing scientific rationalism in the first volume of his triptych on the nature of truth; he must also assuredly have in mind the implicit rationalism in the neo-Scholasticism of the early part of the twentieth century. Indeed, while there are numerous references to Aquinas's study of truth (*De Veritate*) throughout the first volume of *Theo-Logic*, the only secondary source cited is Josef Pieper's *Philosophia Negativa*, a book that sets out to show just how different Aquinas's understanding of truth is from that of his neo-Scholastic interpreters.[19] Pieper's thesis, which is presupposed in Balthasar's book, is that the thing which makes reality knowable, that is, the fact that 'things come forth from the eye of God' and 'partake wholly of the nature of the Logos', is the very thing which makes reality never *exhaustively* knowable.[20] In other words, created things have a share in the inscrutable light from which they were created. All knowledge of an object, then, invites further investigation. The longest section of the first volume of *Theo-Logic* is, in fact, the section entitled, 'Truth as Mystery'.[21]

To this central Thomistic insight, Balthasar adds his own what might be called *nuptial* insight. Insofar as all beings are 'beings for themselves', they are free and must freely offer themselves to be known. At the same time, the subject must freely open itself up to the offer of the object. Balthasar, no naive realist, speaks of truth as a love event between the subject and the object in order to guard against either a false objectivism or a false subjectivism. Both subject and object contribute freely to the truth-event. Certainly Balthasar gives the object priority over the subject, but he insists that truth can only arise on account of the active receptivity of that subject. As he puts it:

> Insofar as the disclosure of being is a property objectively inherent in being itself, the knowing subject is obliged to conform itself to this disclosedness. That is, knowing the truth happens when knowledge, by virtue of an 'adeqation' to the thing as it really is (*adequatio intellectus et rei*), lets itself be determined and measured by the thing. A proportion has to be achieved between subject and object, and the decisive measure of the proportion lies with the object. On the other hand, the purpose and mission of the subject is not simply to be a kind of machine for recording objective states of affairs. Subjectivity in the full sense includes freedom, self-determination, and creativity *ad extra* ... Although the object remains the measure by which truth is measured, the agent of the measuring is now the subject, and this activity of measuring is a spontaneous, creative achievement.[22]

In fact, Balthasar will go so far as to say that the disclosure of being only makes sense if it is directed at a knowing subject, that the object's final meaning then, in a sense, lies in the subject, 'which therefore contains the measure of the object'.[23]

The point to be emphasized in the present context, then, is that, against any naive realism that would suggest that truth could ever be contained in a final way in a system or a set of propositions, Balthasar reemphasizes the notion of truth as the unveiling of being as a whole. This both makes knowledge possible and precludes its finality.[24] Next, by calling attention to the crucial role played by both the subject and the object in the act of knowing, Balthasar can highlight two aspects of knowledge which modern thinkers tend to overlook: namely, that all true knowledge stems from love – for an object must willingly give itself to a subject and a subject must make itself freely available for the object – and that all knowledge presupposes faith, in that the subject must, in a sense, surrender itself before the evidence of reality. In this manner, Balthasar refuses to allow the hard sciences to determine our final understanding of the nature of truth. This also enables him to reject the modern dichotomy between faith and reason: because reason itself is marked by a give and take which necessarily entails love and trust, reason exceeds that which occurs in the cold objectivity of the scientist's gaze.

At the other end of the philosophical spectrum from naïve realism, however, stands idealism in all its forms. Indeed, since the time of Descartes, philosophy seems doomed to ricochet between the extremes of empiricism and idealism, both of which assume the alienation of the subject from the external world. In the face of such an alienation, Balthasar is going to insist upon our common belonging in being, a common belonging which helps to overcome not only this alienation, but also the modern notion that knowledge is power over the external world. If naive realism downplays the role of the subject, idealism tends towards its exaggeration.

Part of the problem, in Balthasar's view, is the skeptical starting-point of modern philosophy and the foundationalist endeavors which such a starting-point encourages. As Balthasar insists, one should no more wait to philosophize until one has proved the existence of truth (beyond any possible doubt) than one should wait to fall in love until one has proved the existence of love. Just as one can only learn about love in the process, Balthasar insists that in order to understand truth one must 'start by diving into the current'.[25] Both love and truth demand, at their beginning, an act of faith. But such an act of faith – of 'self-abandoning confidence' – is not irrational; it is rather the prior condition of any certainty about the rational at all.[26] And this is precisely where Balthasar's inter-personal approach wishes to complement the transcendentalist approach mentioned above: for Balthasar, reason, like faith, requires a primary act, not of grasping, but of 'letting be'. The foundationalist starting-point of modern philosophy, on the other hand, has doomed it to failure from the beginning because it short-circuits the question of the being of the world.

> It has often happened in the history of epistemology that the conditions of knowability are either deduced from those of knowing or are simply equated with them, as if ontology were nothing more than a projection of the structure of knowing upon being … But … [b]eing's laws, which are not necessarily identical with those of knowledge, require an original analysis of their own.[27]

But modern philosophy's inability to deal adequately with the polarities of the subject and the object, the ideal and the empirical, and so on, have also to do with its attitude towards the relationship between philosophy and theology. The introduction of the idea of a transcendent and creator God into the Western philosophical tradition by way of Christianity left an indelible mark on the history of philosophy. The knowability of the external world was rooted, in this Christian philosophy, in the fact that things were first known by God. The archetypes for all things were held in God, and the fact that things exist at all is rooted in the fact that they have their being and truth from God. Modern philosophy tries to carry on without this context of Christian belief, but it really never succeeds in doing so. It continues to draw on much of this Christian heritage, even while it denies it is doing so.[28] It is only inevitable that once the role of the Infinite Subject – God – has been introduced into the philosophical playground, it will have to be replaced once it has been exiled. And modern philosophy eventually did this with the Self. In other words, modern philosophy paved the way for a loss of distinction between what is created and what is artifact.[29] Now, even the external world is understood as artifact and this gives the subject absolute control over that which it studies. It became common for modern philosophers to insist that only that which is made can be known, and since there was a de-emphasis on the world as creation – that is, as a reflection of the intelligence of God – it was left to the subject to *determine* the nature of things. In the light of all of this, Balthasar refuses, even in *Theo-Logic*, which is the closest he comes to a sustained work of philosophy proper, to do philosophy as if there were no God of Jesus Christ. In fact, Balthasar insists that it is no longer possible to do philosophy in a neutral key because it will now always be marked by either belief or unbelief:

> The world as it concretely exists is one that is always already related either positively or negatively to the God of grace and supernatural revelation. There are no neutral points or surfaces in this relationship. The world, considered as an object of knowledge, is always already embedded in this supernatural sphere, and, in the same way, man's cognitive powers operate either under the positive sign of faith or under the negative sign of unbelief. Of course insofar as it works in a relative abstractness that prescinds from creaturely nature's embedding in the supernatural, philosophy can indeed highlight certain fundamental natural structures of the world and knowledge, because this embedding does not do away with, or even alter the essential core of, such structures. Nevertheless, the closer philosophy comes to the concrete object and the more fully it makes use of the concrete knowing powers, the more theological data it also incorporates, either implicitly or explicitly. After all, the supernatural takes root in the deepest structures of being, leavens them through and through, and permeates them like a breath or an omnipresent fragrance. It is not only impossible, it would be sheer folly to attempt at all costs to banish and uproot this fragrance of supernatural truth from philosophical inquiry; the supernatural has impregnated nature so deeply that there is simply no way to reconstruct it in its pure state (*natura pura*).[30]

Balthasar makes no apologies, therefore, for continuing to speak, in the great tradition of Christian philosophy, of human knowledge as a participation in divine knowledge. The fact that things can be known is rooted in the fact that they were created out of the divine knowledge. And this goes back to a previous point which was made against naive realism. *Both* naive realism *and* idealism encourage an understanding of knowledge as the subject's dominance over the object, and this leads to the conceptualization of being so bemoaned by Heidegger and others. To repeat what was said before, the mystery of the world is coextensive, for Balthasar, with the rationality of the world.

A few final points should allow us to round out this sketch of Balthasar's view of knowledge. First, knowledge begins, as Aquinas insisted, with beings in the world. One comes to a knowledge of being in general not directly, but rather indirectly, through its presence in beings. Next, because the subject's knowledge of being is always mediated through beings, philosophy must be careful to avoid the perennial temptation to downplay the importance of the particular. It must also overcome its suspicion of the historical. Not only is being only unveiled in particular things at particular times, the subject's knowledge of truth is always also located within a particular time and place. Such situatedness never allows the subject's grasp of being to equal that of absolute being itself, Hegel notwithstanding. And this has everything to do with what Balthasar calls the personal or intimate nature of truth.

> The perspectival character of truth is not simply a temporary condition that can gradually be sublated and synthesized into a total standpoint by an intensive information, by a sort of thorough reconnaissance of the land of truth (as Hegel, for example, attempted to do in his *Phenomenology of the Spirit*). Such an attempt would lead, like abstract scientific thought, albeit in a more subtle way, to the vaporization of the positive element in perspectivity: the intimate character and personality of the truth. It would presuppose that the thinker's standpoint could after all coincide with the absolute standpoint, that the individual thinker was secretly identical with the world spirit that runs through all standpoints . . . Apart from Christian revelation, there is only one way in which the thinker in the world can progressively lay hold of the truth: by taking seriously the personal situation in which he finds himself, on the one hand, and the inconclusible dialogue with all the perspectives surrounding him, on the other.[31]

More will be said about the 'perspectival' nature of truth shortly, but notice, first, that each aspect of the truth that has been discussed to this point highlights the importance of dialogue in truth's discovery. This is so because only a view of truth which acknowledges *both* its mysteriousness *and* its objectivity can really account for the importance of genuine dialogue. A false subjectivism – and it is precisely modernity's subjectivism which postmodernity, in spite of its critique of Enlightenment rationalism, seems incapable of supplanting – renders genuine dialogue superfluous for a number of reasons. First, *the* model for truth during the Enlightenment was that of the hard sciences. Indeed, truth was *reduced* to that which could be ascertained through the scientific method.[32] Next, the *ultimate* questions are necessarily removed from public discussion on account of the fact that they cannot be answered with the kind of certitude found in the hard sciences. Unfortunately, even while Liberal regimes refuse to have public discussions about final ends and ultimate goods, they must assume some notion of the good in order to make even the most mundane of public policy decisions.

Finally, this goes back to what Adrian Walker has called the liberal model of dialogue. This model is premised upon the modern fact/value distinction which insists that truth concerns the facts of science, while 'values' are private and subjective. Liberalism, in such a view, must create a 'neutral' space in which isolated (and alienated) individuals can work out their own notions of the good life. Notwithstanding the absolute impossibility of any such thing as a 'neutral' political space, dialogue under such auspices can only concern trivialities for the simple reason that it has already been determined that there can be no objective truth with regard to the good and the beautiful. And, as Alasdair MacIntyre has pointed out, all who question the validity of the notion that questions of the ultimate good are private, are not welcome to the dialogue. To switch from the political to the religious, the liberal model of religious dialogue invites all religions to dialogue, provided that all of them are willing to see themselves as a particular example of a more general phenomenon. If a religion thinks that it is true or unique, it is excluded from the dialogue. And this is why Balthasar says that under such conditions there can never be a genuine competition of catholicities.

But a false objectivism is no better off. Once it is forgotten that truth is not contradictory to mystery, it becomes possible to bottle the truth up into a system, replete with all of the right propositions. This false objectivism which comes under fire in Balthasar's treatise on truth is not only guilty of a forgetfulness of mystery, however, it is also guilty of ignoring the situated and perspectival nature of truth. We should, therefore, return to our discussion concerning the perspectival nature of truth. In one of the most provocative sections of *Theo-Logic I*, Balthasar speaks of the 'mobility of the idea'. While it is certainly the case that the world and the things in the world are determined by certain universal laws which transcend the individual instances of such things, it is also the case that the 'idea' (*ideos*) of things – speaking in the language of classical metaphysics – is colored by its instantiation in each particular thing and its individual history. Furthermore, the knowledge, say, of this particular fern cannot be exhausted in terms of its 'fern-ness'. There is always what Balthasar refers to as a 'remainder' which is not reducible to the universal idea of a thing, and this accounts for the particularity of truth. This 'remainder' by no means militates against the universality or rationality of truth, it simply points to the fact that 'the individual can never be transposed without remainder into universal terms'.[33] And this becomes increasingly the case as we progress from simple organisms to free and self-conscious beings. And this means, furthermore, that as one moves from the study of relatively simple things – e.g., rocks or molecules – to more complex things – e.g., animals or human beings – knowledge in terms of universals is even less adequate to the entire truth of the thing. This is precisely why the scientific method becomes less appropriate as a total way of knowing as one proceeds up the chain of being. Finally, it should be pointed out that as one moves from knowledge of simple things to knowledge of free subjects, it is not that there ceases to be universal truth, it is rather that the universal truth concerning the latter require a certain eye that is capable of seeing or perceiving the universal *in* the particular.[34] This helps to explain why it takes a sort of *finesse* to understand human nature – a finesse that a

Shakespeare or a Dostoevsky seemed to possess in spades – which is not required in, say, botany.[35]

Such situatedness of truth, then, gives an urgency to dialogue which might be lost on the naive realist. If there is a real mobility of the idea, then knowledge is never something that is over and done with. There is always further truth to be mined, greater depths to be explored. This is especially true in the case of the spiritual subject who actually has a role (freedom) in the manner in which the 'idea' unfolds in its particular case. And the unfolding of a destiny must always take place with a community of fellow travelers.[36] The first aspect of the truth, then, that Balthasar wishes to emphasize against false objectivism has to do with its 'situatedness'.

If truth is always situated, for the finite knower it is also perspectival. When people today speak of perspective, they are often speaking from the position of a postmodern skepticism which denies the inherent rationality of being. Such a position, in what cannot help but amount to a contradiction, has, indeed, become a sort of 'ism' in our day. But Balthasar's emphasis on perspective is not rooted in being's irrationality; it is rooted, rather, in the necessary interplay between essence and existence. Again, it must be re-emphasized that knowledge occurs for Balthasar at the intersection of a subject and a particular object. Access to an essence is always mediated through a particular existent, and the truth event which results takes place before a particular knower. Balthasar refers to this particular confluence of essence, existence and subject as a 'constellation'.

> This constellation places both being and truth in a determinate state that, while in itself caused by general forces, nonetheless channels their operation toward the production of a unique outcome. If we picture the subject as occupying the center of this constellation, we realize that the subject therefore sees truth perspectivally.[37]

It is as if the knower is situated in the land of truth and is necessarily looking at it from a particular place and angle, making it possible to speak, in a not merely pejorative manner, of 'personally colored world views and *Weltanschauungen*'.[38]

That it is not possible to get a bird's-eye view is a reason neither for despair nor for skepticism because there are numerous ways in which one can fill out one's own perspective. The chief of these, the reader could have guessed by now, is conversation with other worldviews and perspectives. But the key to Balthasar's understanding of this process is that such conversation can be fruitful precisely because 'all individual standpoints participate in a single truth' such that it is 'possible to compare them, to coordinate them, and to order them to a unity', even if a never fully attainable one. The truer the worldview, in fact, the more capable it is of integrating various partial perspectives. The one thing that needs to be emphasized – and it should be remembered at this point that Balthasar is prescinding here from an explicit appeal to revelation – is that it is never possible to escape in a definitive way – *à la* Hegel – one's perspective and become one with the absolute Subject.[39] And it is these two just mentioned points that mark the heart of Balthasar's philosophy of dialogue: first, the closer to the final truth that a worldview draws, the more it is able to incorporate other points of view – a robust sense of truth, that is, is not opposed to a robust openness to dialogue – and second, a hiatus from the particular in order to evaluate all particulars is untenable for the simple reason that finite beings can only see something from this or that particular, or, otherwise put, for the finite subject the bird's-eye view is a chimera.

III. A Theology of Dialogue

All that has been said to this point is presupposed in Balthasar's theology of dialogue. If Balthasar was somewhat suspicious regarding what he often called the overhasty ecumenism of post-Vatican II Catholicism, it was precisely for its tendency to bypass the 'scandal of particularity' by building church unity on a transcendental unity of religions. In order to clarify Balthasar's theology of dialogue we will now look at Balthasar's understanding of the nature of doctrine and his ecclesiology. The thesis which is being presented here is that, in spite of an ostensible suspicion with regard to the official ecumenism of his later years, there is a consistent interest in church unity that pervades the work of Hans Urs von Balthasar. More specifically, and this is not to deny an intense interest in Orthodox–Catholic dialogue, or even a broader dialogue with the world's religions, Balthasar wanted to construct a fully Catholic theology which also reflected the positive aspects of the spirit of Protestantism. This has been suggested by Christoph Schönborn, but as the following quote makes clear, it has yet to be fully appreciated:

> Von Balthasar's closeness to the Reformation too lies in this pointing toward the obedience of faith, practiced in retreats and reflected upon repeatedly in the theological work. He says himself: 'It is here, too, that we come closest to the sense and inspiration of the Reformation, from Luther to Barth.' Too little attention, in my opinion has been paid as yet to the supreme significance of von Balthasar's work for a profound reception of the 'inspiration' of the Reformation. Here lies a great ecumenical task waiting to be done![40]

It is precisely the task of this present work to show the 'profound reception of the "inspiration" of the Reformation' in Balthasar's work. Because

Balthasar never wrote the intended volume on ecumenism which was to conclude his *Theological Aesthetics*,[41] we will have to distill these principles from rather disparate sources.

A. Difficulties with Official Ecumenism

The principle, discussed in the previous section, that the most openness is to be found precisely where Christianity makes its strongest claim for particularity, must be kept in mind not only where Balthasar is concerned with other worldviews and religions, but also where dialogue is proposed between Catholics and other groups of Christians. Any attempt to bypass this 'scandal of particularity' is, by definition, no longer Christian in its thrust. What has just been stated in terms of principles can be seen more clearly in Balthasar's reaction to any overhasty ecumenism. In his short work *Convergences*, Balthasar has this to say about the current ecumenical dialogues, in particular those between Catholics and 'Evangelicals'[42]:

> A word about the Evangelical-Catholic controversy in general is appropriate here. The present ecumenical dialogue, although it is frequently understood as a cooperative search for Christian truth in focus on the mutual Lord, is understood also as a radical reduction of the allegedly 'essential', along with the elimination of all dispensable additions which disturb the understanding. It is clear that the Catholic partner will draw the shorter straw under these conditions, for the Reformation already lightened the ship of all its alleged 'ballast' four hundred fifty years ago, and today, in the face of the events within the Catholic Church, it speaks, not without satisfaction, of a 'need to catch up'… Against all this, attention must be drawn to the following point: Just as biblical theology is highly complex and cannot be reduced to a 'systematic' denominator, so ecclesiastical theology, which has only to mirror biblical theology and make it ready for the proclamation of the gospel, is not constructed of short-sighted formulas and hastily set up as a 'system', but requires an obedient consideration of all aspects, as well as the capacity not to disregard what is supplementary (to the fullness of Christ!) within the necessary gradation.[43]

Almost all the essential elements of Balthasar's negative reaction to overhasty ecumenism are contained in this quote. In the first place, there is the central difficulty that those things which define a Catholic over and against any of the variety of Protestant groups are the very things which are often relegated to the periphery in the various dialogues. On the one hand, there is a certain prudence and logic here which Balthasar appreciates[44] based on the notion of a 'hierarchy of truths'. This enables the Catholic and his interlocutor to find a common ground upon which to build. On the other hand, a difficulty arises when this ordering is allowed to give the impression that the Protestant position is the right one from the outset, that, indeed, the doctrines regarding Mary, cooperative grace, the Petrine office and the like are all undesirable accretions to that which is essential to the Christian faith.

In keeping with this first difficulty lies a second: an increasing inability to see just how the Catholic 'surplus', what Barth has called the Catholic 'and', is related to that which is more generally agreed upon as central. In this quote Balthasar warns us that we should not understand the Church's articulation of its doctrines along the lines of a system, in which certain parts are easily dispensable and others are basic denominators. Here, again, Balthasar is presupposing a certain 'aesthetic' sensibility as he articulates it in the first part of this trilogy. According to such an understanding, 'form' (*Gestalt*) is not understood in such a way that the external expression of a thing is a dispensable pointer to the essential, invisible mystery which lies beyond it. If that were the case then one could begin with a general awareness of mystery, or a general religiosity, and then examine the various articulations of this experience in the light of this originary experience. Instead, for Balthasar, our experience of mystery is *made possible by* and is *given its normative expression in* that which is concrete, i.e., in the epiphany of Christ. These apparently external details, the 'periphery', are ordered to the mystery, not in a mechanistic but in an organic and intrinsic way. Insofar as they are truly indispensable parts of the Christian mystery, they are living appendages which are organically connected to their living source.

B. The Nature of Theology and Dialogue

It has been rightly said that Balthasar's theology is radically 'revelocentric', but this should not be understood to imply that Balthasar rejects either theological foundations or the necessity of communicating the faith to a 'secular' world. It is simply that Balthasar rejects any strategy of correlation that would involve downplaying the supernatural or 'from above' dimension of genuine Christian theology. Not only does such a strategy not do justice to historic Christianity, it is also bad philosophy, for, as Balthasar has shown, even the 'truth of the world' is marked by a give and take that provides a necessary pre-understanding for the Christian understanding of revelation. Already in philosophy, that is, there are themes such as gift (revelation), mystery and faith which correspond to and provide the necessary pre-conceptions for a fully Christian understanding of these things. Balthasar's theology of dialogue, then, is very much in keeping with his philosophy of dialogue and this is especially apparent in his understanding of the nature of doctrine.

The twin dangers of modern theology parallel the philosophical extremes discussed above in terms of false objectivism and false subjectivism. In theology these extremes become propositional fundamentalism on the one hand and, to borrow from George Lindbeck, 'experiential expressivism' on the other. In order to preserve the objectivity of doctrine against the vicissitudes of time, the former emphasizes the need to have clear, timeless and binding doctrinal statements in conjunction with a strong teaching authority, located for Protestants of this persuasion solely in the Bible and for Catholics in some combination of Scripture, Tradition and the Magisterium. While the strength of this position lies in its ability to protect doctrinal orthodoxy from the encroachments of the perennial *Zeitgeist*, God's infinite mystery is all too often sacrificed at the feet of doctrinal certitude. On the other end of the spectrum lie the various forms of doctrinal liberalism, and it could be argued that behind the appeal to experience in such approaches lies the noble and quite traditional desire to protect God's transcendence from human rationality. Indeed, Balthasar will go so far as to commend Paul Tillich – against Barth! – for such a desire.[45] But a danger lurks here also: a simple juxtaposition of mystery and doctrinal formulation appears to have more in common with Gnosticism than with a faith that insists that the God of Christianity is a God who speaks.[46] In other words, modernity seems locked in a battle between a propositionalism which denies mystery and an experientialism which denies objective truth.

It should be remembered at this point, Balthasar reminds us, that the same centuries which gave us the Nicene and Chalcedonian formulas were the very ones who never ceased to emphasize – sometimes to an almost Platonic excess – the ultimate incomprehensibility of God. *Si comprehendis non est Deus*, says Augustine, in perfect company with the Fathers of the East. In these matters, Balthasar follows Erich Przywara and Gustav Siewerth in their insistence that God's transcendence grows proportionately with his immanence and that the more God reveals himself, the more he remains unknown. It was Przywara who called attention to a forgotten aspect of Catholic theology which was to become axiomatic for Balthasar, namely, that the analogy between God and the world which makes God-talk possible contains an ever greater dissimilarity.[47] Moreover, such a 'greater dissimilarity' does not cease to exist when one moves from so-called natural theology to positive theology – or, from the *via negativa* to the *via positiva* – because the God who is revealed in Jesus Christ is even more incomprehensible to human reason than the God of the philosophers. Again, against the modern tendency to oppose doctrine to mystery, Balthasar will wish to insist that it is precisely in the Church's teachings that the true mystery of God is preserved. In such teachings we have true knowledge of God, but such knowledge should never be understood to exclude the 'ever greater dissimilarity' just noted.

These basic ideas provide the foundations of Balthasar's understanding of the place of doctrinal formulations and magisterial pronouncements. At its heart, it must be remembered, Christianity is not primarily a doctrine or set of teachings, but a person, or, perhaps better, an event. It is only subsequently something written down,[48] and even then this writing is always there at the service of the event and never claims to exhaust it.[49] Scripture itself is written in such a way as to testify to the infinite mystery of the Christ event, which is precisely why four Gospels are required to give witness to Christ and why any false harmonization is ruled out. The truth of Christ is such that it can only be given witness to in a 'symphony', and symphonies cannot be understood in the manner of mathematical formulas. Scripture, then, is not an end in itself but is rather a means – in a way analogous to the sacraments – to the very activity of God on our behalf. Balthasar is careful to preserve the distinction, therefore, between Christ who alone is the 'Word of God', and scripture, which is the Spirit's testimony to that Word.[50] This is not to decry scripture, it is simply to say that scripture is there to make present something that ultimately transcends it.

It is precisely this understanding of scripture that paves the way also for the Catholic understanding of Tradition. Tradition is simply the progressive understanding – under the guidance of the Spirit – of the one 'Word' who is testified to in scripture. And this 'Word' is rooted in the fact that in the Triune God, the Son is eternally the expression of the Father. 'Since God has in himself the eternal Word that expresses him eternally, he is most certainly expressible; and since this very Word has taken human form and expresses in human acts and words what it is in God, it is capable of being understood by men.'[51] Tradition is the Catholic way of testifying to the fact that the things which are revealed in scripture cannot be exhausted in human language, nor understood all at once.[52] On the other hand, it is important to emphasize that Tradition makes no attempt to add anything new which is not already implicit in the event which gives rise to scripture.[53]Tradition is simply the progressive deepening, under the guidance of the Spirit, of the Church's understanding of what is testified to in scripture

But this still leaves the question of the role of doctrinal statements in Balthasar's theology. To go back to the 'ever greater dissimilarity' discussed above, Balthasar is insistent that God remains totally other even when revealed. If Gustav Siewerth wanted to trace the origins of theological rationalism to nominalism, Balthasar will wish to go back even further to the christological councils of the early Church.[54] And it is here, already, that a twofold danger emerges with regard to doctrinal definitions. First, there is a danger that the formulas attract so much attention to themselves that they actually prevent the seeker from pressing on towards the mystery which they are intended to protect. In other words, knowing the definition becomes a substitute for knowing – in the mystical sense, now – Christ.[55] Second, all doctrinal definitions arise out of a conflict with heresy, such that the danger is to state the final position in a one-sided manner against the heresy in question. 'In other words, the error is always a partial one, and so the corresponding dogmatic truth is in danger of being partial too insofar as it contents itself with merely the contrary.'[56] But now the paradox of Balthasar's understanding of doctrine comes in. Contrary to various forms of doctrinal liberalism, Balthasar does not, at this point, dismiss the need for doctrinal statements, nor does he deny their normative nature. On the contrary, understood in their proper light, doctrinal statements become valuable precisely in their *service of* the mystery of God's self-revelation in Christ. Far from being a 'hellenization' of Christianity, the doctrinal statements of the great early councils actually preserve Christianity from a false Platonism, for it is precisely Arius's views which betray a compromise with Platonic rationalism. The 'homoousios' of Nicea is precisely there to preserve the incomprehensibility of the biblical God who comes to us in Jesus Christ.[57]

If doctrinal statements and magisterial pronouncements, then, are not an attempt to deny but rather to highlight the 'ever greater dissimilarity' between God and our understanding of him, neither are they a barrier to genuine theological dialogue. If the scriptures which give witness to Christ do not mark an end but rather a beginning of our quest to know God, neither do the doctrinal definitions of the Church mark an end, but rather, also, a beginning. Indeed, by protecting the mystery of the Word, they actually enable us to talk about the one thing which can help bring unity, Christ. For Balthasar, there is no other path to unity, for Christ is God's manner of dialoguing with the world. Dialogue now serves two purposes. First, it is our common pressing on in love to know Christ, a task which will never be complete. Second, it enables us to avoid the danger of the one-sidedness mentioned above, which is always the danger of doctrinal formulations. And if this was a danger even in the relatively united Church of the early councils, how much more so in a divided Church? And now Balthasar speaks directly of dialogue with Protestants:

> For Catholics, this dialogue has two aspects, which must be seen simultaneously. On the one hand, the non-Catholic Christian communities stressed certain basic evangelical truths and kept them in their exodus from the Catholic Church, in which these truths were obscured and not reinserted with sufficient balance by the extreme contrary positions that were taken during the subsequent confrontations (catchword: 'Counter-reformation'). In this case Catholics must listen to those who point out a piece of the totality of faith which is missing or not sufficiently

realized. On the other hand, a member of the Catholic Church must be aware that his 'separated brothers' can alert him only to things that have always rested in the fullness of his faith, things which were merely lost or forgotten through negligence and guilt.[58]

Both aspects are crucial here: first, the retrieval of a balance which has been distorted in various overreactions; and second, the notion that whatever the Catholic learns from her Protestant interlocutor was part of the original fullness of truth which Christ entrusted to his Church. Protestant tradition, that is, can no more introduce anything novel than can Catholic.

For the Christian, then, Christ is not just a model of dialogue, he is path upon which to dialogue. In other words, just as Balthasar's understanding of the analogy of being is rooted *in* his Christology – rather than arrived at prior to it – so his understanding of dialogue is rooted in Christ as the second person of the Trinity, in Christ, that is, insofar as Christ is the Father's self-expression. The Church, as the body of Christ, has no other basis for dialogue, whether we are speaking *ad extra* or *ad intra*, than Christ, who is the personification of the union between the divine and human, without confusion or mixture. As David Schindler has put it:

The Church can and must extend an invitation to dialogue always and to all persons. The warrant for and sense of this are to be found in the very substance of Jesus Christ, as understood from within the very heart and authoritative center of the Catholic tradition. Jesus Christ is the divine *Logos*: in him is founded the dialogue ('dia-logos') which God has initiated with the entire cosmos (Col. 1.14–18). The fundamental mission of every Christian, therefore, through forgiveness and conversion by the power of the Holy Spirit, and by virtue of the liberation from sin whose paradigm is given in Mary (cf. *Redemptoris Mater*, 37), is to enter this dialogue which God has initiated with every creature in Jesus Christ. The terms in which the *process* of dialogue is to be conducted are thus given from the beginning and all along the way precisely from within this *christological substance*. Christ is both the (objective) truth and the (subjective) way (829).[59]

As Balthasar often emphasized throughout his work, where the organic link between the various articles of faith and their source in the central mystery of Christ is lost, the fullness of the faith is always in danger. This can happen in the Fundamentalist direction by equating the mystery of faith to a set of propositions in a mechanistic way, or, in the Liberal direction, by reducing what is essential to the level of something pre-thematic or, ultimately, subjective. Or, to borrow from Schindler again:

High christological substance which is invoked without noticing that its content consists precisely *in* the process of dialogue (Christ's dialogue with the Father, and with all of creation from and for the Father, through Mary and in the Spirit) in the

> end becomes 'objectivistic' (wrongly exclusivist)... Dialogue carried on without this high christological substance in the end becomes vague and sentimental – 'subjectivistic' (wrongly inclusivist).[60]

The major points of this section, then, are these. Revelation, according to Balthasar, should not be understood primarily in either propositional or experiential terms, but rather in dramatic/aesthetic terms. In the personal realm there is a simultaneous revealing and concealing that guards against a false doctrinal rationalism on the one hand and a false doctrinal subjectivism/historicism on the other. The God of Christianity is eternally expressed in his Word, a Word which became flesh and which is testified to in the word of scripture. This aspect of Balthasar's theology accounts sufficiently for the propositional aspect of revelation: the God of Christianity, in short, is a God who speaks and who takes up human flesh and human language in order to make himself known. On the other hand, even as Jesus Christ reveals the Father, he reveals what is quite simply incomprehensible. Indeed, the incomprehensibility of God is not only not obliterated when the Word becomes flesh, it is actually deepened, for who could have guessed the God whom Jesus reveals and who can grasp such a God even now. Even as Jesus, that is, makes God known – the proper objectivity – he only highlights our inability to grasp or comprehend this God – the proper attention to mystery. Doctrine, then, serves the purpose of preserving precisely this relationship. Far from eliminating the mystery or the 'ever greater dissimilarity', true doctrine helps to preserve such mystery in the face of all attempts at a false rationalization. True dialogue, therefore, is not dialogue that occurs outside of high christological content, for it is only such content that enables the only quest for unity which, for Christians at least, will do.

C. Biblical Theology and Dialogue

This notion, that unity can only be found in high christological content is made most clear in Balthasar's Old and New Testament theologies. Indeed, the unifying perspective which the risen Christ gives to the two Testaments offers a perfect model for genuine Christian dialogue in Balthasar's view. This is the theme taken up in the important work *Convergences* where Balthasar is interested primarily in the fragmented nature of modern theology, which is made manifest in the split between theology and spirituality, in the reduction of theology to another scientific discipline, or, finally, in the current dissection of the Bible into various theological communities which are then played against each other. With regard to the second of these Balthasar reminds the reader that the discussion surrounding theology as a 'science', which consumed much of the Middle Ages, was by no means unvariegated. Even in the synthesis reached by Thomas Aquinas, the scientific nature of theology must be qualified in two regards. First, according to Thomas's understanding, all sciences proceed from certain pre-scientific 'first principles' which make the process of investigation in that science possible. In other words, there was something akin to faith even in the non-theological sciences.[61] Secondly, and this is a point that is often forgotten or underestimated in many current discussions regarding the nature of theology, the scientific nature of theology vis-à-vis the other academic disciplines is only an analogous one. For Balthasar this means that the thing which makes theology unique is as important in Aquinas's discussion as that which makes it similar. Positively put, a faith decision lies at the bottom of theology which roots all of its subsequent investigations in a way that is analogous to other disciplines in the academy, but also in a way which is unique and rooted in the gracious gift of God.

When applied to the study of scripture as it is currently carried out in the academy, the same general rules apply. That is, at the root of the investigation of *this* text must be a method which corresponds to its object.[62] As with any science, there are decisions made prior to the investigations which are carried on in that science which figure into the obtained results, and offer them a unifying point of view. This has been shown to be true even in the so-called 'hard' sciences, and is even more so the case in the '*Geisteswissenschaften*'; but with regard to the study of the Bible there is also the aspect of faith to be taken into consideration. The 'decision' which lies at the foundation of this science leaves us with two possibilities: either we allow the many words of scripture to find their point of unity in the person of Jesus Christ, or we make the principle of our research 'historical man' (*der geschichtlichen Menschen*) and 'his understanding of himself' (*Selbstverständnis*).[63] There is no 'neutral' standpoint in this regard. With regard to the issue of unity, the manner in which one investigates the Bible becomes especially important in that this text lies at the root of the varieties of Christianity. Indeed, the ecumenical dialogues have been correct in the common insistence that any hoped-for unity must be founded upon this text.

It is at this point, however, that a new problem presents itself. In the first place, Balthasar acknowledges that the current historical investigation of scripture has offered us a whole new dimension in our understanding of the Bible, showing that even in the New Testament texts there are a variety of approaches to the central phenomenon of Jesus Christ which parallel the current ecumenical dialogues. Yet, if the assumption is made from the outset that these various perspectives in the New Testament find their source solely in humanity's self-understanding, then there is nothing beyond them to serve as a point of reference. What we are left with is a variety of articulations of the human predicament which are, for the most part, indeterminable. This recognition of the variety of 'theologies' within the New Testament itself, and the subsequent attempt to build an ecumenical synthesis thereon, dates back to Schelling, but the unity achieved is only external, and tenuous at best.[64] The unity that stems from such a situation would parallel the kind of contractual, political unity that is present in modern, liberal regimes. But, certainly, this will not suffice for the unity that is called for in the Church.

It is important to recall at this point that the unity of the Church is premised upon the unity which exists between the persons of the Trinity, and that this union is only made possible in Christ. To return to biblical theology, Balthasar finds an analogy, as we have already mentioned, between the current ecumenical dialogues and the variety of biblical theologies, and hopes that the study of scripture, in the way that he has conceived it, will shed light on the current situation. His method is an attempt to integrate the best of the approach of the Church Fathers with the findings of modern exegesis. That is, he thinks that the 'christocentric' approach to scripture of someone like an Origen need not exclude the modern historical approach. In fact, Origen's ignoring of the human element led him to what Balthasar calls a Docetic approach to scripture, which needs to be balanced by the modern historical understanding.[65] On the other hand, the modern approaches which bracket the divine element from the outset, whether out of a lack of faith or as a methodological strategy, will necessarily miss that aspect which alone can unite all of the fragments of scripture into a whole. This lack of a sense for 'the one thing necessary' will necessarily affect the way in which even the part is treated. The basis for Balthasar's approach is christological: just as the human nature and the divine nature coexist without confusion or division in the one person of Jesus Christ, so in scripture the Word of God is entrusted, through the Holy Spirit, to the words of human beings. To ignore either element is to lapse into a misunderstanding of the nature of the text.

In the Old Testament we have a variety of figures who shed light on our concept of God. First, we have Abraham, who stands as a reminder to all of Israel that God freely elected them out from among the nations on the basis of his love alone. Next we have Moses, who stands as a reminder to the people that their end of the Covenant is to keep the law of God, by which they are to prove themselves worthy of their election. Then there are the Prophets, who collectively speak of a time when Israel will regain its land, receive the Law into their hearts, and gather under a new king whose kingdom will have no end. Balthasar also mentions the apocalyptic and wisdom strains of the Old Testament. None of these strains, taken in itself, is adequate to contain the mystery of God's dealings with Israel. Nor can they all, taken together, form a coherent picture, because they, in some cases, mutually exclude each other. How does one reconcile, for instance, the image of the Davidic King with the image of the Suffering Servant? Balthasar juxtaposes these various strands of Old Testament theology in terms of 'figures' (*Bilden*) incapable of coming together to make up a final 'form' which can express the full mystery of God.[66]

Of course Balthasar is building up here to the fact that it is Jesus Christ alone who fully unites all of the fragmentary aspects of these Old Testament theologies into his person; this is certainly nothing new in the history of Christian thought. What is interesting about Balthasar's approach, however, is the implications which he draws from this phenomenon. In the first place, Christ does not fulfill the various strands of the Old Testament in such a way that he renders them obsolete: indeed, they will become part of the permanent language required to tell Christ's story. In Jesus Christ, in fact, the temporal value which they had in their previous context will be gathered up and given an eternal value, in a way analogous to the manner in which grace perfects without destroying nature. The second point to be mentioned here is that Christ unites these strands in a way that could have never been anticipated from the various, and often contradictory, figures in themselves. He can do this because he, alone, can represent both the divine and human ends of the Old Covenant: that is, both the Abrahamic and Mosaic aspects of Old Testament theology. He is at once the divine initiative which comes to humanity freely and graciously, and the human response to this covenant which makes up the intention of the Mosaic Law. In the former, he is the illustration of the fact that God is in essence self-giving love (i.e., Trinitarian). But, at the same time, Christ represents the fact that no degree of human estrangement from God, even to the degree of the God-forsakeness of sin, death, and Hell, can ultimately overcome the love of God 'which surpasses all understanding'. This bringing together, in one 'figure', the divine and the human goes beyond anything that could have been imagined in the Old Testament.[67]

This is the central mystery, a 'wordless event', which stands at the heart of the Old and New Testaments, and at the heart of all true theology. If the various figures of the Old Testament are incapable of containing this mystery because of their transitory and contradictory nature, neither can the various words of the New Testament exhaust it. The New Testament must be understood, in Balthasar's view, as the translation of the '*logos sarx*' into the '*logos rema*'.[68] Each of the New Testament theologies is an attempt to account for this central mystery, and each does so in such a way that they can never be separated, but must be allowed to complement one another. If it is the advantage of modern exegesis to call attention to the distinguishing characteristics of the various New Testament 'schools', it was the advantage of the exegesis of the Church Fathers never to lose sight of this central, unifying mystery.[69] If these two types of exegesis can be brought to complement each other, we will have a new basis for the ecumenical dialogues. That is, we must be prepared to acknowledge the essentially 'wordless' and 'timeless' (i.e., eschatological) event at the root of all biblical theologies,[70] which, at the same time, serves as the foundation for the Church, in order to allow it to serve as the unifying point of all of our ecumenical quests. Because of the mysterious character of this event we need all of the perspectives of the New Testament in order to gain an adequate witness to it. This allows for a legitimate plurality in the Church's theology which can only be threatened by a naive equation of any one expression with the fullness of truth.[71] At the same time, however, it prevents an illegitimate 'pluralism' which would want to find a common basis for unity outside of this central mystery – e.g., in a pre-thematic religious experience at the root of all religious expression. This discussion of Old and New Testament biblical theologies allows Balthasar to come full circle to his discussion of unity in the Church. The same Christ who had the power to unite all the disparate elements of Old Testament theology, also serves as the basis for unity in the Church. To equate any one of the New Testament witnesses with the totality of this mystery would be to give a one-sided view. Earlier in this essay Balthasar used the example of a kaleidoscope, wherein one 'segment' is given the appearance of a 'rounded off' form with the aid of the internal mirror. The same can happen in theology when one aspect of the biblical witness is given precedence over other aspects. In the current division in the Church there is this precise tendency to give precedence to one truth over and against others. The Catholic finds herself in the awkward position of defending the 'periphery' in the face of the Protestant call to the 'one thing necessary'. A twin danger presents itself at this point. For the Protestant that danger consists in a failure to realize that while it is, indeed, the nature of all true reform to recall the Church back to its center, it is unbiblical to exclude those elements which legitimately stem from this center. Balthasar gives the example of James's understanding of faith *and* works, insisting that the priority of the former need not exclude the necessity of the latter. For the Catholic, the danger consists in so defining itself in terms of this periphery that it ceases to see how these things are living offshoots of the center. Dialogue with the Protestant, who really comes to the dialogue as a Protestant, benefits the Catholic by bringing this center back into the light. The proper response from the Catholic does not consist in dispensing with the alleged 'ballast', but in re-integrating it with its center. It consists in an *Einfaltung*.[72]

D. The Ecclesiological Basis of Dialogue

Finally, a word about Balthasar's ecclesiology is in order. There was a pronounced tendency in the Protestant Liberalism of the nineteenth century to paint a portrait of Jesus as liberating individual against the cult of Israel. If Israel was concerned with religious externals, rituals and a rigid moral law, Jesus, it was maintained, was here to emphasize the importance of interior over exterior, individual piety over cultic worship and ritual. Already in *The Babylonian Captivity of the Church* Luther had excoriated the late medieval Catholic Church for an extreme externalism which amounted to an alienation between the individual believer and God. In this treatise, for instance, Luther is not so much opposed to the doctrine of transubstantiation as he is to the Church's right to impose such doctrines on its members when they are not taught explicitly in scripture. For his own churches, Luther would allow members either to embrace transubstantiation or not, as long as they did not deny Christ's real presence in the Eucharist. I raise these two historical examples at this point simply to call attention to a perennial Protestant (and, one could add, also Orthodox) concern that Catholic ecclesiology is overly concerned with the external and the juridical at the expense of the true interiority which gives rise to externals in the first place.

Throughout the essays in *Spirit and Institution*,[73] Balthasar examines these concerns in a straightforward manner, making it very clear that they are not simply to be dismissed. In fact, it could be argued that it is in his ecclesiology that Balthasar's aesthetic sensibilities bear their greatest ecumenical fruit. Again, such an assertion may appear strange to those who think of Balthasar as a theological conservative who tends to support the Church's teachings on any number of controversial issues, the ordination of only males to the priesthood and the ban on artificial contraception to name only two. But upon closer inspection it becomes clear that Balthasar's ecclesiology, while emphasizing the genuine importance of the Church's teaching office, is equally concerned that sheer juridical power, when divorced from the spiritual gifts at its roots, has no basis whatsoever in either the New Testament or the early Church. Indeed, it is the strength of Balthasar's approach that he refuses to emphasize institution at the expense of pneumatology, or pneumatology at the expense of institution. Where there is real, ongoing life, Balthasar insists, there can be no simple juxtaposition of inner and outer. The Protestant critique, then, becomes justified only when the Catholic allows the externals, the institution, to become a substitute for the authentic work of the Spirit. It is also this demand that inner and outer must always go together in a living organism that keeps Balthasar from explaining the current divisions in the Church in terms of the invisible and visible Church.[74]

Balthasar articulates the tension in the Church, between its mysterious, invisible character and its structural, visible character in terms of 'bride and institution'.[75] In a provocative essay entitled 'Office in the Church', Balthasar offers a meditation on the call to Christian discipleship. Christ insisted that his followers, originally the Twelve, but eventually all who would follow, take up their crosses just as he would take up his. The utter seriousness of Christ's call reaches a crescendo in the 'Sermon on the Mount', especially when the disciples are called to be 'perfect as their heavenly Father is perfect'. The 'dialectical Protestant' treatment of this command draws attention to its inimitable nature. It is offered, so the argument goes, simply to draw attention to the infinite chasm between the master and his disciples. The Catholic, on the other hand, has always insisted that this call demands a response: it is a call to *follow*, to imitate. Balthasar sees truth in both of these perspectives: true, there is an incommensurability between the call to perfection and those to whom the call is made; true, also, there is an urgency in this call which demands a response. On the Protestant side there has been a tendency to ignore the fact that Christ really is offered up as a model to his disciples; on the Catholic side there has been a tendency to downplay the inimitability of Christ's example. At this point Balthasar examines the various attempts to deal with this call to imitation: from the earliest phase which emphasized imitation through literal martyrdom, to a second, 'ascetic' phase which, building on various forms of Platonism, emphasized the overcoming of the passions (*apatheia*). A third phase, built on medieval notions of chivalry, culminated in Ignatian obedience; and a fourth phase, in reaction to a worldly and wealthy Church, linked imitation closely to poverty (St Francis). Finally, a fifth phase, marked by Luther, turned this following into an inward state, as opposed to any external form. This latter is echoed in the writings of Pascal and Kierkegaard. Each of these approaches, while containing great resources for renewal in the Church, is not without its weaknesses. There is an overly negative asceticism which marks the earliest period of the Church, borrowed from the Platonism of the time, which fails to do justice to the inherent goodness of the material world and our bodily existence. Francis's understanding of the importance of poverty, which was always cognizant of the fact 'that what mattered were the heart and the spirit prompting it',[76] became overly literalistic and one-sided in many of his followers. The same can be said of Ignatius's focus on obedience, which, while in itself a magnificent portrayal of gospel discipleship, can degenerate into an obedience 'detached from this inner disposition and seen simply as a tool for the use of the hierarchy'. And finally, Luther's division between internal justification and external discipleship, which was correct in its attempt to return to the spirit which inspires our following of

Christ, can all too easily lapse into a dialectic between external and internal that does not do justice to the idea of Christian discipleship. 'Form became exterior representation, in opposition to inwardness.'[77]

All of these various interpretations of Christ's call have significance for our understanding of ecclesiology. The Protestant dialectical understanding of this command has too often led to a juxtaposition of internal and external, the consequences of which Dietrich Bonhoeffer is famous for noting. In terms of ecclesiology, this can easily degenerate into a relativization of the external, official, visible form of the Church, in favor of the internal, invisible, personal aspect of the Church.[78] On the other hand, this call to imitation can degenerate in its 'Catholic' form into a mere external following, into the kind of legalism which George Bernanos was quick to denounce.[79] Ecclesiologically speaking, this results in a focusing on structure disconnected from its spiritual roots.[80] All of this translates into a failure to integrate successfully the 'Marian' and 'Petrine' aspects of the Church, and a Petrine Church which is severed from its Marian roots will be forced to rely increasingly upon the juridical. It is against this which Luther (justifiably!) reacted.

Against an overemphasis on hierarchical structure, Luther insisted on the priesthood of all believers. Balthasar wishes to do justice to Luther's concern in his insistence that Christ's call was not directed merely at the twelve – the future 'hierarchy' – but to *all* who would come after him. This general call will then take on different forms in the varying states of life, but the call itself is offered to all.[81] He also wants to do justice to the Reformation concern that this call is, humanly speaking, impossible to follow. In his solution, Balthasar attempts to transcend the either/or nature of this dispute: it is precisely where Christ is most inimitable that he calls for the closest imitation. However, Balthasar acknowledges that this following is, humanly speaking, impossible, because it requires a change of disposition in the disciple that the disciple is incapable of achieving. It is precisely at this point that Balthasar emphasizes the Marian aspect of discipleship, and, with this, the Marian dimension of the Church. Marian discipleship is not one that grasps at achieving Christ-likeness. Instead, in Mary's response to the annunciation lies a tacit acknowledgement that she is not equal to the task to which she has been called. It is in this childlike acknowledgement that lies the key to becoming a disciple of Christ: receptive faith, *indifferentia*. It is precisely on the basis of this willingness to forfeit all that is rightfully called one's own that a space is made for the indwelling of Christ; acknowledgement of one's own poverty becomes the basis for one's richness in Christ.

> This form of Christ has its source in the, so to speak, material, feminine principle of the surrender of faith, 'leaving all things', and in the formal, male principle of

> grace giving itself and imprinting itself on the believer, in whom it is a participation, in Jesus Christ, in the life of the Trinity.[82]

Or, again:

> The faith that 'leaves all' is, however, not one's own achievement. It is preceded by redemption through the blood of Christ, God's taking possession of man, the fact that 'you are not your own' (1 Cor. 6.15, 19)... his humiliation is the condition for his elevation by God.[83]

Mary's response to the annunciation, made possible by the prior grace of God, marks the beginning (a *typos*) of a grace-endowed partner for God's covenant. In this sense, Mary stands as the origin or *typos* of the Church, in that she is the embodiment of humanity's Yes to God. This should make it very clear that, for Balthasar, the origin of the Church is not human but divine; yet it is the divine working through and with the human by grace. The importance attributed to the necessity of this human partner makes it impossible for Balthasar to relegate the Church, including its structure, to the *merely* human realm. The fact that Mary's Yes is the origin of the structure of the Church makes clear that the Church, including its structure, has its source in the grace of God. It also shows that this institution, in all of its 'bodiliness', is an indispensable means to that very grace.[84]

Balthasar draws the following conclusions with regard to the relationship between the bridal (Marian) and institutional (Petrine) aspects of the Church: (1) On the basis of the incarnational aspect of Christ's mission, and his bodily resurrection, there can be no legitimate separation between the visible and invisible. Because Christ has a bodily constitution, 'the "Bride" who is this Man's partner, as a social entity, must have a bodily constitution ... [because] where there is real, ongoing life, *there is never any opposition between life and form*'.[85] (2) The events of Christ's life, especially those surrounding his death and resurrection, are intended to be ever-present events for the believer. Indeed, the fact the Church is born from these very events means that 'the abiding structure of offices in the Church (the "institution") means that we are guaranteed the possibility of participating in the original event at any and every time'.[86] (3) The presence of subjective holiness in the Church, and this goes back to our discussion of the call to discipleship extending to each one of us, presupposes an objectified holiness which exists in the Church *as* Church. Again, this holiness is based on the prior act of grace on Christ's part which raised up and sanctified Mary's response: it is from here that the source of the Church's holiness stems.[87] (4) It is part of the institutional Church's mission to call her members to the way of the cross, and it is through the heeding of this call (i.e., the way of the cross) that these members obtain an 'existential knowledge' of the Church's teachings which is equal to that of the Church's teaching authority.[88] Balthasar is emphasizing the importance of real obedience and real assent versus the blind obedience and notional assent (Newman) that has occasioned so much criticism of the Catholic Church. In this regard, Balthasar can sound as 'individualistic' as a Kierkegaard in his insistence that there is no substitute for the individual's response to Christ, especially not the Church, which is there to make this call present. (5) Finally, and we would do well to allow Balthasar to speak for himself here:

> [This relationship between the bridal and Petrine] can be explained by reference to the tension between the 'episcopal' and the 'prophetical' office, as set forth by Newman. Tradition and the instinct of faith are of the essence of the whole (Marian–Petrine) Church. But the episcopal office has to guard the authenticity of the 'prophetical' sense of faith that is alive in the whole; it must evaluate it and keep it pure. On the other hand, the episcopal office, for that very reason, has to pay attention to this 'prophetical' office of the whole Church, and when necessary it must learn from it . . . [89]

This excursus on Balthasar's ecclesiology, which in no way is intended to give an adequate overview thereof, is intended to show why there is no possibility of attributing the existing divisions in the Church to the level of the visible Church, while taking refuge in the invisible Church. On the basis of the intimate link, outlined above, between these two aspects of the Church – and this goes for the Catholic as much as the Protestant because he is partly guilty for the existing division – any division in the structure of the Church cannot help but affect the Church in its very essence. In addition, this excursus gave us a glimpse at Balthasar's ecumenism in action. While insisting on the absolute necessity of the Church's external structure as an integral part of its nature as Church, Balthasar admits that there has been a tendency in certain periods of Catholicism to forget the intimate link between the Church's structure and its source in the Triune God. In such times the externals (i.e., 'ballast') of the Church really can become barriers between the Christian and Christ, or, the structure of the Church can be seen as a substitute for the personal faith of the individual Christian. Luther's criticism of such externals, especially in his *Babylonian Captivity of the Church*, as well as Kierkegaard's alleged individualism, can, at this point, have a positive role within Catholic doctrine, provided they are integrated in a positive manner.

IV. Conclusion

This brings us to some final considerations regarding Balthasar's view of ecumenism. At the heart of Balthasar's concern is the passionate belief that if ecumenical dialogue is to have any success it must stem from the center of the faith. That is, it must stem from the fact that the Church is already one on the basis of its origin in the life of the Trinity; it must stem from the fact that any division in the Church is a scandal to the one faith that it is supposed to manifest to the world; it must stem from the fact that no one historical expression of the Christian faith can be equated with the faith itself, realizing that those who felt the need to separate themselves from the Catholic Church did so on the basis of convictions that came from the heart of the Church's faith; and, finally, it must stem from the fact that the 'object' which is at the center of this faith is a 'form' that requires the pluriform perspectives of the Old and New Testaments to give it adequate witness. No one aspect of this witness can claim to exhaust the meaning of this figure: there can be no Paul without James, no Peter without Mary, no John without Matthew, Mark and Luke, and so on. Within this diversity of witnesses lies the ground for a legitimate *plurality* in the Church, but the fact that these witnesses are complementary witnesses to the one figure at the center of our faith prevents any illegitimate *pluralism.*

For Balthasar, then, the best means to Christian unity stems from the heart of the faith, from Jesus Christ. 'Such theology is ecumenical, because it is fascinated only by its "object" and because, for this reason, it wants to lead only to this object.'[90] Because the Church's unity stems from this 'object', any attempt to build unity on purely human or practical considerations, or any attempt to found unity on anthropological grounds, is bound to fail. This is why the short work *Convergences* is so concerned about the various divisions in modern theology. Whether we are talking about the division between theology and sanctity, or between the various specializations within theology as it is taught in the academy today, or between the various New Testament theologies, Balthasar wishes to see all these things brought back together in their common focus on Christ. He has demonstrated that this cannot be done as long as theology is pursued in a disinterested manner, as if one's decision for or against Christ made no difference. This is why Balthasar was so insistent on the fact that Catholics cannot be really prepared to dialogue with their separated brothers and sisters until they have worked harder towards unity in their own house.[91]

It seems quite clear that Balthasar understood his own work in the light of this last sentence. If Balthasar was not involved to a great degree in the official ecumenism of his later years it was not because he did not think reuniting the churches an important issue. Rather, Balthasar understood that as long as the Catholic Church was unsure of its own theological bearings, it was hardly ready to engage those on the outside. It will be the central task of this study to show that Balthasar's call for a 'christocentric' revolution in Catholic theology was initiated for the twofold reason of providing this basis for Catholic unity, while, at the same, providing the groundwork for the dialogue that must take place with Protestantism. In other words, I want to argue that Balthasar's work in Catholic 'foundations' was already done in the light of an engagement with the Reformation, so that when Catholic theology entered into that dialogue it would be prepared in advance to do so. As I mentioned above, Balthasar's attempt to engage in a christocentric Catholic theology is also relevant to the more recent divide in Christian theology between the disciples of Karl Barth and the disciples of Karl Rahner. In what lies ahead, we will examine the theological approaches of Martin Luther and Karl Barth in the light of Balthasar's theological project, and then we will show how Balthasar takes up this christocentric style of theology in his critique of the 'cosmological' approach of the Church Fathers and the 'anthropological' approach of modern theology.

2

Balthasar on Luther's *Theologia Crucis*

I. Introduction

A study which intends to bring Balthasar into dialogue with Protestant thought has the advantage of being able to resort to his lengthy, in-depth study of Karl Barth, undoubtedly the most important representative of Protestantism in the twentieth century. But before we examine Balthasar's treatment of Barth it will be helpful to examine the origins of the Protestant critique of Catholic theology as it appears in the theology of Martin Luther. A number of factors, however, make such an examination difficult. In the first place, Balthasar never directly confronts Luther in the detailed manner in which he does Barth. Furthermore, where Balthasar does address Luther's theology, it is typically in brief sections of larger works which are not primarily concerned with understanding Luther's thought in and of itself. To make matters even worse, in those places where Balthasar does confront Luther's theology he relies, extensively, on the work of two Luther scholars whose work has been less than positively received by the rest of the scholarly community – including Catholic scholars.[1]

Another difficulty revolves around the work of Luther himself, and the almost limitless possibility of construing his work in terms of the interests of the reader. In the scholarship one finds the Reformation Luther, the modern Luther, the medieval Luther, the Catholic Luther, the mystical Luther, the nominalist Luther, the realist Luther, and so on. Part of this variety can be attributed to the fact that the people who study Luther are engaged in theological situations of their own in which one of these 'Luthers' is more appealing than another. For instance, during the nineteenth century, when it was the fashion to show how entrenched the Middle Ages was in idle speculation, it was important to show that Luther was a radically novel thinker, uniquely capable of presenting authentic Christianity in the midst of Scholastic speculation. More recently, however, in light of the critique of Protestant Liberalism from thinkers like Karl Barth, it has become important to Luther scholars to show that Luther, far from being the father of modernity, was thoroughly a man of the Middle Ages.[2] More recently still, one finds the Luther who arises from the ecumenical dialogues. Consider, in this latter regard, the work being done by a group of Finnish Luther scholars who have been in dialogue with the Orthodox Church.[3] Here, those aspects of Luther's theology which emphasize the real presence of Christ in the life of the believer – ontological realism – against any purely forensic understanding of justification, are central to the interpretation.[4]

On the other hand, although it is true that Balthasar identifies Barth as *the* representative Protestant thinker, he does recognize the importance of addressing the origin of the Reformation's concerns. In fact, he understands his short work, *Love Alone*, as well as his 'theological aesthetics', as a response to these concerns. Furthermore, Balthasar understands Luther's theological enterprise as an attempt to heal the rift between theology and sanctity, a rift that had become increasingly gaping in the late Middle Ages. This attempt to overcome the separation of theology and sanctity is a common concern of Luther and Balthasar, and, although they find somewhat different solutions to this problem, they are both interested in seeing theology return to its source: the Word of God as it is received in faith. For Luther, this means attempting to overcome the extrinsic relationship between the Christian faith as it was experienced in the life of the ordinary believer, and the manner in which this faith was being scrutinized in the late medieval university. Luther's theology must be understood as an attempt to salvage the otherness and distinctiveness of the Christian faith in the midst of this philosophical encroachment

In what follows, then, we will examine Luther's theology of the cross, especially as it appears in the *Heidelberg Disputation*, but also in terms of its effect on Luther's understanding of faith and the righteousness of God. For Luther, issues of 'theological method' are never separated from properly soteriological issues. Of course this will require a brief discussion of Luther's theological *Sitz im Leben*, especially as it regards late medieval nominalism. Because Balthasar does not offer a basic examination of Luther's thought, this will fill the gap that he presupposes in his mostly sketchy discussions of Luther's theology. After presenting the origins of Luther's theology on its own terms, we will examine Balthasar's criticisms of certain aspects of Luther's thought. This chapter, like the next on Karl Barth, will serve as a preparation for the second half of this study wherein we will examine Balthasar's attempt to integrate the legitimate concerns which flow out of these Reformation projects into a Catholic theology for the new millennium. Although he will have several criticisms of the approaches of both Luther and Barth, he never loses sight of the legitimacy of their concern to protect the free revelation of God from all forms of Promethean presumption.

II. Nominalism and Luther

Important to Balthasar's understanding of Luther's theology is the precise role that Luther plays in the passage to modernity. If Balthasar's chief theological contribution is to be found in his attempt to overcome the separation of nature and grace that marks the beginning of modernity, and the segregation of the transcendental attributes of being which accompanies this separation, it is important that we properly characterize Luther's role in this historical transition. Balthasar would agree with Louis Dupré that the transition to modernity should not be located, as typical historiography has done, with the Renaissance, nor as Heidegger and the Postmoderns would have it, with the turn to the *logos* in Plato, but with the 'radical Aristotelians' of the High Middle Ages. The question which betrays the very heart of this new philosophical approach concerns how far reason can move towards the ultimate meaning of the universe without the aid of revelation. In order to situate Luther's theology, then, we must understand it in the context of a new approach to theology that was growing in influence in the late medieval university, the so-called *via moderna*. As will be shown, this new theological attitude arose in direct response to the exaggerated claims for reason made by those influenced by this 'radical Aristotelianism'.

If early Luther scholarship tended to exaggerate Luther's adherence to nominalism, more recent Protestant scholars have tended to nuance this relationship. There is also another dynamic in understanding Luther's relationship to nominalism, however, and that is the assessment that is given to nominalism itself. This assessment has tended to break down along Protestant and Catholic lines. The Catholic approach, which finds its most outspoken representatives in Étienne Gilson and Henri de Lubac, presents nominalism as the breakdown of the 'Thomistic synthesis'. The greatest failure of nominalism, according to this view, is its inability to construe correctly the relationship between God and world. First, there is the tendency to emphasize God's 'otherness' to such a degree that the world takes on an autonomy that it never had in the thought of, say,

Augustine and Aquinas. This novel understanding is rather more skeptical of the ability of the 'cosmos' to manifest God, paving the way, at least, for an understanding of nature as 'purely natural', something which is to be exploited for the sake of humanity's comfort. Next, there is a tendency to relegate 'this-worldly' concerns to the realm of reason and 'other-worldly' concerns to the realm of faith and revelation in a way that is unprecedented in the history of Christian thought. In short, nominalism is painted as a villain, the precursor to modern secularism.

Protestant scholars, on the other hand, following the lead of Heiko Oberman, have recently begun to offer a more positive assessment of nominalism.[5] According to this view, which we will examine at more length below, nominalism is an attempt, on the one hand, to salvage the theological enterprise from increasing philosophical encroachment, and, on the other hand, to answer the difficult questions about the relationship between divine and human freedom which had yet to be satisfactorily addressed by the Church at that time. With regard to this latter question, Oberman insists that the attempt of Biel to deal with these issues was perfectly in keeping with the perimeters of the Catholic theology of his day, and that, even after the Council of Trent, they were not explicitly condemned. While it is not necessary for our purposes to evaluate Oberman's work, it can be said that the truth about nominalism probably lies somewhere between these two views. While what follows will largely be based on Oberman's study of Gabriel Biel, de Lubac's and Gilson's critique of a rising dualism between the orders of nature and grace should be kept in mind. Again, the Protestant defense of certain aspects of nominalism is often rooted in the twin desire to highlight the necessity of revelation on the one hand and to emphasize the proper autonomy of the secular order on the other. The Catholic critique is often directed at the false autonomy of natural order articulated in various secularist worldviews.[6]

If anything can be said about the variegated theological scene of the late Middle Ages, it is that nearly everybody wanted to be thought of as an 'Augustinian'. The situation at this time was so diverse that Jaroslav Pelikan entitled the first chapter of his volume on the Reformation as, 'Doctrinal Pluralism in the Later Middle Ages'.[7] In this chapter he goes on to point out that, '[t]he growth of medieval theology can be seen as a series of "Augustinian syntheses" ...', and that 'in this sense everyone was an "Augustinian"'.[8] Of course this 'pluralism' arose out of disagreements concerning just what constituted Augustinianism. One school of thought that came about as a result of these discussions is commonly called 'nominalism', and one of its chief theological representatives is Gabriel Biel. It is nearly impossible to understand Luther's theological writings apart from their uneasy relationship to this school of thought.

As mentioned above, another name often given to nominalism by historians is the '*via moderna*', the 'modern way'. This name is intended to distinguish it from the more traditional style of medieval theology – the *via antiqua* – which was associated with the disciples of Thomas Aquinas and Duns Scotus. Adherents of this more traditional school adhered to philosophical realism:

> They held that universal concepts (*universalia*) are more than just human tools to inventory the extramaterial world, but are the expressions of reality itself, indeed that final, higher reality behind all individuality.[9]

In contrast to their realist counterparts, the nominalists denied that such 'universal concepts' were an inherent aspect of the universe, but claimed instead that they were projections upon reality by the human mind. Any knowledge that one may have of these universals is really the result of a mental abstraction from the concrete world of individually existing things. If the purpose of the older school was to make a connection between God and the world, on the grounds that all things owed not only their existence but also their very capacity to be known to the fact that they were originally ideas in the mind of God, the nominalists were intent upon highlighting the absolute otherness of God vis-à-vis the things of this world. Again, it must be remembered that nominalism was directed at the exaggerated claims made by certain philosophers and theologians regarding the sufficiency of reason alone to know God.

As a part of this general concern to distance God from the objects which he created, came a further concern to bring into bold relief the basic weakness of all human reason. If human reason had typically made its most exaggerated claims in the area of metaphysics, nominalism was quick to insist that reason should be limited to those things which can be tested by the senses, quick to insist, that is, that 'all philosophical speculation about the world must be tested by means of experience and reality-based reason …'.[10] It does not take a great deal of foresight to see the effect that this would have on the subsequent study of nature. Soon it would be a commonplace that philosophical knowledge should be derived from the experience of individual objects, while only scripture-based theology should have the right to speak of the non-material world.

Because the classical approach to philosophy was marked by just these sorts of metaphysical speculations, however, the nominalists were forced to take a rather negative view of tradition. A final attribute of this style of thought was, in fact, its relative mistrust of knowledge derived from tradition. Even the precursors of one's own school were not to be trusted without further investigation. One nominalist at the University of Erfurt – Luther's place of education – commented accordingly: 'However important you are, my answer must be: Even great men are sometimes careless and negligent enough to make assertions and statements of which they are not certain.'[11]

These are the general contours, at least, of the basis of the philosophical differences between the *via moderna* and the *via antiqua*. Many of the distinctive elements of nominalist thought were derived from the works of William of Occam (Ockham), but the main theologian of the movement was, likely, Gabriel Biel. This is not to give the impression that 'nominalism' was a tightly defined school of thought, without significant differences from thinker to thinker. The classification, 'nominalist', is simply used by historians to identify certain characteristics of thought which distinguish thinkers of the *via moderna* from the *via antiqua*. While not suggesting that there was a *uniform* school called 'nominalism', it is possible to identify certain such characteristics from its representative thinkers, such as Gregory of Rimini, Pierre d'Ailly, Marsilius von Inghen, and Gabriel Biel, the 'second Occam'. The best way to do this is to examine some of the key terminology of these thinkers, and the manner in which they use it.

One of the key problems for nominalist thought centered around the relationship between God's absolute power (*potentia absoluta*) and God's ordained power (*potentia ordinata*). Although one can find this distinction even in the writings of Aquinas, it takes on a unique theological significance for the first time in the writings of Duns Scotus and William of Occam, where it is used to signify the difference between the power of God as it exists in itself, subject only to the law of non-contradiction, and the power of God as it is operative in the world as it is. In terms of the relationship between philosophy and theology, this distinction has the effect of drastically limiting philosophy's jurisdiction to this-worldly things. The realm of God's *potentia ordinata* is the proper arena of theology alone. If there has been a tendency to equate nominalism as being overly skeptical in this regard, Oberman insists that the nominalists had theological reasons to place such a limitation on philosophical speculation.[12] The impression should not be given, however, that Biel and company denied all knowledge of God to natural reason. On the basis of natural reason one can know that God exists, and even that he is loving and wise. It is true, nonetheless, that this knowledge of God is not innate, but is learned by the *homo viator* through sense experience and abstraction. Indeed, Biel will even say that it is based on a combination of sense knowledge and faith, that it is not *per se nota* (innate). Therefore, while the nominalists are willing to acknowledge a natural knowledge of God, there is a tendency to downplay the immediacy of this knowledge, and even to elevate the necessity of faith at its base. Such a restriction of metaphysics, while not denying the possibility of natural knowledge of God, places it on more historical and empirical grounds, and thereby paves the way for a highlighting of the historical, concrete revelation of God in scripture. This results in the placing of a greater rift between reason and faith than certain theologies of previous eras had admitted.[13]

In the area of theology proper the relationship between the *potentia absoluta* and the *potentia ordinata* takes on a further significance. One of the most controverted theological problems in the late Middle Ages concerned the tension between the justice and grace of God, and the bearing of this tension on the moral accountability of human beings. It is in its attempt to address this question that nominalism becomes most significant for any discussion of Luther's theology, for it is in response to this form of soteriology that Luther presented his unique understanding of justification by faith. Biel, Rimini, d'Ailly and other like-minded theologians worked out their understanding of God's salvific activity in terms of the above distinction between God's absolute and ordained will. In this context they made a further distinction between '*merit de condigno*' and '*merit de congruo*', the former referring to 'full merit', or, that merit which corresponds to the standard of God's justice. Such an act must be performed in a state of grace, and is thereby worthy of divine acceptance. *Merit de congruo*, on the other hand, is that form of merit that only meets the standard of God's mercy, the *misericordia dei*. This latter form of merit is achieved on the basis of pure nature (*ex puris naturalibus*) and concerns one's ability to adhere to the law of God, whether natural or revealed. Although the acts derived from this state of nature are not worthy of merit in terms of God's absolute power, on the basis of God's mercy he deigns to accept them according to his ordained power.[14]

In spite of the fact that one can never satisfy the absolute standard of God's justice, that is, can never merit God's reward in the proper sense, by 'doing what is in one' (*facere quod in se est*), one can merit God's reward according to his mercy. This phrase – *facere quod in se est* – is a favorite among the nominalists and refers to the preparation that can be made for God's grace on the basis of doing one's best to adhere to his commands. Although such activity is not worthy of God's reward in an absolute sense, he does deign, out of mercy (*misericordia dei*), to reward it with the gift of first grace out of his ordained will. 'The tension between God's love and justice is relaxed insofar as the set order is governed by a mitigated form of God's justice.'[15] To clarify this, it should be mentioned that, according to Biel, there are two eternal decrees which come from God. The first has to do with the eternal transition from God's *misericordia* to his *iustitia*. According to this movement, God has chosen, in terms of his contingent will, to subject himself to contingent laws which allow him to accept the one who 'does what is in him'. In all of this, God's absolute will is protected by the arena of his ordained will. The second decree has to do with the same movement from God's mercy to his justice, but this time in terms of the temporal order. God deigns to accept the activity of humanity so that he can reward them with his grace. This movement is from the Incarnation to the last judgement. Once God has accepted the one who has done what is in him, God now expects that one to bring forth acts of love. This means that the one who now acts on the basis of God's grace can merit God's rewards out of justice, and not simply out of mercy.[16]

The question that comes to the center here is what a person, on the basis of nature alone, can contribute to his or her eternal salvation. According to the nominalist perspective, the one who is in a state of 'pure nature' can prepare for first grace in terms of *facere quod in se est* (doing what is in one). Of course a question remains as to who is in such a state. According to the nominalist, only Adam, prior to being infused with 'original justice', was in a state of pure nature. The rest of humanity, subsequent to the fall, is now in a state influenced by the effects of sin. Nonetheless, the influence of sin does not destroy humanity's ability both to know the good, and to make a choice for or against it. In other words, the difference in situation between the state of pure nature and the state of sinfulness does not have a marked effect on Biel's speculations into these issues. If humanity was free to choose between good and evil prior to the fall, this choice is only made more difficult subsequent to it.

> All these obstacles, due partly to man's created condition, partly to the consequences of his initial disobedience, do not, however, diminish the liberty of the will to choose freely between good and evil; they only diminish the ease with which the good acts are elicited.[17]

The difficulties with such a position, theologically, should be obvious; yet there is considerable disagreement over the degree to which Biel and those like him are guilty of Pelagianism. According to Oberman, the nominalists, because they attribute to the human being who is not yet in a state of grace the ability to merit first grace, are Pelagian. George Tavard, however, has insisted that such a charge ignores the difference that the distinction between God's potential and ordained will make in this regard. According to Tavard, the nominalists should not be accused of Pelagianism, because even this first grace is merited, not really on the basis of the value of one's work, but on the basis of God's mercy to accept these works.[18] Harry McSorley, in his study of Luther's doctrine on justification, has identified Biel's and Occam's positions as Semi-Pelagian, on the basis that, in spite of the fact that the nominalists do not maintain that one can merit God's grace according to *merit de condigno*, they still speak of the possibility of meriting first grace on the basis of *facere quod in se est*, apart from the assistance of first grace.[19] A great deal of this debate comes down to semantics and how one interprets the distinction between God's ordained and absolute will. While it would certainly be mistaken to identify the nominalist position with that of Pelagius, who would have maintained that on the basis of the gift of free will alone human beings can merit eternal salvation, it would also be a mistake to treat it as an adequate Catholic view. Not only is it significantly different from the positions of Aquinas and Augustine, it is also not sufficient in terms of the position articulated at Trent.

This brief discussion of late medieval nominalism serves the purpose of preparing the reader for Luther's early disputations, where he both responds to the difficulties, as he sees them, in the position of Biel and Occam, and betrays some of the influence of the *via moderna* on his own thought. The university of Erfurt, where Luther received his philosophical and theological training, while not committed to a particular school of thought according to its statutes 'was nonetheless considered a stronghold of the *via moderna*'.[20] In fact, only four years before Luther enrolled at the university, two of its faculty members, Jodokus Trutfetter and Bartholomaeus Arnoldi held a disputation in front of the entire university in which they presented the basic ideas of nominalism. The most pronounced theme which kept resurfacing in their disputation was this:

> All philosophical speculation about the world must be tested by means of experience and reality-based reason, regardless of what even the most respected authorities might say to the contrary.[21]

While it would be a mistake to overestimate Luther's commitment to nominalism – as we shall see he radically critiqued the nominalist view of salvation – there were certain elements of this school of thought which continued to influence him throughout his theological career. In the first place, there was the subordination of reason to experience. In the second place, there was a fundamental separation between God's word and human reason.[22] In short, God's word, reason, and experience belong together; God's salvation, scripture, and faith belong together. That the nominalist influence upon Luther was a mixed one, however, is verified in the following comment which he made in 1520: 'I demand arguments, not authorities. That is why I contradict even my own school of Occamists, which I have absorbed completely.'[23]

III. Luther's New Approach to Theology

It is in this late medieval context that we must understand Luther's famous *Disputation Against Scholastic Theology* (1517) and his *Heidelberg Disputation*

(1518), and it is here that the basic contours of Luther's entire theological approach emerge: first, justification by faith alone against any trust in human freedom or works, and second, the theology of the cross, against any attempt of human reason to make a claim upon the being of God. In the earlier disputation Luther establishes the following theses in response to the theology of Biel, Scotus and Occam:

> Thesis 10: One must concede that the will is not free to strive toward whatever is declared good. This is in opposition to Scotus and Gabriel.
> Thesis 13: It is absurd to conclude that erring man can love the creature above all things, therefore also God. This in opposition to Scotus and Gabriel.
> Thesis 20: An act of friendship is done, not according to nature, but according to prevenient grace. This in opposition to Gabriel.
> Theses 26 and 27: An act of friendship is not the most perfect means for accomplishing that which is in one. Nor is it the most perfect means for obtaining the grace of God or turning toward and approaching God. But it is an act of conversion already perfected, following grace both in time and by nature.
> Theses 29 and 30: The best and infallible preparation for grace and the sole disposition toward grace is the eternal election and predestination of God. On the part of man, however, nothing precedes grace except indisposition and even rebellion against grace.
> Theses 54 through 56: For an act to be meritorious, either the presence of grace is sufficient, or its presence means nothing. This in opposition to Gabriel. The grace of God is never present in such a way that it is inactive, but it is living, active, and operative spirit … This in opposition to Gabriel. It is not true that God can accept man without his justifying grace. This in opposition to Ockham.[24]

This list of theses from Luther's early disputation is offered here, not because it is representative of Luther's mature theology, but because it brings into bold relief the early stages of Luther's theological concerns in the context of the general opinions of the day. Two things should be noted about the above theses. The first, and most pronounced feature is their utter contempt for the notion that one can prepare for the first grace of God's by 'doing what is in one' (cf. theses 26 and 29). The other thing to be noted is that there is really no trace yet of any juxtaposition of faith and works. In fact, Luther speaks mostly about 'grace', and in this context he is quite clear that when grace is present in the believer it is active. In other words, the precise relationship between law and gospel, faith and works that Luther works out in his studies of Romans and Galatians is not yet articulated.[25]

It is in the *Heidelberg Disputation* (subsequently HD), however, that the basic outline of Luther's later theology begins clearly to emerge, more so even than in the more famous ninety-five theses.[26] Speaking of this disputation, Heinrich Bornkamm has called it the most influential of all of Luther's disputations,[27] and Gerhard Forde said that the theses 'are almost a kind of outline for Luther's subsequent theological program'.[28] Walther von Loewenich has also dispelled the nineteenth-century myth that the 'theology of the cross' which Luther articulates in this disputation is to be attributed only to the early Luther, while he was still under the sway of the mysticism of the late Middle Ages.[29] All of these authors agree that the style of theology that Luther articulates in this disputation is the style that will manifest itself in his subsequent theological work, despite developments on particular issues. Von Loewenich has demonstrated, more specifically, that the 'theology of the cross' is taken up in the more mature works of Luther in terms of the 'hidden God' (*The Bondage of the Will*) and in terms of his understanding of the relationship between reason and faith, and faith and experience. Luther's disputation opens with an assertion that he is not relying on his own wisdom, but that the 'theological paradoxes' which he is about to present are derived from, 'St. Paul, the especially chosen vessel and instrument of Christ, and also from St. Augustine, his most trustworthy interpreter'.[30] Forde begins his study by recalling Bornkamm's interesting analysis of the structure of HD in terms of two pillars: the first pillar is the pillar of the law, which Luther insists is powerless to assist humanity on its way to righteousness; the second is the love of God, which does not find, but creates what is pleasing to it. The way from the law of God to the love of God passes through the cross.[31] The first part – theses 1–12 – of HD deals with the futility of human works and the law in terms of overcoming sin and attaining righteousness. What is interesting about Luther's argument in this section is not so much that he attacks the sinfulness of humanity – even his opponents did this – but that he attacks humanity's goodness. We have already seen how theologians in the late Middle Ages, like Biel, wanted to find a point of continuity between God's righteous demands and human deeds. Even if they stated that God only deigned to reward humanity's efforts on the basis of his mercy, it was still human goodness that was being rewarded. Luther takes the radical position in these early theses that it is precisely human goodness that is most susceptible of being mortally sinful. This is because human goodness cannot help but be co-mixed with pride, and pride is the chief sin for Luther throughout this disputation.[32]

The second thing which makes the first part of HD interesting is that one can see, in a nascent form, the notion of *simil iustus et peccator*. Luther states explicitly that even the works that God does through a person are 'not merits, as though they were sinless'. In other words, he does not deny, yet, the meritorious nature of the good works of the righteous, only that they are sinless. In the explanation for this thesis Luther says the good works of the saints are meritorious for them only because of the fear of their humble confession. He compares God's use of human beings to a skilled laborer's work with a dull hatchet. Even though the agent is skilled, the instrument is imperfect. The final thing to be noted about this first section is its view of the law: in spite of the inherent goodness of the law, it is powerless to help human beings in their quest for righteousness. Indeed, according to Luther, making reference to Romans 5.20, the law actually exacerbates the problem. The point of the first part of the treatise, then, is not to undermine humanity's ability freely to choose goodness; it is to point out that, due to the sinfulness of humanity and the absolute righteousness of God, all of what is best in us is still drastically short of the standard of God, and that even our best efforts are co-mingled with pride. This is why the law is not able to help in this regard: because it remains external to us, it cannot remove the pride at the source of all of our works.[33]

The next section of HD deals with the problem of the free will and its relationship to one's eternal salvation, and is an explicit refutation of the nominalist notion that one can prepare for first grace 'by doing what is in one'. Again, the emphasis is on humility. According to Luther, the very thought that one could freely prepare for first grace betrayed great hubris, because it placed God at the debt of the one striving. Luther likely considered meaningless the nominalist distinction between God's ordained and absolute will. In any case, Luther is prepared for the objection that such pessimism concerning humanity's ability to prepare for first grace could lead to despair or quietism, for he responds that such a realization of the futility of one's works arouses 'the desire to humble oneself and seek the grace of Christ' (Thesis 17).[34] In other words, Luther wants to assure his reader that he is not encouraging people to give up, only to despair of their own abilities, including their own freedom, so that they will rely on the grace of Christ.

Up to this point, Luther's disputation has been directed, again, against certain late medieval notions of the relationship between God's grace and human effort. Although it moves beyond the *Disputation Against Scholastic Theology* in some matters of detail, for instance, in its treatment of the works that are achieved through the assistance of grace, and in its emphasis on humility, it is still directed against the same theses of Biel, Occam, d'Ailly, *et al.* At this point, however, the disputation takes a slight turn in order to address the abilities of human reason to know God and the things of God. Here, Luther is much closer to his nominalist forerunners, except that he tends to base his understanding of the limits of reason more on scriptural than on philosophical grounds. In this next section, in other words, Luther draws the implications of his teaching on human goodness and freedom into his discussion of the competence of human reason.[35] Theses 19–24, then, address the issue of the theology of glory versus the theology of the cross.

It was mentioned above that nominalist thought in general tended to be more skeptical with regard to natural knowledge of God than the *via antiqua* had been. Luther inherits this skepticism and places it on a theological foundation in his theology of the cross. The point of such a move is not to downplay the abilities of human reason as much as to highlight the otherness of God. Luther makes an interesting juxtaposition in this section of the famous text of Romans 1.20 with that of 1 Corinthians 1.25. The former text is part of the much-quoted passage of Paul that was used to establish the validity of 'natural theology'. Luther, however, after referring to the part of the text that claims that the Gentiles knew about the invisible attributes of God through the things that God created, mentions verse 22, which states: 'Claiming to be wise, they became fools.' Immediately Luther makes reference to the Corinthian passage in which Paul states that God's foolishness is wiser than humanity's wisdom. Luther's purpose in bringing these texts into contact in this manner is surely to demonstrate that he is aware of the classical text used in the Middle Ages to support natural knowledge of God: Romans 1.18. In fact, he is quick to point out that it is not knowledge or wisdom in itself that is evil – these, too, are gifts from God – but that human beings, without the theology of the cross, make the worst use out of the best things (cf. Thesis 24). This deserves further explanation.

IV. Luther's Theology of the Cross

Although Luther's theology of the cross is presented most clearly in this early disputation, von Loewenich has argued convincingly that Luther never abandoned the central insights articulated at this early stage. What are those central insights? Again, it must be pointed out that these theses concerning the theology of the cross (19–24) must not be understood apart from the context of the larger disputation. If the context is ignored, it is easy to miss the link that Luther is making between 'doing what is in one' and 'thinking what is in one'. In both cases, Luther is challenging the exaggerated claims that were being made in the late Middle Ages concerning humanity's natural abilities. As von Loewenich puts it, 'Reason is about as helpful in leading us to God as the Law.'[36] This is, perhaps, the shortest possible summary of Luther's position as articulated in this disputation.

> The first two theses of this section are stated accordingly:
> Thesis 19: That person does not deserve to be called a theologian who looks upon the invisible things of God as though they were clearly perceptible in those things which have actually happened [Rom. 1:20].
> Thesis 20: He deserves to be called a theologian, however, who comprehends the visible and manifest things of God seen through suffering and the cross.

As was mentioned before, Luther makes reference to the classic Romans text that was usually invoked to support natural knowledge of God, but instead of quoting the verse usually quoted, he refers to the fact that although certain ones did know about the invisible attributes of God, they did not acknowledge him as God, 'but their foolish hearts were darkened'. Luther draws the conclusion that although it is possible to know about God through nature: (1) it is only the 'invisible' God that can be known, and (2) humanity will inevitably make the worst possible use of such knowledge. Concerning the first of these, Luther's point is that the God who can be known about through his creation is the God who hides himself, the God who would only show Moses his 'back' parts.[37] The invisible attributes of God are here contrasted with his visible attributes, such things as his humanity and his cross, etc., all things which appear to be foolish in the eyes of the 'wise'. In other words, human beings would find it easier to talk about attributes of God such as 'virtue, godliness, wisdom, justice, goodness, and so forth', but because they misused such knowledge, God chose to reveal himself in things which humiliate them, things which would turn their wisdom into folly. That is the chief point of this section of HD: if you want to know about God, look to the cross, for that is where he desires to be known.

We have already stated that this early notion of the theology of the cross is developed later in Luther's idea of the hidden God. David Steinmetz has pointed out that Luther intends his doctrine of the hidden God in two ways: first, God is hidden outside of his revelation in Jesus Christ in such a way that what can be known about him through nature and reason is useless to the sinner; second, God continues to hide himself in revelation, hiding himself in the very act of revealing himself.[38] The first serves the purpose of radically downplaying the importance given to natural theology in certain forms of medieval theology, the second serves the purpose of protecting the inscrutability and otherness of God even in his self-revelation in Jesus Christ. Once more, this should not be taken to mean that Luther is a skeptic; his disdain for natural theology is not based on his maintaining that God is not present in his creation, but on the fact that God is so transcendent that, outside of Christ, human beings do not know what to make of such knowledge. Steinmetz puts this accordingly:

> The transcendence of God is not equivalent to his absence. On the contrary, transcendence means that, while God is present in every creature that surrounds me, his presence is inaccessible to me apart from his Word.[39]

This also serves the purpose of focusing theological discussion on those things which have been clearly revealed in God's Word. This became especially important in the debate with Erasmus because Erasmus kept pointing to the fact that it would be unjust for God to condemn some to Hell apart from their free will. Luther responded that such concerns on Erasmus' part were speculative, that he was seeking explanations for things that were God's business alone. In this context Luther was always telling his hearers not to concern themselves with the hidden God of predestination, but with the God who comes to them in the loving person of Jesus Christ. It was necessary, in this context, to know *about* the hidden God, but to *know* the revealed God of Jesus Christ.[40]

The theology of the cross serves the purpose, then, of protecting God from the encroachments of human beings into his freedom and transcendence. This has both soteriological and theological implications: in terms of the former, it means that God's will to save is based on his grace alone, not on what we have done to prepare for it; in terms of the latter it means that the knowledge of God that amounts to anything in our standing with him is derived, not from our search for him, nor from the knowledge of him we derive from his works, but from his gracious coming to us in the person and work of his son, Jesus Christ. We will address the degree to which this approach to theology parallels that of Balthasar momentarily, but first it is necessary to examine, briefly, the development of Luther's thought on justification as it appears in *The Freedom of a Christian* and the Galatians commentary of 1535.

V. The Righteousness of God

The theme of God's righteousness clearly served as the impetus for Luther's early break with late medieval nominalism, but he developed his understanding of it in his later confrontations with Catholic theologians as well. As the early shape of this discussion centered around the question of preparing for first grace – and here it must be conceded on all sides that Luther was closer to the Catholic tradition than his nominalist opponents – in later discussions Luther's position became more precisely defined, addressing the Catholic notion that faith must be formed by love. In this discussion Luther clarifies his position on the relationship between law and gospel, the relationship between faith and works, and finally the relationship between faith and love. In its most basic form, Luther's position can be captured in the early lines of his treatise on Christian freedom: 'A Christian is a perfectly free lord of all, subject to none. A Christian is a perfectly dutiful servant of all, subject to all.'[41] Luther is now beyond the question of merely what one can do to prepare for first grace, and the theme of humility no longer has the central place that it had in his early disputations. The question now is this: What is the basis of my being declared righteous before God?

It is well known that Luther claims, in his later reflections on his work, to have had a theological breakthrough concerning the Pauline phrase 'righteousness of God'. According to Luther's later recollections, this phrase, which had once been a source of terror to him, interpreted as that righteousness whereby God judged sinners, became a great source of comfort when he discovered that it meant that righteousness which God attributes to the sinner on the basis of his or her faith in Christ.[42] In *The Freedom of a Christian* Luther expounds on this understanding of righteousness in terms of a series of pairs: commandments and promises, works and faith, law and gospel, outer man and inner man, love and faith, bondage and freedom. The conclusions he draws from these pairs is relatively simple: since the scripture can be divided into two parts – commands and promises – it is only left to determine which part fits which situation. The commandments of scripture are intended to reveal to us the will of God; they tell us what we ought to do in order to be righteous; yet they do not empower us to perform what they command us to do. It is here that the promises of scripture fit: they tell us what is available to us in Christ if we have faith in him. 'Believe in Christ and the commands are fulfilled ... Promises give what commands demand.'[43] The purpose of the commands, in this view, is to press upon the hearer the need for Christ.

The question which this immediately raises for Luther's opponents is this: Does not this insistence that one need only believe in Christ in order to be declared righteous promote a certain idleness? But Luther is quite clear at this point that what is given to us in Christ is really given to us; we are really given Christ in our faith, so that his qualities are now imparted to the soul of the believer. 'Just as heated iron glows like fire because of the union of fire with it, so the Word imparts its qualities to the soul.'[44] There are many other quotes throughout this treatise which should dispel any notion that Luther's understanding of justification is merely forensic. Accordingly, Paul Althaus can state, 'It should also be noted that according to these passages, the word not only declares that man is righteous but also gives him a new being.' And later: 'Faith therefore does not justify by itself but only because Christ makes himself present in us through it.'[45]

Yet neither should we forget that this righteousness, for Luther, is still an 'alien' righteousness: it is Christ's, and in relation to it the believer is completely passive. The reason for this has to do with Luther's notion of the *fröhliche Wechsel*, the 'joyful exchange'. Here Luther draws heavily on the imagery of the marriage that occurs, through faith, between the soul and Christ:

> Christ and the soul become one flesh ... Christ is full of grace, life, and salvation. The soul is full of sins, death, and damnation. Now let faith come between them

> and sins, death, and damnation will be Christ's, while grace, life, and salvation will be the soul's.[46]

It is in this manner that Luther can say, at one and the same time, that the righteousness that the believer has in faith is really present in him, yet it is not his. Furthermore, the judgement that God makes of the believer is not based on the degree to which his 'outer man' has been made to conform to his 'inner man', but is based solely on the presence of faith, and therefore Christ, in the believer's soul. Thus gospel, justification, Christ, faith and the inner man go together, while law, sanctification, works, love and the outer man go together.

Here Luther thinks he has found Paul's middle ground between works righteousness and antinomianism. He avoids 'works righteousness' by attributing justification to the faith that receives the benefits of Christ. He avoids antinomianism by insisting that true faith will always issue forth in works, in the love of God and love of neighbor. It is only that one must not place one's confidence in these latter. 'He needs neither laws nor good works but, on the contrary, is injured by them if he believes he is justified by them.'[47] So, faith does not free us from doing good works, but it does free us from false notions about such works. Such paradoxical statements lead Althaus to the following conclusion: '[Luther] says that good works, the "works of grace," are necessary. At the same time, he refuses to characterize them as necessary for salvation and for justification.'[48]

Already in this treatise on Christian freedom Luther has insisted that salvation is by faith alone, and he has alluded to the fact that the love that follows from this faith is on the works side of the equation, that justification is based upon our faith alone and not on the love that will automatically issue forth from true faith. It is not until the 1535 Galatians commentary that Luther fully articulates his response to his opponents' suggestion that faith without love is incomplete, formless. In an incisive article on Luther's notion of justification in the 1535 Galatians commentary, Peter Manns addresses this dividing issue between Luther and his interlocutors.[49] Although many people have tried to trace Luther's departure from the Catholic understanding of salvation to his treatment of the relationship between faith and love/works, Manns insists that Luther's polemical context must be kept in mind. His main point is that, considering the fact that most of Luther's opponents held to a heretical view – and this is by Catholic standards – of the role of works in the salvation process, Luther's almost obsessive desire to protect justification from any dependence on human works is justified. And this must be remembered even if one must finally acknowledge that Luther went too far in distinguishing faith and love.

It is in this 1535 commentary that Luther makes his clearest statements concerning the relationship between the law and the gospel. To the law corresponds what Luther calls active righteousness: prior to faith the law serves the purpose of keeping societal order in the face of sinful humanity, and also of pointing out to the conscience its sinfulness and hopelessness before God. After faith, the law serves the purpose of assisting the believer in the continued mortification of the flesh that is still required even after one's justification. Because the believer remains *simul iustus et peccator* (simultaneously justified and sinner), the believer must actively pursue what he has already passively received. Again, one's justification depends only on one's trust in Christ, not on the degree to which one has progressed in making this an external reality. Luther identifies this dual situation of the believer in terms of two kinds of righteousness: the first is passive, and merely receives what Christ has already accomplished, the second is active and consists in mortifying the sins that remain in the flesh. Luther's concern here is always pastoral, and he exhorts Christian teachers to comfort the anxious Christian by bringing them 'from the Law to grace, from active righteousness to passive righteousness, in short, from Moses to Christ'.[50]

Two difficulties arise in this regard: first, in this polemical situation in which Luther wants to safeguard justification from the necessity of active righteousness, he relegates love to the side of the law, to the side of active righteousness; secondly, he uses a rather unfortunate christological illustration to make his case. With regard to the first of these, according to the tradition of Thomas Aquinas, or, in Luther's day, Cajetan, love itself was understood as one of the theological virtues, or, as a gift of God given to the believer, and so was not understood as a human work. In the case of the second of these, in Luther's insistence on distinguishing between 'absolute' and 'incarnate' faith, relegating the passive righteousness by which we are saved to the former, and the active righteousness by which we mortify the flesh to the latter, he used the doctrine of the two natures of Christ to make his case. Luther insists that just as everything divine was attributed to the man Jesus on account of his divinity – here Luther is drawing on the patristic notion of the communication of attributes between the human and divine Christ – so everything that is attributed to the working Christian is accountable to his faith.[51] Congar has drawn attention to the problems with this use of Christology, not the least of which is a basic denial of salvific efficacy to the humanity of Christ. Completely lacking in such a construal is the patristic notion that what is assumed by Christ is redeemed precisely because it is assumed, or – at the risk of being anachronistic – the insistence of *Gaudium et Spes* that in uniting himself with human nature, Jesus somehow united himself with each and every one of us.[52] Congar's conclusion is that this is the basis of Luther's refusal to speak of human cooperation with the work of God. Yet Peter Manns is quick to point out that it is really not fair to Luther to take this passage on Christology, which is obviously used in a polemical situation, as representative of Luther's typical Christology. He goes on to show that elsewhere, in fact, Luther's Christology is much more 'orthodox'.[53] It is only that,

> whenever Luther confronts the problem of justification as a case of applied Christology as he did here, he is apprehensive of endangering both the divinity and grace with a 'monophysitical' or 'monistic' attempt at a solution.[54]

VI. Balthasar and Luther

Although Balthasar's theological setting was radically different from Luther's, both men were, in a sense, reformers, and both men saw the key to reform in a renewed focus on the person and work of Christ. We have already examined evidence of Luther's reaction to late medieval Scholasticism, but let us now listen to Balthasar's recollections concerning his own theological training:

> My entire period of study in the Society [of Jesus] was a grim struggle with the dreariness of theology, with what men had made out of the glory of revelation. I could not endure this presentation of the Word of God. I could have lashed out with the fury of a Samson. I felt like tearing down, with Samson's strength, the whole temple and burying myself beneath the rubble.[55]

Balthasar's complaint with regard to his Jesuit training was, in short, that the glory of Christ was being obscured by a philosophical system that did not do justice to God's self-revelation in Christ. In fact, theological method was determined long before theological content was given a serious consideration. Neo-Scholasticism never imagined, in Balthasar's view, that the traditional Chalcedonian Christology might shed light on, for instance, the relationship between philosophy and theology. With Luther, then, Balthasar called for a new and radically christocentric approach to theology.[56]

However, lest we too get 'carried away by ecumenism', it must be noted that Balthasar's theological aesthetics is a two-edged sword, and, as such, it cuts both ways. If theological aesthetics makes it possible for Balthasar's so-called Fundamental Theology to proceed under a certain christological light, it also makes it possible for him to insist on a real analogy between inner-worldly beauty and the revelation of God's glory in Christ. To recall what was said in Chapter 1 about theological aesthetics, Balthasar understands Christianity as mediating between the two historical tendencies toward the mythological and the philosophical. The mythological view of the relationship between God and world has the advantage of bringing out the personal nature of God, and the fact that God is involved with the fate of humanity. In the words of Balthasar:

> The first image of God, that of *myth*, could be described as the religious projection of the primal experience of loving common humanity, though undeniably interwoven (and not a little obscured) by the existential feelings that man has in face of the strangeness and superior power of nature and of Being as a whole … This God is understood … as a somebody, as *one* in a manner that is not the object of conscious reflection …[57]

Although there are many advantages to this understanding of God, it is limited by its anthropocentrism, that is, by the fact that its image of God hardly exceeds that of the whimsical behavior of a mere mortal writ large. Herein lies the origins of the battle between the poets and philosophers in antiquity, which culminated in the expulsion of the poets from Plato's *Republic.*

On the other side of this equation lies the image of God in the philosophers. Acknowledging the great diversity among the ancient philosophers as to the supreme being, the difference between the philosophical and mythological understanding of God lies in the tendency of the former to think of God in terms of absolute being. From the time of Parmenides, Greek philosophy concerned itself with the unity, eternity and infinitude of that which is. Speculation concerning such all-encompassing being led to a denial of the reality of the world of matter and change in Parmenides' philosophy, but even Plato and Aristotle did not fully escape his conclusions. Both Plato and Aristotle, that is, are concerned to define their 'gods' in terms which transcend the conditional world, and it is here that they understood the gods of Homer to be lacking.

> The primary dualistic division of Being into an immortal world of the gods and a mortal world of men … reduces the divine in its power and freedom to an inappropriate finitude and keeps it dependent on something dark and ineffable that is antecedent to the split into two worlds (*moira*).[58]

It is this subjection of the gods to the all-encompassing realm of good and evil that proves unsatisfactory for Plato and Aristotle; it is no accident that Plato essentially defines his 'god' as the 'Good'. Again, however, there is a price to be paid for the removal of God from the world of change, from the world in which humanity strives to live the good life.

> This absolute can indeed still be the cause of all that exists in Plato as the 'ideal of the good' (*Republic* VI, 505A) and the sun that casts its rays everywhere (ibid.,

> 508B), by 'towering above reality in sublimity and power' (509C), but it can no longer be conceived as personal love (except once again in the myth of the *Timaeus*, for example).[59]

What is gained by removing God from history, as it were, is lost in not being able to explain the loving or donating aspect of all reality, and this forces Plato to lapse, from time to time, back into myth to supplement his philosophical speculations. Even as Plato banishes the poets, he must incorporate them.

All that can be said at this point regarding Balthasar's solution to this classical dilemma is that his theological aesthetics, based as it is on the fact that the Christian God became an actor in the human drama, attempts to do justice to the partial truth of both of these approaches. This will be taken up later in more detail, but it is being introduced now in order to set up Balthasar's response to Luther's theological approach. Once more, what Balthasar endorses regarding Luther's theology is his insistence that it is the free activity of God which constitutes the basis of the Christian religion, and the fact that this activity culminates in the death and resurrection of the Son of God, events which are not only inaccessible to human reason, but even appear to it as foolishness. As to the other aspect of theological aesthetics, however, the notion that the concrete can really manifest the eternal, that God need not fear the legitimate accomplishments of nature because he is its source and end, and that, furthermore, as a result of the incarnation, God has totally transformed nature to its very core in such a way that it can now serve as the medium of that which is divine, Balthasar finds Luther to be wanting. In order to unpack this criticism, however, we must look further at Balthasar's explicit criticisms of Luther's work.

VII. Balthasar on Luther's Soteriology

We have already examined the fact that Luther's central theological concern centered upon the need to protect the free and gracious decision of God to justify the sinner from any attempt to explain this salvific act in terms of human accomplishment. If human beings can do something to elicit God's first act of mercy, then salvation itself is dependent upon human capacities rather than on the grace of God, so the argument goes. This central concern was, according to Balthasar, a reaction to the late medieval lapse into semi-Pelagianism, which was, furthermore, the logical soteriological consequence of the 'non-dialectical schemata of Neo-Platonic aesthetic metaphysics'.[60] This metaphysical 'schemata' equates the world with the appearance of the non-appearing, so that the realm of creation touches the realm of the deity 'ontologically, ethically, and mystically', culminating in the contemplation of the supratemporal world of ideas. Soteriologically, this 'continuum' between creation and creator is just what Luther could not abide because it denied the gratuity of God's gift of salvation. According to Balthasar, Luther wanted to recover: (1) the free creator God in the face of any form of emanationism, (2) the even less comprehensible redeeming God, who turns to the sinner without any previous achievement on the sinner's part, an act that can be received only in faith, and (3) the *absconditas Dei sub contrario*, the fact that God chooses to veil his appearance to his creatures under things which are contrary to his nature, that is, in the manger in Bethlehem, in the rejected prophet, and, ultimately, on the cross. 'In this light, we can understand Luther's attack on the "whore" Reason, which aesthetically attempts to achieve a harmony between divinity and humanity.'[61]

Balthasar, accordingly, situates Luther's theology in the context of the late medieval mystical theology which was reacting to the Gnostic tendencies of certain forms of late medieval Scholasticism. In his discussion of 'Metaphysics in the Modern Age', Balthasar explicitly identifies Luther as the theological heir of the 'metaphysics of the saints', and more particularly, of mystics such as Catherine of Genoa.[62] In other words, Luther is the recipient of a breakdown of the Thomistic synthesis in which the tendencies between rationalism and fideism become ever more pronounced, and, with these, the gulf between theology and sanctity. *Saint* Catherine of Genoa; *Doctor* Gabriel Biel.[63] Once the balance which Thomas had achieved is lost,

> there are only two possible ways forward: either to formalize Being to the extent that it becomes the comprehensive concept of reason ... and thus expressly or by implication to concede to reason the oversight and control of Being.[64]

Or,

> simply to identify [Being] (once again) with God, as Meister Eckhart does, thus setting his stamp upon the conceptual model of late-medieval mysticism and to a large extent upon that of its spiritual descendants ... But if in the development of the Scotist model reason gains the upper hand over God, then in the logic of the Eckhartian model it is difficult to see how there can exist a world outside of God.[65]

As we shall see, it is an abiding concern of Balthasar that the 'Eckhartian model' had an adverse effect on the theology of Protestantism from its very beginning, and that neither the theology of Luther, nor that of Barth is totally without the deleterious effects of this metaphysics. It could be argued that Balthasar's conceptual construal of history into such neat categories does not do justice to the novelty of individual thinkers, but nowhere does Balthasar reduce Luther's, or Barth's, thought to the 'system' of a Meister Eckhart. He only suggests that Luther's theology was not without its tendency to denigrate the created realm to such a degree that all that was left was the pure actuality of God, and this to such a degree that it is now difficult to see any continuity between the work of God in creation and his work in redemption.

To recall the suggestion above that Balthasar thus situates Luther in the theological wake of Catherine of Genoa *et al.*, Balthasar sums up the latter's 'metaphysics' accordingly: 'God is Being and the self-diffusive Good who gives form to all things. The creature, of itself, is nothing, indeed sin …' He quotes her statement that, 'All the glory is God's, all the malice is man's.' And later, 'I see clearly that all the good that is in me or in any other creature and even in the saints is God's alone.' No one can deny that statements such as these recall Luther's notion of the 'alien' righteousness of Christ, in the face of which the believer is purely passive.[66] Typical of the late medieval mystical solution to the problem of God's justice and mercy is Catherine's emphasis on the simultaneity of one's unworthiness and worthiness before God, of the simultaneity of God's judgement and love. Balthasar sums up this train of thought accordingly.[67] To allow things to stand in such a paradoxical tension is one of the traits of the spirituality which stems from Eckhart's work, and is a sign that spirituality has been largely severed from the theology of the schools. Before returning to this theme, we must take up Balthasar's explicit critique of the soteriological direction which this type of thinking takes in Luther's work.

In Balthasar's treatment of soteriology in *Theo-Drama* IV, he identifies five characteristics of the New Testament presentation of Christ's atoning death, maintaining that all of these five elements must be brought together in any adequate theology of atonement. The *first* thing to be noted is that it is Jesus who is both given up, out of the love of the Father (John 3:16), and who gives himself up: he is both 'lamb' and 'priest'. *Secondly*, this giving up of himself is taken to the level where he actually *exchanges* places with us. This was known, by the Fathers, as the *admirabile commercium*, the 'happy exchange', which attempts to incorporate the biblical notions that he became poor so that we could become rich, and the like. *Thirdly*, this death in our behalf results in our 'negative' liberation *from* sin, which leads directly to the *fourth* aspect: our liberation from sin has its 'positive' counterpart in the gift of the Holy Spirit, which restores our lost freedom. *Finally*, all of this stems from the fact that God is, in his deepest nature, infinite love, and it is on this basis that he is willing to give up his son for us.[68]

Balthasar goes on to trace the historical development of the Church's soteriology with the following introductory statement:

> These are the dangers to be avoided. 1) No aspect must be allowed to dominate and so diminish the significance of the others. 2) The full content of the central assertion (which is the goal of all five aspects) may not be replaced by some alleged equivalent that is more 'intelligible' to the spirit of a different epoch but in fact lacks the center of gravity of the biblical assertion. 3) The tension that exists between two aspects must not be slackened, let alone dissolved, in the interests of an illusory synthesis: rather, it must be endured. The history of soteriology gives us examples of all three dangers. With regard to the first danger, there was a theology of the 'exchange' which failed to do justice to the first aspect; a theology of liberation which failed to pay sufficient attention to aspects 1, 2, and 4; and a theology of reconciliation which did not take aspects 1 and 2 seriously enough.[69]

After giving a fairly close examination of the way in which these themes are played out in the theology of the Fathers and then in the Middle Ages, Balthasar turns his attention to the approach taken by Martin Luther under the heading, 'substitution'. In the face of such philosophical/psychological models as Karl Rahner's model of 'solidarity',[70] Luther's model of substitution 'strikes like a thunderbolt'. Simply put, Luther pays almost exclusive attention to the fact that Christ, in his crucifixion and resurrection, stood in the place of humanity, so that what was ours, sin, death, poverty, etc., became his, and what was his, righteousness, life, wealth, etc., became ours.[71]

While it is true that in highlighting this '*fröhliche Wechsel*', Luther is recalling the patristic notion of the *admirabile commercium*, the emphasis is no longer on the exchange of the divine and creaturely nature. 'The aspect of divinization is relegated completely.'[72] Yet nobody takes more seriously than does Luther the notion, articulated most clearly in 2 Corinthians 5.21, that Christ became sin so that we might become righteous. What makes this even more shocking, according to Luther, is that Christ does not simply experience our experience of sin, for when we sin we never fully understand the entire gravity or full implications thereof; instead, Christ, who was sinless according to his life, became sin with full knowledge of the utter God-forsakenness that belongs to this state.[73] The alert reader may begin to glimpse, at this point, the origins of Balthasar's difficulties with a construction which focuses all of its attention on the exchange aspect of the atonement, and this, not in terms of Christ's giving us a share in his divinity, but, primarily, in terms of his taking on our sin so that we might be attributed his righteousness.[74]

The difficulties which Balthasar sees at this point echo those of Congar mentioned in the previous section: that is, Luther's Christology, rather than determining his soteriology, rather derives from it. This forces Luther to speak of Christ as the origin of the *simul iustus et peccator*. Christ's humanity, in this context, is given a purely passive role in the salvation process. Here Balthasar also mentions Luther's depiction of Christ's humanity serving as the bait which the devil is duped into taking, only to find out that he cannot abide the divinity, which remains hidden.[75]

This depiction both motivates and derives from Luther's understanding of two kinds of righteousness which was discussed in the previous section. Luther is so concerned with protecting the realm of 'justification' from any dependence upon 'sanctification' that he is forced to separate the unified process of grace: 'Artificially, but very deliberately, the unity of grace – which justifies *and* sanctifies – is torn asunder.'[76] And, therefore, the unity of Christ as *sacramentum* and *exemplum* is also torn asunder. The justified sinner is left in a situation which can only be expressed in paradoxes, and this follows from the fact that Christ himself is at once,

> the poor and the rich, the strong and the weak, the confused and the composed, the sad and the merry, the forsaken and the powerfully protected, the rejected and the chosen, and ultimately, fearful man and God – all these meet in one and the same Person.[77]

Missing here is the connection between Christ's incarnation, with its soteriological implications, and his passion. The entire patristic and biblical notion that the work which God began in creation is now given its true form in Christ, 'the recapitulation of all things', is either missing or radically downplayed in this view. As a result of Luther's unwillingness to speak of any continuity between creation and redemption, and this stems from an insufficient distinction between creatureliness and sinfulness on his part, it is difficult to see how the person who is justified is really the same person whom God created. 'We can no longer tell whether man, who is both a sinner and righteous, is one or two; we can no longer tell whether he is a subject enjoying continuity.'[78]

Of course such an interpretation would eliminate the aesthetic sensibilities of a Balthasar from the realm of legitimate theology. For Balthasar, where there is true life, there can be no opposition between form and appearance: this is the heart of the aesthetic approach. Because Luther focused so heavily on the contrast between faith and works, and Balthasar admits that his semi-Pelagian adversaries are partly to blame for the position which Luther finally took, it was impossible for him to articulate consistently the essential unity of the life-giving Spirit and the fruit which it produces. It is here that Balthasar wishes to suggest a move beyond the categories of either Luther or his contemporaries, a move away from the juridical, extrinsic categories of merit and the like, toward the more organic categories of the scriptures.

Let us be clear at this point: Balthasar is not saying that Luther was wrong in his insistence on the priority of grace in the salvation process; on this point he was right and his nominalist adversaries were wrong. Balthasar's difficulties arise with Luther's separation, no doubt elicited by the polemical situation in which he found himself, of the act of faith, which leads to justification, from the subsequent act of love (i.e., works) which contributes to our sanctification (i.e., active righteousness). This is made clear in what Balthasar says in the following:

> If Christ's obedience was the expression of his perfect love for the Father and for men … then Christian *following in faith*, too, can find its *ultimate meaning only in love.* Luther got this elementary idea wrong, unfortunately, when he created antithetical pairs of concepts: faith–justification and love–work.[79]

For Balthasar, as for Ignatius, and it would be difficult to exaggerate the degree to which Balthasar's soteriology is Marian–Ignatian, faith is already the first movement of love:

> Against [Luther's understanding], Ignatius understands faith … as a movement of love that makes directly toward the person of Jesus, hears his call to follow him and answers by 'leaving all and following'.[80]

This refusal to separate the first act of faith from the discipleship which issues from it, even if for theological reasons, is a consistent aspect of Balthasar's critique of Luther's solution. Once again, and in keeping with the same theme, Balthasar states,

> The deepest deficiency in Luther's construction is that it makes far too wide a separation, for polemical reasons, between justifying faith and love (which is assigned to the 'works'); for it is not obvious why the original pure faith, which as such is based on pure grace, should not already be the first act of the unconditional gift man makes of himself to God, the act that is the basis of everything else.[81]

The fact that this first act of 'pure faith', which contains in itself the first movement of love for God on the believer's part, is based on 'pure grace', and not on any prior decision or activity, should assuage any fears that Balthasar is endorsing a 'works righteousness'. This is made clear throughout *Theo-Drama* IV in terms of the fact that finite freedom is always operative *within* the realm of infinite freedom. In a discussion of Kierkegaard's *The Sickness unto Death*, Balthasar notes that human beings are a riddle to themselves, for while they contain a 'natural desire' for God, they are incapable, in their autonomy, to grasp the one thing that will fulfill them. Here is the great paradox which marks all human existence: it is only in giving up one's claim to self-fulfillment that one is ready to touch one's true end.

> [Kierkegaard] shows that created freedom cannot be brought to a state of 'balance' between its opposing elements unless it recognizes its creatureliness, its 'transparency,' allowing God to shine through.[82]

It is not necessary to bring in de Lubac's treatment of the nature–grace problematic at this point, but it should be said that Balthasar agrees that one does not have to posit a supernatural element in order to explain humanity's natural desire for God.[83] We will discuss this at greater length in the next chapter.

The point to be made at this time is that far from having a claim on the grace of God on the basis of some previous action, human beings, who already long for God on the basis of creation, must despair of their own efforts if they are to be united with this God, on the basis of supernatural grace. The key notion here is that of 'indifference', and it is here that Balthasar thinks that he can do justice to Luther's concerns without abandoning the Catholic concern for the necessity of faith being formed by love. In the mystical insistence on the priority of contemplation Balthasar thinks that he has found an alternative to the nominalist's 'doing what is in one' on the one hand, and Luther's '*sola fide*' on the other. This primarily contemplative viewpoint was championed, almost exclusively, by the mystical tradition in the late Middle Ages,[84] and,

> is later given the more scriptural expression in Ignatius of Loyola that at the origin of every differentiated task given to a Christian life there must stand an act of absolute *indifferentia* (i.e., *indifferentia* in immediacy to God) that is above all the pure readiness for everything, the pure act of allowing validity to everything that God can dispose in his word, and thus stands very close to Luther's pure faith.[85]

What flows out of this primary stance of readiness is based purely on grace (the stance of readiness is itself already the result of God's previous activity), resulting in the fact that 'the useless sinner, contrary to all expectations, should become usable for the Lord thanks to the pure grace of the Cross (and not to any synergism!)'.[86]

VIII. Balthasar on Luther's 'Fundamental' Theology

What has been said so far concerning Balthasar's assessment of Luther has to do with the issues surrounding soteriology, and makes no claim of being an exhaustive treatment, for this would require a much fuller discussion of the relationship between nature and grace, the nature of human freedom, the role of Mary–Church, and the like; instead, we have merely attempted to address those aspects of Balthasar's soteriology which come directly to bear upon the questions raised by Luther in the previous sections.

The complete ramifications of this 'aesthetic' approach for the nature of theology will emerge fully only in the next three chapters, but we can at least try to tease out some of the implications from this approach as they relate to Luther's understanding of the nature of theology. In other words, it is time to shift attention, albeit briefly, from issues of soteriology to the implications that these issues have for Fundamental Theology. It has already been shown that Luther's understanding of the relationship between natural theology and positive theology flowed quite directly from his understanding of the relationship between works and faith, nature and grace, law and gospel. While Luther does not deny that there is a knowledge of God available to human beings through creation, he is equally insistent that such knowledge does human beings little good in their presently fallen state; that is, they will either make an idol of it which they can manipulate, or they will come face to face with the invisible God, with whom Luther wants nothing to do![87] This is in complete accordance with Luther's teaching on the law and its relation to the gospel: all that the law can do is to terrify its recipient into the gracious arms of God. This recalls, also, the above discussion of Luther's theology of the cross. As Althaus points out:

> Luther feels that since man's fall into sin true theology is possible only as theology of the cross ... Luther can say that the wisdom with which man learns to know God in his works is, in itself, just as good as God's law. Like all good gifts, however, this one is used by the sinner to exalt himself. Therefore only the theology of the cross now leads to a true knowledge of God.[88]

This summary by Althaus is illustrative of the difference between Luther's theology of the cross and Balthasar's. Before concluding this chapter it will be helpful to look at Balthasar's understanding of the relationship between the cross and its implications for theo-logic. It must be remembered that for both thinkers the cross is central to all true theology.

In *Mysterium Paschale*[89] Balthasar explicitly takes up the theme of the theology of the cross in terms of its effects on human knowing. It will be helpful to keep in mind the role that the cross is given in Luther's theology, and von Loewenich's assertions that this approach is not to be relegated to the early Luther. Instead, as von Loewenich has shown, it lives on in his notion of the hidden God and the notion that God reveals himself *sub contrario*. Like Luther, Balthasar's theology of the cross is intended to cut across all human attempts to approach God from 'this side'. The cross confounds all of our human expectations regarding the nature of God and what God should do in our behalf: it is 'foolishness to the Gentiles' and 'a stumbling block' to the Jews. Indeed, Balthasar castigates much previous Catholic theology for attempting to harmonize human reason and God's self-revelation while ignoring the full implications of the cross.[90] In order to correct such an omission, Balthasar insists that God is revealed to us fully only in the event of the cross. He begins his discussion by laying out the implications of the 'hiatus' that occurs when Jesus Christ dies:

> If without the Son no one can see the Father (John 1.18), nor anyone come to the Father (John 14.6), and if, without him, the Father is revealed to nobody (Matthew 11.27), then when the Son, the Word of the Father is dead, then no one can see God, hear of him or attain him.[91]

The remainder of this chapter of MP is a discussion of various attempts to bridge this hiatus. The first thing to be noticed is the role that the hiatus has in itself: it is precisely the radically unbridgeable nature of this event that 'makes the eyes of faith take notice'.[92] And yet if we rest content with the unbridgeable nature of it, that is, if we are to rest content with Luther's *sub contrario*, it becomes impossible to explain the continuity between the crucified and risen Lord.

> If we rest content with the simple *sub contrario*, then we shall be forced to take the path that travels from Luther to Hegel. A purely dialectical Christology becomes transformed into a sheerly 'philosophical' dialectic, into a 'worldly' discourse.[93]

What is intended, in Luther, to guard against any merely human way to God, through works or reason, becomes itself the key to all theological riddles. The 'analogy' presupposed in the Chalcedonian formula is replaced by Luther's '*simul–et*'. Balthasar quotes Eric Seeberg accordingly:

> It is, then, in Christ that Luther discovers the fundamental law which holds good in life: he is simultaneously cursed and blessed …, simultaneously living and dead, simultaneously grieving and joyful. In him is prefigured the great 'simultaneously' which constitutes the fundamental idea of the doctrine of justification – simultaneously just, and a sinner … – which is so easily and quickly distorted into a 'one after the other' … In Christ, we see the way in which God acts at large, namely, in opposition to reason, evidence and so on.[94]

The danger of Luther's approach is that it fails to appreciate fully the *revelatory* aspect of the cross, that on the other side of this event, and even in the event itself, there is a light that is shed on the entirety of human experience, so that Balthasar can say:

> But if it is true that in Luther's *sub contrario* the 'absolute paradox' (of Kierkegaard) comes to expression, there can be, nonetheless, no resting with this static form of expression. The paradoxical formulation has, rather, an inner dynamism which manifests itself in purposiveness (became poor, *so that* you might become rich). This finality kindles a kind of light in the darkness of rational incomprehensibility. This light is the light of love … [95]

The tightrope which Balthasar is trying to walk here is between a view that would, on the one hand, see the cross as simply another example of a general truth – i.e., that God is always, already reconciled to the world

– and a view which, on the other hand, would fail to see that the glory of God is revealed precisely in this event of self-giving, that the most intimate *truth* about God and humanity is revealed here and is not to be derived outside of this event.[96]

What this implies about our knowledge of God is something that is expressed quite radically in Balthasar's thought: while there has been a tendency in Christian history to understand God in terms of the static philosophical concept of being, thus making it difficult to account for the Trinitarian, self-giving nature of God, and while Luther would rather wish to drive a wedge between the knowledge of God obtained through creation and the knowledge obtained through the cross, Balthasar wishes to understand all being in terms of this event. In other words, between the extremes of understanding God in terms of this-worldly reality, and suggesting a dialectical relationship between this-worldly reason and God's reason, Balthasar wishes to allow our conception of reality itself to be modified by the event of the cross.[97] Ultimately, Balthasar is portraying a christological understanding of the analogy of being.

> If we take a retrospective glance at what has been said above about the Kenosis and the Lamb slain in heaven (namely, Christ as archetype of man), we should realize that those representations which see in the Cross of Christ a principle that founds, and hold [*sic*] together, the cosmos do not necessarily abandon the terrain of Christian theology. This is just what Augustine says in the *De Civitate Dei* X. 20 in describing the meaning (the fulfillment) of the world as the attachment of humankind as a whole to the eternal sacrifice of adoration offered by Christ to the Father.[98]

Here we see Balthasar's attempt to keep the patristic notion of Christ as 'recapitulation' together with a focus on the uniqueness of the event of the cross. The only bridge over that hiatus which Balthasar depicted at the beginning of this chapter, then, is the word of Christ itself; all previous conceptions of God must pass through the purifying fire of this event: 'Remember how he told you, while he was still in Galilee, that the Son of man must (*dei*) be delivered into the hands of sinful men, and be crucified, and on the third day rise.'[99] That is, even for those who were closest to Christ in his earthly life, it was only possible to understand his person and mission in the retrospective gaze of the cross. In the post-resurrection 'eyes of faith', therefore, the possibility of a genuine 'theology of glory' begins to emerge, and, here, Balthasar is willing to give Barth the last words:

> [H]is single work which must not be parceled out into different stages or times in his existence, but which, in this two-fold form, fills and constitutes, rather, his *entire* existence. Ask yourself if this does not correspond better to the New Testament witness about Jesus Christ. Where and when is he not both the humiliated One and

> the Exalted One: already exalted even in his humiliation, and still the Humiliated One even in his exaltation? For example, in Paul: the Crucified who is *not yet* the Risen One, or the Risen One who is not *precisely* the Crucified?[100]

Or, finally, Barth celebrates a genuine '*theologia gloriae*':

> A *theologia gloriae*, celebrating what Jesus Christ in his Resurrection, received for us, and what he is for us as the Risen One, would have no meaning unless it also contained within itself the *theologia crucis*: the praise of what he has done for us in his death and of what he is for us as the crucified. But no more would an abstract *theologia crucis* have meaning. One cannot celebrate in proper fashion the passion and death of Jesus Christ, if this praise does not already contain in itself the *theologia gloriae*: the praise of him who, in his Resurrection, receives our justice and our life, the One who rose for us from among the dead.[101]

The preceding section can be summed up by saying that the difference between Balthasar's and Luther's theologies of the cross hinges on their respective understandings of the relationship of the event of the cross to the very nature of God. Although Luther is not consistent in doing so, he often implies that the God that we encounter in the cross is different than God as he is in himself. Such an understanding of the relationship between natural knowledge of God and that knowledge derived from the cross derives from Luther's soteriological understanding of the relationship between law and gospel. What Luther fails to see in both of these cases is that both the law and creation already have a certain gratuitous character which reveals something of the eternal nature of the Triune God. With Luther, Balthasar wishes to use the cross to judge any merely human approaches to God; yet Balthasar sees that it is precisely in the cross that the true glory of the invisible God is manifest, a glory which is already present in creation. In fact, already in creation we encounter a God who is always, already self-giving love. This is true even if it would have never occurred to us outside of the cross.

The discussion, started above, about the concept of God obtained in mythology versus the concept obtained through philosophy, can be resumed now in that Luther's concept veers too much in the direction of mythology, in that it fails to integrate adequately the God of the cross with the God of creation, the economic with the immanent Trinity. Conversely, any theology which would refuse to allow the event of the cross to modify our preconceptions of God would veer too far in the direction of the God of the philosophers. It also would fail to integrate adequately the economic with the immanent Trinity. In Balthasar's view, on the other hand, something of the very nature of God is revealed in the cross, something intrinsic to who God is, something which could not have been ascertained from our side apart from this revelatory event.[102] We will return to Balthasar's *theologia crucis* in Chapter 5.

IX. Evaluation and Conclusion

The present chapter is an attempt to bring the thought of Balthasar into contact with that of Luther, a task which is, as was mentioned at the outset, rather daunting. Our approach, however, was not so much to compare Luther and Balthasar on various issues in theology, as to create a confrontation of their respective theological approaches, 'methods', if you prefer. This meant getting to the heart of Luther's theology in his original concern over justification by faith alone. It was maintained that this initial concern, and the way that Luther finally resolved it, became the animating force of his entire theology. As we showed, for instance, his unique construal of the relationship between law and gospel provided the point of departure for his understanding of the relationship between nature and grace, natural and revealed theology. At least this was Balthasar's way of approaching Luther's thought.

We should also recall that Balthasar, following especially the scholar Theobald Beer, understood Luther's treatment of the 'happy exchange' (*fröhliche Wechsel*) to be central to his entire theological program. A question could certainly be raised at this point as to whether such an approach to Luther's thought does justice to its full complexity. In his review of Beer's study, Jared Wicks summarizes Beer's conclusions accordingly, raising questions of its fairness:

> Chapter 4, on Luther's Christology, is the centerpiece, revealing the deeper roots of Luther's other themes. Early on, Luther called attention to the dualism marking the moment of redemption itself: Christ on the cross *simul mortus et vivus*, a situation that explains the anthropological *simul peccator et iustus*. Luther articulated a complete causality of Christ's divinity in redemption: the humanity only passively absorbs the hostile negativities of sin, death, and wrath, while the divinity exhausts and overcomes all their deadly power. Luther neglected the patristic interpretation of Philippians 2.5–11, and consequently showed no continuity between the incarnation and the redemption, neglected the subsistence of the Logos in the nature assumed, and attributed no ongoing role to the humanity in salvation ... But all through [Beer's] work one finds crucial lacunae, distorted interpretations, and neglect of Luther's context. Beer reaches his devastating verdict on Luther only by applying inappropriate norms ...[103]

Certainly these criticisms also touch upon Balthasar's reading of Luther. Yet the following can be said in its defense. In the first place, Wicks assumes, because of a somewhat confused notion of ecumenical dialogue, that Beer's criticisms imply an end to Lutheran–Catholic dialogue. True dialogue, however, presupposes that one should attempt to understand the point of departure between one's own thought and that of one's dialogue partner. In other words, serious questions regarding the other's approach, in the light of scripture and tradition, is a crucial aspect of all true dialogue, against a view that would wish to discuss the other's thought only in places where there are similarities. In other words, true dialogue is possible only when both partners are willing to modify previous views on the basis of the encounter with the other.

Secondly, Balthasar is not interested merely in the historical Luther; rather, in keeping with Gadamer's principle that the history of a thing includes the 'history of its effect',[104] Balthasar is addressing issues that continue to be points of difficulty between Catholics and Lutherans. In other words, while it may be legitimate to accuse Beer of 'applying inappropriate norms' to Luther in a purely historical study, one which attempts to use Luther's thought for current theological questions is not only entitled to, but *must* apply all current theological insights to the task. Balthasar is not interested in simply ascertaining Luther's theology in the light of its historical context, he is interested in making an assessment of it in the light of the current theological situation. In this regard, Balthasar will be just as critical of various Catholic thinkers as he is of certain aspects of Luther's thought. Because theology develops over time, all past theology will have to be judged by current theological norms, just as current theological norms will have to be judged in the light of the past. Balthasar is engaged in hermeneutics, not historical reconstruction. In order to engage in a dialogue such as this one, it is necessary to hold one's interlocutor to theological norms that that person may not have been aware of in his day, not least because that person's theology is being used in the present![105]

Having said this, it is possible to question certain aspects of Balthasar's interpretation of Luther. In the first place, as we said in the beginning of this chapter, lacking is an overall study of Luther that attempts to do justice to his thought on its terms. Such a study is a prerequisite to making contemporary theological evaluations. Even if Balthasar were going to rely on secondary studies for this preliminary task, he could have supplemented Beer's and Hacker's with more mainstream studies. This means that there is some legitimacy to the criticism that Balthasar seems to assess Luther's theology in terms of its worst moments, or, at those times when it is most polemically engaged. One thing that could be emphasized, for instance, which Balthasar tends to downplay, is the degree to which, for Luther, Christ is really present to the soul in faith. This would address the issue of divinization which Balthasar sees lacking in Luther's theology. More recently, there has been an attempt, by certain Lutherans and Luther scholars, to find the 'catholic' Luther. Usually this means looking at those places where Luther is either distancing himself from the 'radical reformers', or, at least, those places where he is not responding to his Catholic accusers. In this attempt they too have judged that certain aspects of Luther's thought need to be supplemented and even corrected by a more 'catholic' understanding of Christianity, and even by the more catholic moments in Luther's own theology. This would include certain emphases found in the early Church which Luther either overlooks or ignores in the light of his polemical situation. This attempt should be welcomed by Catholics who are interested in dialogue with this branch of the Reformation.

On the other hand, we can say that many of Balthasar's criticisms of Luther, especially those which question his mere juxtaposition of law and gospel, have been borne out by contemporary biblical exegesis. We need not get into the entire recent development, which centers on figures such as E. P. Sanders and James D. G. Dunn, to note that: (1) The Jewish conception of the law was not such that it could be equated simply with the late medieval understanding of merit. Indeed, as Sanders has shown, in the Jewish understanding of Torah there is always the acknowledgement of the utter gratuity of God in his election and his giving of the Law on Sinai. As Balthasar says,

> [T]he Catholic starting point in loving obedience seems to do more justice to the fundamental aims of the biblical revelation ... than that sharp dialectic that Luther unfolds on the basis of the Letters to the Galatians and to the Romans to cover the whole of the Bible. The antithesis between Old Covenant as law and New Covenant as grace through faith in Christ is untenable; for not only is the covenant with Abraham based on pure faith (as Paul, too, says), but likewise the mutuality between God and the people in the Sinai covenant is based on the one-sidedness of God's gracious initiative, and the Qumran documents have shown us that the Pauline formula of the 'justification of the lost sinner through the grace of God alone' occupied a central position there and waited only for the insertion of the name of Jesus as the one who carried out the divine gracious will to the full.[106]

(2) It was a mistake on Luther's part simply to superimpose his problem of the terrified conscience onto Paul's problem of how the Gentiles are to be included in God's covenant with Israel.[107] While, again, this is to impose a later theological standard onto Luther, this is necessary in the light of the current Catholic and Lutheran attempt to sort out this issue of justification.[108]

The point, then, of bringing Luther into contact with the thought of Balthasar is to illustrate the way in which Balthasar's thought is able to take up Luther's legitimate concern, that of protecting the freedom and gratuity of God's self-revelation in Jesus Christ from any attempt of 'whore reason' to create a god in its image, while avoiding certain of its shortcomings. What is being suggested, and this will become more clear as our study evolves, is that it is the particular strength of a theological aesthetics that it can do justice to the priority of the concrete, historical manifestation of God in Jesus Christ, without thereby depreciating the value of the knowledge of God that is derivable from his manifestation in creation. In order to establish this, however, it is necessary to address the rather tricky issue of the analogy of being, and this will require an examination of Balthasar's dialogue with Karl Barth.

3

Balthasar on Barth and the *Analogia Entis*

I. Introduction

Looming large in the background of the previous chapter's discussion of Martin Luther was the question of the analogy of being. We have already noted that Luther was not opposed to the notion that there was a natural revelation of God in his creation; what distinguishes Luther from, say, Thomas Aquinas, is the emphasis which he places on the fact that in the concrete world of human sinfulness such 'natural' knowledge will always be put to the worse possible use by human pride. The fact is that Aquinas also knew of the effects of sin on human thought; it was simply not something which he placed at the center of his investigations concerning the knowledge of God. Furthermore, even if Aquinas is somewhat more optimistic with regard to what is now called 'philosophical theology', he would have been quite perplexed by the later Scholastic notions of 'pure reason' and 'pure nature'. In short, he knew quite well that reason always operates within the one, concrete order of salvation history. If, prior to Aquinas, all thought was undertaken in relation to this concrete order, in such a way that everything that was brought into the purview of the Christian thinker was investigated in the light of the order of creation, fall and redemption, and after Aquinas a radical rift developed between the orders of nature and super-nature, there has been an incessant danger in subsequent history of reading this rift back into Aquinas.

Luther himself was interested in healing the damaging effects of the above-mentioned rift, but he sought to do so, not so much by showing that God is the only, true end of all creation, but by protecting the sovereignty of God (and this implied human thought about God as well) from the influence of an increasingly autonomous human reason. 'Where are we to find God?' he asked. Answer: In the person and work of Jesus Christ. It is here that Balthasar is closest in spirit to Luther. Yet Balthasar has the advantage of hindsight. By so distinguishing between the God revealed in Jesus Christ and the God revealed in and to a radically fallen nature, Luther willy-nilly contributed to the full autonomy of the realm of human reason, which, if it was still under God, was an abyss away from the God revealed in the cross. This, coupled with the further insistence that the God revealed in nature can only be dialectically related to the God revealed in Jesus Christ, did not succeed in preventing, but in fact may have contributed to, the modern dualism between faith and reason and nature and grace.[1]

This is precisely where Balthasar's interests in Barth are to be located. Balthasar perceives a common goal in the work of Barth and de Lubac: namely, an attempt to overcome the disastrous effects of modern secularism by overcoming the split which had developed since Thomas Aquinas between nature and grace. In fact, in 1950 Balthasar wrote the following to de Lubac:

> I am finishing my Karl Barth, which is basically a discussion between him and you. I would like to dedicate this book to you, he owes you almost everything. Don't lose courage, continue to work as if there were nothing, so many friends surround you and will want to help you. I am doing what I can to make your influence spread in German countries.[2]

In this chapter I shall examine, then, in the following order: (1) the general problem of the analogy of being, especially as interpreted in the works of Gilson and de Lubac; (2) Barth's early theology in terms of his response to Protestant Liberalism; and, finally, (3) Balthasar's interpretation and assessment of Karl Barth's theology especially as it appears in, *The Theology of Karl Barth*.[3] This will enable us to determine the precise effect of the engagement with Barth on Balthasar's aesthetic approach to theology, for it is in Balthasar's attempt to do justice to Barth's concern that theology be radically focused on its object, while at the same time trying to avoid Barth's tendency toward 'christomonism', that Balthasar developed his particular style of theology.

The purpose of the present chapter, briefly, is to demonstrate the fact that Balthasar's study of Barth is not intended to be merely a historical introduction to Barth's thought. Instead, Balthasar sees an approach to theology in Karl Barth that, in spite of its often severely anti-Catholic tone, is in keeping with the basic concerns of de Lubac, and other Catholic theologians whom Balthasar identifies as 'christocentric'. Put rather generally, there is the shared conviction among these thinkers that the best way for Christianity to address the problem of secularization is not to present itself in terms of what it holds in common with the general religious and humanistic concerns of humanity, for this would be to confirm, even prior to a serious engagement, Christianity's basic irrelevance to modern humanity; instead, Christianity must, once again, make a case for the *universal* significance of the *concrete* person and work of Jesus Christ. In order to understand fully the implications of this statement, however, we will have to proceed with the task outlined above.

II. The Analogy of Being

Two people stand out – perhaps above all others – in the twentieth century in the attempt to rescue Thomas Aquinas from his neo-Scholastic interpreters: Étienne Gilson and Henri de Lubac. Gilson's contribution was primarily in the area of the relationship between philosophy and theology, faith and reason; de Lubac's was primarily in the area of nature and grace. Yet both of their treatments, not entirely independently,[4] draw strikingly similar conclusions: that from the time of Cajetan onward, Thomas was understood in a dualistic manner, such that the realms of faith and reason, nature and grace were neatly compartmentalized, and faith and grace were understood as extrinsic additions to the intrinsically complete realms of reason and nature. Both of these thinkers concluded that such a dualistic understanding failed to do justice to the fact that Aquinas saw knowledge of Christ in faith, and life in Christ through grace, as the only true end of humanity: i.e., that humanity had a single end – the beatific vision.

With regard to the analogy of being, this plays out accordingly. Analogy originated with the Greeks as an attempt to overcome the contradictions inherent in the respective philosophies of Heraclitus and Parmenides. The former placed the emphasis of his philosophy on the concrete world of change, thereby determining that being (that which is) is in a constant state of flux. In one of his fragments, Heraclitus puts this accordingly:

> The same thing is present living and dead, awake and asleep, young and old; for the latter change and are the former, and again the former change and are the latter.[5]

Parmenides, on the other hand, rather than understanding being in terms of the world of change, understood the world of change in terms of being. Parmenides' insight was that there is nothing more basic to reality than that it is, and that being must therefore be infinite and unchanging. Because he made no distinction between being and existence, Parmenides was forced to conclude that the world of change (i.e., the material world) was an illusion.

Both systems, according to the Greeks that came after them, led to obvious and insurmountable difficulties that could only be overcome on the basis of the concept of analogy. In short, Plato, Aristotle, Plotinus, *et al.*, all insist upon gradations of being. For Plato this means that the realm of ideas or 'proto-types' is the realm ontologically *prior* to the realm of concrete existents. The realm of ideas has the highest level of being, and the visible realm relates to this as copy to original. For Plotinus this is worked out in terms of the One, which alone truly is, and the various gradations of being ever emanating from this One. There is an analogy, then, between the being contained in the material world of change (Heraclitus) and the being of the unchanging, immaterial One (Parmenides).[6]

When this Greek way of thinking was encountered by the Christian theologian, most systematically in the work of Thomas Aquinas, it was radically transformed in view of the doctrine of creation. It became impossible to view analogy primarily in terms of a gradation of being, implying that the universe exists as an emanation from the 'stuff' of the One. The obvious difficulty with this view, from the Christian perspective, is that it implies a certain necessity to creation: the One necessarily overflows into the being of the cosmos. Or, in Aristotle's view, the universe itself is viewed as eternal. According to the Christian view, by contrast, God creates the world freely, at a certain point in time, and not out of the 'stuff' which God is. The universe is neither eternal nor a necessary emanation from the being of God; God utterly transcends his creation.

Aquinas's treatment of Aristotle is incomprehensible apart from his distinctively Christian understanding of creation. Gilson never tired of pointing out the transformation of Aristotle's thought at the hands of Thomas.[7] For Aristotle, the most primal category is essence, or what makes a thing belong to a certain category. For instance, what is most important about a bear is its 'bear-ness'. This essence is what persists in spite of any accidental differences between individual bears. But this is not true for Aquinas: building on God's revelation of his name to Moses in the book of Exodus – 'I am' – Aquinas understands the act of being (*esse*) as the most important aspect of a thing. For instance, although a bear is a bear because its essence dictates that it should be, a bear *is* because of an act of being. For Aristotle, 'form' determines what a thing is; he knows of no act superior to form. But Aquinas posits above the form an *act* of that form, and is, to this degree, no longer an Aristotelian.[8]

With regard to analogy, this implies that the Christian understanding is significantly different from its Greek forerunner.[9] In Aquinas, a real distinction is posited between being and essence, and, as a result, between being being and having being. Creatures are a mixture of *esse* and *essentia* which makes their very being analogous. In the first place, it suggests that they are contingent: they may not have existed. The fact that they do exist, however, implies an analogy to God. Moreover, in their very similarity (as existing) they are even more dissimilar (in their actual existence/contingency – *essentia*). This is why Erich Przywara was constantly insisting that the 'self-manifestation of God in creation is never an exhaustive one'.[10] The doctrine of analogy, understood in this way, is used to preserve the *distinction* between God and the world in the very similarity. This should also make it apparent that Aquinas's understanding of analogy was never a 'neutral' one, that is, one derived from 'pure reason', for it was intimately connected to the doctrine of creation.

In terms of nature and grace – and now de Lubac's concerns come to the fore – this means that the neo-Scholastic notion of 'pure nature' cannot be based on the writings of Thomas Aquinas. This also explains why Gilson was immediately congenial to de Lubac's presentation of Aquinas in his controversial *Le Mystère du surnaturel*.[11] According to Gilson,

> the doctrine of creation is bound to modify the notion of metaphysics itself, in that it introduces into the realm of being a first cause to whose causality everything is strictly subjected.[12]

And this has immediate implications for humanity's final end. As Gilson puts it,

> This is why, in Thomas Aquinas' own doctrine, inasmuch as he wants to know reality through its first cause, since God is that first cause, man *naturally* desires, as his ultimate end, to know God.[13]

This affirms de Lubac's insistence that, according to Aquinas, human beings have one, ultimate end, which is the beatific vision.

For de Lubac, this implied a fundamental paradox lying at the very root of the human person. That paradox as Balthasar presents it is this:

> How can man in his natural order be interiorly ordered to the fulfilling order of grace, without in the least possessing this latter in anticipation, that is, without being able to claim it for himself?[14]

But de Lubac also knew that this paradox was traceable to Aquinas himself when the latter states that a being who is striving for a perfect good, even if it requires help to reach this good, is more noble than a creature who strives for a lesser good, which it can reach by its own efforts.[15] For de Lubac, then, human beings are fundamentally ordered to an end that surpasses their natural grasp.

What was revolutionary about de Lubac's approach was its insistence that it is ultimately impossible to understand humanity apart from Jesus Christ, that anthropology could only find its solution in Christology.[16] Balthasar understood the nature of this revolution very well, and he also understood that de Lubac was merely taking the earlier speculations of Joseph Maréchal on these issues to their necessary conclusions. In other words, what Maréchal wanted to demonstrate concerning human nature on the basis of philosophy – that is, that human beings long for an infinity which eludes their grasp – de Lubac insisted could only be done in theology.

> [Maréchal] is … a thinker who tried to probe in his philosophy the conditions for the possibility of the supernatural vision of God as the ultimate goal of man in his human nature. If this is so, then the question naturally arises whether or not the object of Maréchal's investigations – human nature – is not already in a hidden way a 'theological object.'[17]

Put differently, de Lubac insisted that in order to deal properly with the fact that human beings are ordered to a supernatural end, one must proceed from a 'theological a priori'. Because the story of de Lubac's debate with his critics is now well known, I will not labor over these issues; I only wish to give brief attention to them because they provide a necessary background to Balthasar's study of Barth. De Lubac's reinterpretation of Aquinas was intended to overcome the neo-Scholastic interpretation which insisted that there were two ends for human beings: one, this-worldly end, which could be achieved on the basis of their natural abilities alone, and another, supernatural end, which was attainable only through the help of supernatural grace. According to de Lubac, there is no purely this-worldly goal; instead, in the one, concrete order of salvation-history, human beings are oriented to the beatific vision by their very nature. And this is so in such a way that the final gift of sharing in the life of God is in no way derivable from or owed to the previous gift of desiring to know God. By framing the anthropological question in this manner, that is, by insisting that human beings cannot be fully understood without reference to Christ, de Lubac was giving theology a role that was totally unacceptable to the modern, separatist mindset; it is here that his theology is closest in spirit to that of Karl Barth.

Although it is not necessary at this point to treat another thinker in support of these ideas, it should be mentioned that Barth's early aversion to analogy was somewhat mitigated by his encounter with a Polish-German philosopher who was making a case very similar to that of de Lubac and Gilson: Erich Pryzwara. When Przywara and Barth met, Barth was protesting against a doctrine of analogy which was based on the neo-Scholastic notions of 'pure nature' and 'pure reason'.[18]

III. Barth's Early Theology

This brief examination of analogy is important for it provides the background of Balthasar's study of Barth. Knowing that the debate over the nature of theology between de Lubac and his critics was in the background of Balthasar's Barth project is important for two reasons. First, it helps to explain why Balthasar focused most of his study on the 'formal' aspects of Barth's theology, rather than on the 'content'.[19] Secondly, it illustrates the importance Balthasar placed on getting the right 'method' in theology. Balthasar recognized in Barth's critique of Liberal Protestantism a concern not unlike de Lubac's critique of neo-Scholastic dualism. In other words, it was not primarily to defend the Catholic understanding of analogy to Barth that Balthasar wrote this study. Rather, it was to show his fellow Catholics the dangers inherent in the doctrine of analogy when it is totally removed from the context of theology proper.

In order to understand this comparison more fully it will be beneficial to take a brief look at Barth's early theological development. Barth was trained in the Liberal Protestantism which reigned in Germany from the nineteenth to the early twentieth century. What typified this theology, according to Barth's later reflections, was its willingness to accept, a priori, the ethics and epistemology of Kant. Faith was what was left over, so to speak, after reason had done its work. God did not meet us in the objective world of knowledge or history, but in the interior world of faith and subjectivity.[20] Barth's early theological training came, in fact, from Wilhelm Hermann, who, though he was thoroughly steeped in Schleiermacher and Kant, also gave Barth his christocentric impulse.[21] Barth summarized his own views at the time accordingly:

> In the end it proved that in contrast to the tendencies of my grandfather and my father, I had made myself a committed disciple of the 'modern' school, which was still dominant up to the time of the First World War, and was regarded as the only school worth belonging to. In it, according to the teaching of Schleiermacher and Ritschl, Christianity was interpreted on the one hand as a historical phenomenon to be subjected to critical examination, and on the other hand as a matter of inner experience, of a predominantly moral nature.[22]

In fact, Eberhard Busch is able to weave together a series of quotes from the young Barth (1910) which are quite telling:

> Typical of [Barth's] sermons were remarks like, 'The greatest thing is what takes place in our hearts.' Or, 'To each man goes out the call to be true to himself, namely ... to that model of the best that anyone can become.' He told the congregation: 'Try to become valuable!' Or, 'Dear friend, think seriously about yourself.' As he explained 'Before I can know God, I must know myself.' He introduced Goethe's Faust as 'without doubt a true Protestant.' The congregation learnt that 'Calvin's

> view of the authority of the Bible would be quite wrong for us.' Critical light was shed on the Ten Commandments: 'Sometimes they contain too much for our needs, sometimes too little.' … He attacked the Christ presented by the Chalcedonian Definition to the ancient church: 'I will gladly concede that if Jesus were like this I would not be interested in him.' But, 'If Christ begins to live in *us* … that is the beginning of Christian faith.'[23]

From the time of his service as pastor in Safenwill, in 1911, onwards, however, one begins to see a gradual shift in Barth's theology away from its former subjectivism. This gradual shift was exacerbated when, in 1914, Barth's old theology professors unanimously endorsed Wilhelm I's war policy. Barth's later assessment of this endorsement was that there was nothing objective in their theology which would warrant a 'No' to the 'spirit of the age'.[24] From this point on Barth's own thought reflects an attempt at a reversal from the anthropocentric, subjectivist theology of Liberal Protestantism to a theology which proceeds from its object.[25]

> It was Thurneysen who whispered the key phrase to me, half aloud, while we were alone together: 'What we need for preaching, instruction and pastoral care is a "wholly other" theological foundation.'[26]

The 1919 edition of the Romans commentary was unabashedly directed against the anthropological reductionism of the historical-critical method. Karl Adam compared the appearance of this commentary to a bomb dropped on the playground of theologians. For Barth, the focus and starting-point of theology was no longer to be humanity but God, and his method was to let God speak for himself.

> During the work [on *Romans*] it was often as though I caught a breath from afar, from Asia Minor or Corinth, something primeval, from the ancient East, indefinitely sunny, wild, original, that somehow is hidden behind these sentences. Paul – what a man he must have been and what men also those for whom he could so sketch and hint at these pithy things in a few muddled fragments! … And then *behind* Paul: what realities those must have been that could excite the man in such a way! What a lot of far-fetched stuff we compile about his remarks, when perhaps ninety-nine per cent of their real content escapes us![27]

Although Balthasar will argue for a developmental understanding of Barth's theology, this concern that God is not merely a continuation of the highest human capacities remains a key element in his thought to the end. In this sense, he should be understood as the modern theological heir to Luther and Calvin. This emphasis on the otherness of God is something that can be seen as early as the lectures which make up *The Word of God and the Word of Man*.[28] As Bruce McCormack has pointed out, 'Barth's theological development from this point on represented a more-

or-less continuous unfolding of a single theme: God is God.'[29] And it is here that we should locate his most fundamental break with the Liberal Protestantism that preceded him.

The point to be noted, however, is how similar Barth's critique of the Liberal Protestantism in which he was trained is to Balthasar's critique of the neo-Scholasticism in which he was trained. The tendency of neo-Scholasticism not only to distinguish a realm of pure nature for theological purposes, but to suggest that such a realm existed in fact made it seem possible to proceed from a purely natural standpoint. Apologetics became utterly anterior to and distinct from dogmatic theology, the latter taking over only after the former was well under way. And both systems, the Liberal Protestant and the Catholic neo-Scholastic, failed sufficiently to enlist Jesus Christ as the measure of all creation. All that referred explicitly to Jesus Christ was relegated to the second phase of the theological project: in Liberal Protestantism it had to be tailored to a secular anthropology; in Catholic neo-Scholasticism it appeared to be of only extrinsic interest to nature as such.

The reason for dialogue with Barth, then, is to be found at that point where Barth poses a serious critique of the 'Catholic system'. Barth understood the doctrine of analogy as the Catholic counterpart to Liberal Protestantism's anthropocentrism. Balthasar therefore wishes to appropriate that aspect of Barth's thought which focuses theology on its object, as the following quote illustrates:

> Who but Barth has gazed so breathlessly and tirelessly on his subject, watching it develop and blossom in all its power before his eyes? One would have to go back to Thomas Aquinas[!] to find a similar spirit, one free from the constraints of every tenseness and narrowness, combining superior gifts of understanding with goodness of heart. In Barth, this graciousness occasionally takes the form of a tinge of humor; but more often we see it displayed in his extraordinary sense of timing, of just the right tempo, a sense of due rhythm. Barth really makes us believe that for him Christianity was a radiantly triumphant opportunity. He manages this, not so much because he possesses the gift of style or writes well, but because he bears witness, sober witness, to a reality that epitomizes style, since God is its author. Barth is the very antithesis of Kierkegaard here, who sharply divided the aesthetical from the religious and ethical. But, for Barth, the religious sphere is aesthetical because it is religious, because it is in itself the most authentic.[30]

Here we also see the origins of Balthasar's preference for a 'theological aesthetics'. In any case, both authors show, in a manner which cuts across confessional lines, a preference for theology done from its object, a theology which takes its bearings from God's concrete dealings in history.

IV. Balthasar's Barth

Balthasar, as was mentioned above, treats the development of Barth in terms of three 'phases': the dialectical phase of the Romans commentary, the 'conversion to analogy' phase, which was marked especially by the Anselm study, and a final, 'analogy of faith' phase, which is given full expression in the *Church Dogmatics*.[31] In the early phase Barth charts 'the irreversible movement from a fatally doomed temporal order to a new living order filled with the life of God, the restoration of the original ideal of creation'.[32] The dialectic here is that between the God who is and the creature who has been radically severed from God, that is, the creature who is sinful and transitory. At this stage Barth subsumes every moment into salvation-history in such a way that, 'there is no fall from God in Adam … that does not have its origin at the point where man has been granted life through being reconciled to God in Christ'.[33] Because Barth has failed to make any distinction between nature and grace at this point, he simply equates what is natural with what is transitory, nature with guilt, and *eros* (drive) with decadence. The religious being is the decadent being par excellence in that a human striving for God and a human concept of God become a substitute for God himself.

The atmosphere of this early phase stems from a 'dialectical' understanding of knowledge which proceeds accordingly: (1) the subjective nature of knowledge gives rise to the antithesis (every thesis has an antithesis); (2) the object remains superior and beyond our grasp, and must always stand in judgement of our supposed knowledge of it; and (3) the 'higher' the level of being, the more pronounced the above-stated difficulty becomes. If this 'object' is at the same time a 'subject', then it must disclose itself. Of course this rules out any 'natural' capacity to know God, leaving only the predisposition to receive revelation which is itself a gift, that is, faith. Revelation is the only adequate object for theology thus conceived.[34]

Balthasar has numerous difficulties with this approach. First, and foremost, it collapses everything into God, resulting in what Balthasar, following Erich Przywara, calls 'theopanism'. Barth simply leaves no room for creation to exist outside of God. This is because in this early phase Barth equates creatureliness with falleness, resulting in a radicalism which Balthasar identifies as 'super-Christian, too Christian [*überchristlich*], and thus … unchristian'.[35] Secondly, without a concept of 'nature' outside of grace, it is impossible to conceive of the incarnation. In other words, if nothing which exists outside God has any true existence of its own, how can God make human flesh his dwelling place in the incarnation? How can the classical formula which speaks of two *distinct* natures in one person be maintained? Finally, if creation (nature) is equated with fallenness, grace becomes a necessity, and, therefore, no longer grace. The outcome of all of this is that the creature has no existence of its own outside of God so that it must be either subsumed into God, or dissolved into a contradiction.[36] Wishing to preserve the utter newness and priority of the realm of revelation, Barth ends up by making that realm the only one there really is, and therefore no longer gratuitous.

To Barth's credit, he eventually came to recognize the problems inherent in this radically dialectic approach, and, in order to deal with them, he turned to the incarnation. The breakthrough of this period occurred with Barth's study of Anselm, originally published in 1931.[37] Aware that in his early thought he had tended to swallow the world into God, Barth now set about to salvage the world in three ways. In terms of culture and philosophy, Barth now admitted of 'a potential in the world of nature, history, and reason that sin has not destroyed'.[38] Accordingly, philosophy can have a legitimate and wholesome role so long as it does not attempt to conceptualize the 'whole' which can only be grasped in Jesus Christ. Barth thus excoriates Hegel for anticipating the unity which can only come from God's Word. There is even the admittance, at this stage, that natural theology lives on in a very real way in revealed theology. However, in his ethics and his theology of the Church Barth still found it difficult to allow for any legitimate activity outside of God. Balthasar sums this up accordingly, 'Actualism, with its constant, relentless reduction of all activity to God the *actus purus*, leaves no room for any other center of activity outside of God.'[39]

There was still a lacuna in Barth's theology at this stage making it impossible for him to deal adequately with activity outside of God. It was primarily in the Anselm book that Barth was able to correct this one-sidedness and elaborate his 'analogy of faith'. This will eventually be defined by Barth accordingly:

> By the power of faith and its profession, the Word of God becomes a human thought and a human word, certainly in infinite dissimilarity and inadequacy, but not in total human *strangeness* with its model. The human copy [*Abbild*] is a *real* copy of its divine counterpart [*Vorbild*].[40]

In a very subtle way Barth has shifted our understanding of what the creature has in common with the creator from the realm of 'being' to the realm of human decision and activity, to God's initial activity and the human response to this activity. This is distinguishable from the 'analogy of being' by the fact that it is an analogy 'from above', that is, one taken from the only real order, the order of redemption. It *is* analogical, however, in the sense that it really is human nature and human words with which

God expresses himself. Human nature and creation can no longer be understood in terms of contradiction because they have been 'expropriated' by God in order to express himself. Now Barth can say that only a false god is a threat to what is human; the true God allows humanity to exist as he created it. 'Far from being self-contradictory with the concept of God or shameful to it, the world is his confirmation, set up to give glory to his name.'[41]

It is in the *Church Dogmatics* (especially from the second volume on) that analogy becomes central to Barth's thought, and this means that the central concept, 'Word of God' of the middle phase is now replaced by that of 'Jesus Christ, God and man'. 'Because Christ the redeemer became man in time, creation in its entirety is something good from the outset.'[42] This enables Barth to take a more positive view, for instance, of 'eros', in that 'agape' has within it the potential for humanitarianism. And anthropology can be of assistance to the theologian who wishes to understand that 'continuum' in humanity which we call 'nature'. The key theme of this period is that of 'presupposition': nature is the presupposition for grace. Or, as Barth puts it,

> Creation (that is, the order of nature) is the external ground of the Covenant; and the Covenant (that is, the order of the Incarnation and redemption) is the internal ground of creation.[43]

In such statements concerning creation and covenant Barth is always aware of the two dangers of either deducing anthropology (the realm of nature) from Christology (the order of grace), or attempting to understand the realm of nature without recourse to the realm of grace. Again, the former would be to deny the gratuity of grace, as in the early period, but the latter would be to fall into the trap of nineteenth-century Protestantism. In his attempt to steer a course between this Scylla and Charybdis, Barth admits that one must allow nature a degree of autonomy within the order of grace, that they must be distinguished before they can be related. And yet in order to make sure that this autonomy is not an absolute independence he will say:

> It is not part of the essence and concept of creation that it *must* have this perspective [i.e., that it must be understood in the light of reconciliation]. But in the work of reconciliation and revelation, it becomes evident that it *does* in fact have this perspective.[44]

In other words, in the light of revelation nature is seen in a new light, but this 'new light' does not violate the integrity of creation, because creation itself already points beyond itself to the realm of grace.[45] In the same paragraph Barth can even say:

> [God] has responded to the Fall not only with an act of restoration (*restitutio ad integrum*) but with a revelation of a perfection that was already hidden in the original integrity of creation as such … Looking back with the benefit of hindsight, we can now legitimately ask: What would that first act of creation be without the second act of reconciliation?[46]

Balthasar examines the implications of this shift in Barth's thinking with regard to the following: (1) Humanity as God's Partner; (2) Faith and Reason; (3) Sin; and (4) the Analogy of Being. A brief examination of the second and fourth of these will help clarify Barth's own understanding, as well as provide the basis for Balthasar's criticisms.[47] Balthasar begins this section by stating that, 'epistemologically, the question of the relation between nature and grace … becomes the problem of faith and reason.'[48] This area is important to Balthasar because it is here that Barth has been most misunderstood by Catholics, a misunderstanding which can be captured in one word: fideism. This is based on a twofold misunderstanding of Barth's central intention. First, Barth has been understood in terms of his early work and his exchange with Emil Brunner rather than in terms of the *Church Dogmatics*. Second, the accusation of fideism makes sense only for a thinker who opposes the realms of reason and faith in a way that Barth does not. A thinker like Bautain, for instance, who was condemned at the First Vatican Council, was accused of fideism on the basis of his denial that there could be any 'natural' knowledge of God. But Bautain was basing his reflections on a Kantian understanding of 'pure reason' which, when left to its own devices, collapses in on itself. The contrast here is between a realm of faith, in which we can know God, and a realm of nature, in which we cannot.

For Barth, no such realm of 'pure reason' exists. For him, the problem of 'natural theology' is not that it is not possible, but that it is an abstraction from the one true realm, the realm of God's redemptive plan for his creation. The realm of faith is not a realm opposed to that of reason, it is the place where we truly come to understand. Again, Barth's thought is directed against autonomous, Enlightenment reason. Even the revelation which occurs in 'nature' is intrinsically related to the 'supernatural' because it is possible only in the light of the *activity* of God in creation. If nature speaks of God, it does so because God has acted in history. This means that, for Barth, God's revelation always precedes our perception of it in such a way that philosophy – i.e., knowledge based on 'reason alone' – is only possible as a method. When philosophy gets as far as it can go, it will automatically point beyond itself to revelation.

> Philosophy in this context is to theology as the abstract is to the concrete and possibility is to reality. But so long as it is really the abstraction of *this* concretion, the possibility of *this* reality, it is legitimate and has its own truth.[49]

This makes it possible for Barth to make a more positive assessment of the 'spoils of the Egyptians' than many might expect, and this is because there is no pure reason, no pure nature: 'Man is created and equipped as a creature of nature to encounter and find God in all things.'[50] This also explains why Barth can be so critical of 'natural theology' in one breath, and so unabashedly approving in the next: the problem is not with knowing God from his creation; the problem is with reducing God's concrete creation to the abstract realm of pure nature.[51] It is this insistence upon a concrete understanding of nature as creation that leads to Barth's distinct understanding of the analogy of being. His objection to the concept of analogy can be summarized in the following four statements. First, the decisive element to be mentioned with regard to the relationship between the creature and the creator is not what they have in common, but in what distinguishes them: i.e., God's aseity versus the creature's dependence. Second, the 'analogy of being' subsumes both God and creature under an overarching concept – derived from the creature – and does not, therefore, allow God the freedom to establish his own relationship to the world. Third, the concept of being is derivative of finite beings and is therefore a finite concept, not adequate to include God. And, finally, in the hands of the sinner, this concept becomes an especially dangerous one, allowing humanity to take a place occupied uniquely by God.[52]

'The *analogia entis* must be replaced by the *analogia fidei*, for only the latter can uproot all these dangers and abuses.'[53] The analogy of faith preserves the fact that all human knowledge of God stems from God's prior activity in creation, that humanity gains this knowledge only by freely submitting its own thought to this prior 'revelation', and, most importantly, that humanity must allow the highest moment of God's activity in history – i.e., the incarnation of God in Jesus Christ – to be the measure of all its knowledge of God. What Barth is calling for here is a christocentric understanding of analogy. But this is still analogy, because in taking on human nature God did not destroy this nature, indeed, he took it to its highest end. And, 'it is in Christ that God's revealed presence in history and creation can become an event for the believer.'[54]

At this point, however, Balthasar wishes to draw implications from Barth's thought that Barth is often unwilling to draw himself. For one thing, Balthasar thinks that there is room in the above statements for a 'rapprochement' with the analogy of being, rightly understood, and even room *within* Barth's analogy of faith for the analogy of being. In other words, if we take Barth seriously when he says that the order of nature is the presupposition for the order of grace, he is admitting that there is something in the order of creation which makes it suitable to the incarnation. That means that outside of this christological center there is a 'periphery' which points to and serves as an analogous realm to this center. While Balthasar admits that this realm – that of creation – is understood as 'presupposition' only because of the one order of God's plan of redemption, he insists that this presupposition gives a legitimacy to creaturely knowledge that Barth is often unwilling to allow. The realm of creation 'contains images, analogies, as it were, dispositions, which in a true sense are the presuppositions for the Incarnation'.[55]

V. Balthasar's Critique

Balthasar's critique originates in the fact that Barth borrows much of his vocabulary for discussing the above problems from German Idealism. For instance, Barth constantly speaks in terms of 'Being' and 'Act', always insisting that we must understand the former in the light of the latter, that it must be God's concrete act that determines our understanding of the way things are. Although Balthasar ultimately concludes that this Idealist vantage point – albeit inverted – does not *determine* Barth's thought, he does suggest that it *constrains* it.[56] 'It is not so much a matter of Barth omitting some crucial doctrine as it is a distortion of nuance, an inappropriate coloration to the whole.'[57]

It is in this section that Balthasar raises some of his toughest questions to Barth's theology. The first thing that Balthasar inquires about is Barth's 'christocentrism'. While Balthasar agrees that theology must begin with the concrete realm of what God achieves in and through Jesus Christ, he wonders if Barth's starting-point might not end up as a straitjacket. In other words, by *reducing* creation to a presupposition, does Barth give creation enough breathing room? Does he allow enough of a distinction between the realms of creation and covenant? Again, Balthasar agrees that the autonomy of the created order is a *relative* autonomy, but this is still a real autonomy. The theologian must 'preserve scrupulously all relative meanings ... to avoid any appearance of *deducing* them from their ultimate meaning'.[58] Furthermore, Balthasar insists that in order to measure properly the distance between nature and grace, theology needs the 'open or covert help of philosophy'. It cannot be determined, as it is in Barth, from within theology. All of this is necessary in order to explain the possibility of existence outside of God, and the possibility of a negative stance vis-à-vis God.[59]

This leads straightway to Balthasar's second critique: that Barth cannot adequately account for human waywardness. In Barth's theology there is practically a universalization of Calvin's 'irresistible grace', which is a symptom of Barth's tendency to make theology overstep its legitimate boundaries. He 'sneaks a peak at God's hand', and, in the end, comes near to turning the God of the Bible into the 'innocuous God of Harnack'. In spite of all of his protest to the contrary, Barth, willy-nilly, tends toward subsuming God into a previously constructed system. Where is the freedom of God in such an approach? Of course Balthasar qualifies all of this by saying that this is a 'tendency' in Barth's thought to which he never entirely succumbs; but it is a real tendency.[60]

Balthasar's final critique is simply to apply the implications of these first two criticisms to Barth's doctrine of the Church. It must be remembered at this point that Balthasar has consistently accused Barth of not being able to account sufficiently for the absence of faith. Because Barth wishes to locate all human culture and history *within* the concrete plan of God to unite all things to himself in Christ, he tends to reduce all *human* activity to meaninglessness. What God does in Christ is so determinative that lack of faith is simply the denial of the truth of faith that is actually present. Certainly this makes relative the role of human freedom and the role of the Church. For Balthasar, conversely, the Church is that concrete place in which, through the power of the Spirit, God carries on his work throughout history. By reducing everything to God's activity in Christ on behalf of the world, Barth does not always give sufficient attention to the Church's indispensable role in carrying this love into the world. For Balthasar, the presence of the Father in the visible Christ is a prelude to the presence of the risen Christ in the visible Church. Missing from Barth is a sufficient emphasis on the Church as sacrament.[61] But this should become clearer in what follows.

It must be remembered that even these criticisms occur in a study which is intended to gain a more sympathetic reading for Barth among Catholic theologians. They make up, as such, a rather small portion of the work, and are placed within an overall positive assessment. In the important afterword to the second edition, however, Balthasar mentions two essays,[62] written after the Barth study, which take up the above-mentioned criticisms at greater length, and in more detail. They also occur in the context of Balthasar's own thought patterns and reflect less directly Barth's immense, sometimes overwhelming presence. This independence allows Balthasar to present a more positive alternative to Barth's approach, rather than simply responding to Barth's 'excesses'. Before drawing some cursory conclusions regarding Balthasar's study of Barth as a whole, it will be helpful to examine these essays briefly.

The treatment of these two important essays is in the context of our overall thesis that Balthasar was attempting to offer an alternative to the prevalent approach of Catholic theology which had separated the orders of nature and grace in such a way that the content of positive revelation could only be related to general questions of anthropology, philosophy, ethics, law, and the like, in an extrinsic manner. Here, the general methodological procedure of these various disciplines was already well established before any encounter with the Christian view of things was warranted appropriate. Barth's daring presentation of the Christian faith, with its radical christocentrism, was appealing to Balthasar because it refused to treat questions of a specifically Christian nature as if they were only marginally or secondarily related to the central questions which concern humanity as such. Once creation is understood as a 'presupposition' to the incarnation, the latter must be allowed to illuminate our understanding of the former. The danger in Barth's approach, as mentioned above, was that it threatened to reduce nature to a *mere* presupposition, that is, to something which made of grace a necessity. These two extremes must be kept in mind in what follows.

While Balthasar does not reject Barth's christological starting-point, he will raise questions from time to time about Barth's Christology.[63] This is especially the case in Barth's pointed comments against the Catholic 'and': faith *and* works, Christ *and* Mary–Church, word *and* sacrament, scripture *and* tradition. Balthasar will wish to insist that the Catholic 'and' is already necessitated by a traditional Christology. It is here that Balthasar will wish to speak of a 'christological analogy of being'. This means that Balthasar will be investigating an old set of problems,

> the relations between natural and supernatural revelation, between that given by the very being of things and that given by the word, and all the consequences in the sphere of natural truth (philosophy), natural ethics and law, etc. ... [64]

in the light of a 'generally accepted Christology'. He understands that this goes against the older approach 'which starts from principles drawn from the revelation in creation to arrive at the revelation in the word', but thinks he can demonstrate that such an approach is warranted by the subject matter at hand.

Balthasar now offers a reflection on the nature of scripture which allows him to shed light on the relationship between nature and grace from within a christological context. In what sense, for instance, can we speak of scripture as God's word without denying its properly historical and human dimension. If the tendency of an Origen was to deny the human in order to highlight the divine nature of scripture, it has been the tendency of modern biblical scholarship to reassert the human dimension of scripture at the expense of the divine. In a sense, however, both the modern biblical scholar and Origen treat the relationship between the divine and the human as a zero sum game: if the text is divine, then it cannot be human; if it is a human text, then it is not divine. Balthasar rebukes both positions by reminding us that God – precisely because he is God and not simply another being in the world – is able to make use of that which is human in order to articulate that which is divine, and this without obliterating the human in the process. Just as Christ did not have to cease being human in order to be one with the Father, so the word of scripture does not lose its human dimension when it is taken up to articulate a message that is more than simply human.[65] As Balthasar says, 'the distinction between the testifying word and the word testified to is an incomplete one'.[66] This discussion is offered to balance the Barthian tendency to denigrate the human in order to make room for the divine.

The question that is being asked is this: what does the incarnation imply with regard to the nature–grace problematic which will allow us to assert, with Barth, the relevance of Christ to all things, without swallowing creation up into Christ? Balthasar's answer, in short, is that God is able to speak to us as a man without thereby ceasing to be God, or without doing violence to what it means to be a man. Furthermore, because this God-man, this Jesus Christ, is now the norm for all of humanity, now, that is, that he is the 'second Adam', it is no longer permissible to treat humanity as if Christ did not exist. Again, Balthasar returns to scripture to clarify this relationship: just as the promise of the Old Testament is only understood as *promise* in the light of the New Testament, so the fact that nature has within it the capacity for the divine only becomes conceivable in the light of God's inconceivable decision to unite it with the divine in Jesus Christ. The free gift which God offers humanity in Jesus Christ has become the key to understanding humanity in its very depths.[67] And yet what Christ sheds light on is human nature as it really is, just as the New Covenant shows the true nature of the Old.

This means that Balthasar will be more generous with regard to a genuine human role in the drama of salvation. Christ's human nature is given a real role in the drama between divine and human freedom.

> Because of [Christ's activity as a man], and since in spite of all Christ's humanity must be designated a pure humanity, it could well be maintained that the rest of men become in Christ, competent as regards acts to which they are not fitted by their own human nature.[68]

Here we get to the heart of the difference between Balthasar's and Barth's approaches. If Barth is sometimes willing to allow the activity of God in redemption to shed light upon God's previous activity in creation, he is not always consistent in his application of this to the human dimensions of existence. This accounts for his tendency to be dismissive of human religiosity and his refusal to see Jesus as a religious model.

We are now in a position to draw some concrete conclusions from Balthasar's findings which should help to illustrate the differences between his and Barth's approaches. (1) Pre-redeemed humanity – with all of its religious longings and all of its ethical ideals – need not be seen in a purely negative light when compared to God's definitive activity in Jesus Christ. Instead, Jesus Christ takes up all of these natural longings and capacities and gives them the shape that they were intended to have all along, preserving their own inherent goodness. What must be emphasized here is that these longings are in no way a 'transcendental' apprehension of Christ's 'categorial' gift.[69] (2) Redeemed humanity, given as it is a share in the divine life, is now given a role within Christ's redemptive activities, enabling it to achieve things unthinkable to human nature alone. (3) Because Jesus Christ acted as a human being, thereby changing what it means to be human, he makes it possible for other human beings to join themselves to him in such a way that, in all of their humanness, they can carry on his work. Here Balthasar is speaking of the Church which now, with Christ as its head, makes up the '*totus Christus*', and can be said to be truly holy:

> The holiness attributed by Paul to the faithful is not that of the synagogue, but a participation of that of Christ their head. His death and resurrection, as an accomplished fact, was the grace communicated to them, and this primary grace of Christ became the ethical ideal they were called to realize subsequently.[70]

(4) Finally, it is no longer necessary or even permissible to speak of a radical separation between sacred and secular history. We need not go into Balthasar's theology of history in its entirety to mention the fact that he understands the whole of human history to be impregnated with the Word of God, and that he even ventures the possibility that we may be able, with the eyes of faith, to perceive God's providential activity in world history.

> For the history of the human race, into which the redeemer inserts himself, is not divided into two clearly separate and distinct histories. There is only one history, that of man from paradise to the last day, and its significance is not exhausted in the fact of Adam's fall and the eschatological redemption through Christ. Nor does the divine seed implanted in world history, there to 'die and rise again,' wish to establish its own second history alongside the first, but rather to propagate salvation in the one and only history.[71]

It is possible to summarize Balthasar's position on these matters in the following manner:

> God is under no sort of necessity to make use of man for his own self-revelation; but once he has decided on this and done so in an incarnation, all human dimensions ... are taken up and used to express the absolute personality.[72]

VI. Conclusion: Some Implications of Balthasar's Critique

We are now in a position to draw some conclusions from this rather lengthy discussion. It should be reiterated at this point that our intention was not to present Barth's theology in itself and then Balthasar's response to it. Instead, we were interested in Balthasar's understanding of Barth's theology in order to determine what Balthasar wished to appropriate from this theology for the Catholic struggles of his time. We mentioned at the very beginning that Balthasar understood this study as a way of reintroducing de Lubac's ideas under another name, for it was Balthasar's sincere conviction that in its innermost spirit Barth's insight into the problem of creation and redemption was very close to that of de Lubac. Indeed, it was his conviction that this novel approach, which both thinkers shared, opened up brand new ecumenical vistas between Catholics and Protestants, vistas which had been closed since the time of the Reformation.

In short, the difficulties which arose between the early reformers and their Catholic counterparts directly concerned the relationship between humanity's natural abilities and God's gift of grace. Unfortunately, at the time that these problems arose, the dominant understanding of the problem of nature and grace was a dualistic one. Both Luther and his interlocutors asked the same question: What can unassisted human nature do in order to prepare for God's grace? If their answers were different, their responses were still overly determined by an improper question.

With Barth's later theology a new possibility for dialogue between Protestants and Catholics was opened up because of his willingness to acknowledge the implications which creation and incarnation have for nature as a whole. Even if we agree with McCormack that Balthasar exaggerated the shift which occurred in Barth's thought, we still must insist that there is a shift in tone and emphasis from his early Romans commentary to his *Church Dogmatics*. This shift stemmed from his willingness to understand creation in terms of a presupposition for the covenant, that is, as a necessary precondition for God's work of grace. In this light it was possible for Balthasar to understand Barth's rejection of the analogy of being as a rejection of the idea of 'pure nature'. Once the Catholic acknowledges that even our natural knowledge of God is already the result of God's gift of creation, indeed, a result of the fact that all human beings are ordered in their very nature to be united with Christ, then the analogy of being ceases to be a human attempt to comprehend God.

That there continued to be differences between Barth and Balthasar, however, cannot be denied. Although there was certainly a major convergence in their understanding of analogy, when it came time to apply the 'implications' of this to concrete aspects of doctrine there remained fairly marked differences. Barth did not like Balthasar's attempt to show that the mysticism of Thérèse was 'Evangelical' in its spirit. Barth still feared that the attribution of saintliness to a human being or an institution would inevitably lead to detracting people's attention from Christ.[73] In other words, there is still a refusal, and this stems from Barth's continued doubts concerning the analogy of being, to acknowledge the full implications of God's decision to reveal himself as a human being. Missing is the more Eastern understanding that God unites himself, in the incarnation, to all of human nature, thereby transforming the capacities of that nature. This comes out most clearly in Barth's understanding of the Church, the liturgy, and the sacraments. To elaborate on this would require, however, a full comparison of Balthasar and Barth on these issues, and this we are not prepared to do. We have intentionally remained on the level, as did Balthasar, of formal issues.

The question which remains is what can be salvaged of Barth's work which will benefit Catholicism both in its attempt to articulate its own position and in its subsequent attempt to engage Protestantism. Balthasar raises such a question in the second half of his Barth study. His answer, and this is something which remained with him throughout his work on the massive trilogy, is Barth's christocentrism.

It is possible, at this time, to draw some cursory implications from Balthasar's study. Ultimately, Balthasar's assessment of Barth is a relatively positive one in which he insists that the above-mentioned 'tendencies' need not lead to a constraining system. This is why, I believe, Balthasar kept his study of Barth on the formal level, so that the concrete application of his principles could be made in a Catholic context. Balthasar simply felt that when Barth applied his principles, for instance, to ecclesiology, or Mariology, or the sacraments, he did not follow through with his christological starting-point. Therefore, Balthasar can insist that the 'nature' of Barth's theology does not exclude the 'nature' of Catholic theology. Also, because there is a convergence between Barth's approach and a Catholic christocentric approach on the formal level, there are grounds for hope that there may be convergence on particular doctrinal matters.[74] In fact, the difference between Barth's and Balthasar's formal approach is often less significant than the difference between Balthasar's and that of some other Catholics, or between Barth's and that of some other Protestants.

The crux of Balthasar's critique is simply that Barth is not always faithful to the full implications of his analogy of faith. What Balthasar said earlier about the dignity of creation as 'presupposition', and about the center in Christ implying a periphery which is distinct from Christ, implies that Barth should give creation 'more breathing room' (even according to his own standards). In other words, a christocentric approach to theology need not result, indeed *should not* result, in denying the creaturely realm its legitimate autonomy. What Balthasar suggests is that Catholic theology should incorporate Barth's christocentrism in a way that preserves the distinction between 'nature and grace' established in the analogy of being. This will help to prevent Catholic theology from making the mistakes that it has so often made since the Counter-Reformation:

> In all these systems that have been developed since the Counter-Reformation, we notice a distinct tendency to protect the concept of nature from the danger of Protestant subversion. But the tendency goes so far that post-Tridentine Catholic theologians not only try to set off nature from sin and grace but also feel obliged to prove that the sphere of nature can be isolated and depicted *in fact*.[75]

It is the purpose of the rest of Balthasar's study of Barth to illustrate what such a christocentric Catholic theology might look like. Here the reader is introduced to Catholic thinkers such as Romano Guardini, Henri de Lubac, Erich Pryzwara, Joseph Pieper, and others, all of whom accept the analogy of being as understood in the light of the marriage of the divine and human nature in Jesus Christ. Balthasar concludes this section with the following:

> These sketches of a Catholic christocentrism have shown that this is in no way what makes Protestantism distinctive. ... For it is the opinion that basically goes back to the opinion of the Fathers and of the theology of high Scholasticism. ... It is also not in conflict with the formula of the analogy of being, because the analogy of being, according to Pryzwara, is nothing other than the provisional and abstract expression for this ultimate truth [i.e., the truth revealed about humanity in the hypostatic union].[76]

Before looking at some specific applications of Balthasar's 'Catholic christocentrism', we must first examine his critique of two prevailing tendencies in Catholic theology, one related to the Church Fathers – the cosmological approach – and one related to modern Catholic theology – the anthropological approach. This will be necessary before we can summarize Balthasar's contribution to an ecumenical Catholic theology in the concluding chapter. Necessary for the following reason: if Balthasar is understood only in terms of his response to Luther and Barth, it is impossible to appreciate the degree to which he sought to forge an ecumenical Catholic theology for the next millennium. This new style of theology can only become visible in the course of Balthasar's critique of a tendency in some forms of Catholic theology towards what Jean-Luc Marion has called conceptual idolatry. Conversely, Balthasar's critique of cosmocentrism and anthropocentrism cannot be separated from his equally penetrating critique of Luther and Barth outlined in these last two chapters. It is only if Balthasar's theology is understood as mediating between the sometime Protestant tendency toward 'christomonism' and the sometime Catholic tendency toward 'conceptual idolatry' that his theological aesthetics can clearly emerge. This will hopefully become clear in the final two chapters.

4

The Cosmological and Anthropological Alternatives

I. Introduction

It should be reiterated at this point that Balthasar's engagement with Protestantism stands out in the midst of two other approaches. The strategy which reigned from Trent to Vatican I (often identified as Counter-Reformation) was not as interested in truly engaging the Protestant position as it was in correcting it. The more progressive, modern tactic, conversely, builds its dialogue upon those aspects of the faith in which both Catholics and Protestants can agree, while in varying degrees marginalizing those aspects of Catholicism which set it apart. Balthasar's approach, which begins with the presupposition that the fullness of the faith inheres in the *Catholica*, is rather to allow the Protestant critique to be raised within this fullness, to work, that is, like a leaven in order to preserve the Catholic structure from ossification. This is in keeping with Balthasar's conviction that when the Catholic Church countered the Reformers' errors, it actually denounced aspects which were originally a part of its own fullness.[1]

Rather than entering into the official ecumenical dialogues, which were underway in Balthasar's later years, he chose to bring his own appreciation of Luther and Barth into the service of forming a style of Catholic theology which would reflect the legitimate concerns of the Reformation, without having to sacrifice the 'symphonic' fullness of the Catholic faith. This 'style' of theology Balthasar identified as 'christocentric',[2] and it represents more than a simple return to the Church Fathers. Once the Reformation has taken place, it is no longer possible or even desirable to proceed as if it did not happen. Certain aspects of the Christian faith which were lying dormant in so much of post-Tridentine Catholic theology were being developed in Protestantism, reaching a highpoint, according to Balthasar, in the theology of Karl Barth. Any subsequent Catholic theology which was worthy of the name 'Catholic' could not afford to overlook this development.

In this part of our study, then, we wish to illustrate the manner in which Balthasar allows the distinct voice of the Reformation, even in terms of its focus on the folly of the cross of Christ, to shape his particular theological style. Because this comes out most clearly in his critique of a certain one-sidedness within the 'cosmocentric' and 'anthropocentric' approaches in Catholic theology, we will have to examine this critique in order to understand fully Balthasar's alternative. This will involve yet another examination of Balthasar's polemic against the Maréchalian-Rahnerian answer to modernity, but this time in the light of Balthasar's attempt to do justice to the Reformation critique of 'natural theology'.[3] We will maintain, in fact, that the very impetus for Balthasar's theological aesthetics lies in his passionate concern to reincorporate the Christ-centered, and cross-centered, approach of Luther and Barth into the *Catholica*, without sacrificing Catholicism's legitimate concern to relate the specific elements of the Christian faith in a positive manner to humanity's immortal longings.

Although it is true that the dialogue with Barth occurred relatively early in Balthasar's writing career, the effort to avoid the ever-present danger of subsuming the unique manifestation of God in Christ into a universal human standpoint provides the point of departure for his entire subsequent theology. What is more, Balthasar wishes to give due emphasis to the uniqueness of this revelation in Christ, without thereby forfeiting the Catholic concern, exemplified in Paul's speech at the Areopagus, to show the *universal* implications of this unique epiphany. I will argue that it is only in such an aesthetic approach to theology that one can do justice to God's concrete dealings in history, beginning with Israel, rather, Adam, and culminating in Christ, without thereby forfeiting Rahner's legitimate concern that the Christian faith be related in a positive manner to humanity's immortal longings.

After reminding the reader of those aspects of Luther's and Barth's theologies which Balthasar would like to see given a greater role within the Catholic faith, the chapter will proceed accordingly: (1) Balthasar's critique of the cosmological approach will be examined, as outlined in the small book, *Love Alone*, and developed in several later works. (2) This will be followed by a close look at Balthasar's explicit critique of the transcendental approach, for it is this approach which receives the bulk of his attention in the years following the writing of *Love Alone*. As with the other figures we have encountered in this study, the choice of Rahner in this context follows Balthasar's own lead. While there is no single representative of the cosmological approach as far as Balthasar is concerned, Rahner is singled out in Balthasar's theology as *the* modern representative of a Catholic anthropological approach. I think this is true for two reasons. First, Balthasar had an immense amount of respect for Rahner's gifts as a theologian, understood the influence that Rahner's theology was having and would have in Catholic circles, and was quite sympathetic with Rahner's attempt toward a reintegration of the orders of nature and grace. Secondly, because Balthasar was convinced of the legitimacy of Rahner's intentions, he understood his own theology as striving towards the same goal – again, the reintegration of the orders of nature and grace – without forfeiting the strangeness and uniqueness of Christ in the process. In short, Balthasar felt that Rahner's theology could not fully elude the Barthian critique, but felt that it was possible to pursue Rahner's intentions in a way that could.

II. Summary of Luther's and Barth's Contribution

In the chapter on Luther attention was drawn, especially, to his critique of the human encroachment on the freedom of God, whether this be in the form of human reason's claim to understand God prior to his self-revelation in Christ, or in the claim of human works to righteousness apart from the unmerited gift of God's grace. We agree with von Loewenich, then, that Luther's *theologia crucis* is not something which can be relegated to the early Luther, the Luther, that is, who is still under the spell of the 'mystics', but is a central element in his entire subsequent theological approach. The cross is as much an affront to human works, that is, as it is to human reason. To say that Luther dispensed with a theology of the cross after, say, the *Heidelberg Disputation* would be no less of a mistake than to say that he dispensed with an insistence on justification by faith, for already in this disputation Luther's 'theology of the cross' is directed at the kind of 'works righteousness' found, in his view, in Aristotle's *Ethics*. Luther can therefore say: 'We do not become righteous by doing righteous deeds but, having been made righteous, we do righteous deeds.' And directly following this thesis is one which mentions Aristotle explicitly: 'Virtually the entire *Ethics* of Aristotle is the worst enemy of grace.'[4] This theme continues in the *Heidelberg Disputation* with the statement: 'He who wishes to philosophize by using Aristotle without danger to his soul must first become thoroughly foolish in Christ.'[5]

Attention has already been drawn to those aspects of Luther's theology which Balthasar finds wanting – namely, an extreme focus on the uniqueness of God's activity in the cross which makes it difficult to see the continuity in God's work of creation and redemption – but what is important at this point is the shift in perspective which Luther's theology forced upon the later Middle Ages. God's 'personhood' was brought to the fore in such a way that the existential aspects of the Christian's experience of God could now be made central to the theological enterprise. In short, Balthasar saw in Luther an attempt to overcome the ever-widening gap between theology and sanctity. The focus on knowing God as he is manifest in Christ upon the cross, which had been relegated largely to the so-called mystics in the late Middle Ages, was moved to the center of the theological discussion. Balthasar sees this as a positive shift, as the following, especially pertinent quote should make obvious:

> So all 'Christian culture' remains in an ineluctable crisis: very often, indeed in the best cases, the framework is understood as exhibiting the central mystery which may indeed remain virtually unexpressed – Denys is a good example, for he virtually never speaks of the Cross and Resurrection but regards the whole cosmos as liturgical worship; often the showy splendour of such cosmic and mystical piety leads to a forgetting of Christ, and the world of beauty overshadows the mystery of the biblical glory, and *one must wait for Luther* – whose influence is only slowly beginning to be felt in the Catholic realm – to bring the sharpness of the crisis to consciousness. Yet with the supposed collapse of the 'Platonic' tradition through the rise of the modern natural sciences the question is only shifted: certainly to begin with (with Kant and his various followers) a new anthropocentrism replaces the old cosmocentrism, yet this means no more than taking seriously the freedom of the human spirit and (something that was always known) the teleology of nature at the level of mankind; so the old religious *theios kosmos* and the enthusiasm for it – in Schelling, Darwin, Soloviev, Teilhard de Chardin – must rise up again virtually unchanged, and the question about 'beauty' and 'glory', about oblivion of Christ and consciousness of Christ, be posed again without alteration.[6]

It is not too much of an exaggeration to say that the remainder of this chapter will only be an elaboration of this quote, but our purpose in presenting it now is only to draw attention to that aspect of Luther's thought to which Balthasar responds sympathetically. Against any endeavor to do theology in such a way that God's activity in Christ is understood as only one instance – even if the greatest – of the workings of God in the cosmos in general or in humanity in particular, Luther announces the necessity of the cross. This is central in Luther's view because of the inherent sinfulness involved in humanity's attempts to understand God from his 'invisible' workings in nature. Although Balthasar is not prepared to go as far as Luther in his denunciation of 'natural theology' – indeed Balthasar defends the 'analogy of being' against Barth – he agrees with Luther that every prior conception of God must be measured by the life, death and resurrection of Christ, that *theologia* must always be rooted in *economia*. He also knows, with Luther, that, because of human sinfulness, the manifestation of God in Jesus Christ will usually appear as foolishness unless one learns the 'ignorance' of the cross.

As was pointed out above, however, Luther's theology failed in its refusal to relate the God of Jesus Christ in a more positive manner to the God of creation, the God of the gospel to the God of the law. Put more simply, Luther did not stress sufficiently the universal implications of God's activity in Christ. Balthasar, therefore, will turn to Barth in order to find a Protestant thinker who rediscovers the importance of the 'Cosmic' Christ. In Barth, Balthasar saw an unswerving attempt to remain fixed on the splendid figure of Christ, without thereby forgetting about the world for which Christ came; he found, in short, a Protestant theologian who was ready to appreciate the continuity in God's work of creation and redemption. Barth did this, however, not by proceeding *from* a general presence of God located in nature, accessible to unaided reason, and then *to* God as he is revealed in Jesus Christ; instead, Barth understood the entire creation to be already in Christ, understood, that is, that world history is contained *within* God's one and only concrete plan to reconcile all things to himself. Accordingly, Barth never had to prescind from a Christ-centered perspective in order to pay tribute to the glories of God found in the cosmos at large. This is why Barth could make the quip that in God's presence the angels played Bach, but that *en famille* they played Mozart!

Towards the end of the Barth study, Balthasar raises a question concerning which aspects of Barth's thought are of the greatest service to modern Catholicism. His answer: 'those that involve the foundations for a christocentrism, for the historicity of nature and the created character of worldly truth'. What is most valuable, then, is Barth's insistence upon doing theology from the concrete situation, that situation in which the realms of history and nature are understood in terms of their embeddedness in the overarching order of redemption. That does not mean that the Catholic has to forfeit the notion of the relative priority of creation to covenant in the order of salvation-history, for it is only here that one can speak of a *potentia oboedientialis*; it is simply that one must always keep in mind the fact that such a potential is only possible in the light of the one plan of God in concrete history. 'The first Adam had a determinate nature, but the second Adam is the ground and goal of this nature.'[7] Regarding the notion that this approach might be overly restricting, Balthasar responds:

> [T]his *concretissimum* is also the fullest and richest of realities, which is why it is so inexhaustibly rich in interpretative value. As even it is not mute or a-logical but is the source of all the meaning in existence and nature, justifying and fulfilling them. And within the various interpretations of this event (best circumscribed by the category of contemplation), we find room for the use of universal concepts, categories, properties and finally of Being itself.[8]

As far as Balthasar was concerned, Catholic theology had nothing to fear from such an approach, and, indeed, had already witnessed such, without Barth's occasional excesses, in the Church Fathers and various modern figures in whom Balthasar sees the combination of catholicity and christocentrism.

III. The Third Way: Love Alone

A consistent failure among Balthasar interpreters – even those who wish to grant him a more pronounced role in the current theological landscape – lies in the tendency to see Balthasar primarily as a dogmatic theologian – or, better, an in-church theologian – who eventually came to despair of the possibility of a dialogue with a modernity blind to the glory of God in the cosmos, and so retreated to the work of intra-church polemics. If Rahner and Lonergan, so the story goes, will be remembered for their contributions in the area of Fundamental (read mediating) Theology, Balthasar's niche is to be found in Dogmatic Theology. As such, he will be granted a complementary, but extrinsic, relationship to their work. While there is a certain amount of truth to this interpretation, and even Balthasar suggests in some places that his theology and Rahner's can, at a certain level, be brought into complementary dialogue,[9] there is a danger here of missing the distinct contribution to Fundamental Theology that Balthasar has made. Balthasar is not ignorant of the very real need for a 'fundamental' aspect to theology's overall task, nor is he unwilling to give philosophy its proper role both in the human enterprise as a whole and in theology's endeavor to understand its faith, nor, finally, is he ready to dispense with the urgent task of engaging modernity. Rather, a case could be made that Balthasar's particular presentation of the nature of Fundamental Theology, his understanding of the relationship of faith to reason, and his rather aristocratic manner of engaging modernity has largely fallen on deaf ears – perhaps he would have preferred 'dull eyes' – or was, simply, ahead of its time. In a context which is increasingly being designated 'postmodern', Balthasar's Fundamental Theology is beginning to look more acceptable to many than its transcendental counterpart.

As we will show, Balthasar is just as interested in the truth of Christianity as he is in its beauty:[10] the real question concerns the nature of truth. In the beginning of *Theo-Logik* Balthasar makes this perfectly clear:

> It is a fruit of modern rationalism that we think we can easily relegate the True to the realm of the purely theoretical, in such a way that the Good and the Beautiful get placed outside of the rationally justifiable. These latter are then reduced to the arbitrary and subjective, to the world of private belief and taste. With this, the image [Bild] of Being, the unified view of the world, is torn apart and any genuine

> discussion concerning the truth becomes impossible. Discussion becomes focused on common, trivial, and finally, negligible matters, while the deepest questions of truth, which cannot be dealt with apart from decision and discernment, remain buried in the false reserve of silence. When the True is without decision, then the personal, worldview-determining decision is without truth. Such undermining of the discussion of truth – as will be shown later – is equal to an annihilation of truth.[11]

Even a quick reading of the small book *Love Alone* betrays that Balthasar's suggestion that love has been exiled from its central place in theology has implications both for the theology of the early Church, which often followed the Greeks too closely in speaking of God in Platonic categories, and for modern thought, in which 'truth' has been reduced to the kind of certitude that one finds in the exact sciences. In this sense, a 'theological aesthetics' is intended to counter rationalism of any sort.

> If there were no such thing as the resurrection of the flesh, then the truth would lie with gnosticism and every form of idealism down to Schopenhauer and Hegel, for whom the finite must literally perish if it is to become spiritual and infinite. But the resurrection of the flesh vindicates the poets in a definitive sense: the aesthetic scheme of things, which allows us to possess the infinite within the finitude of form (however it is seen, understood or grasped spiritually) is right. The decision, therefore, lies between the conflicting parties of myth and revelation.[12]

However, because the ancient philosophical worldview understood that the transcendentals of Being belonged together, even the 'idealism' of Plato would never have thought of dissociating truth from beauty. This is why Balthasar can be critical of Dionysius in one breath for neglecting 'positive theology', and in the next breath call him the most aesthetic of theologians. If modern theology's tendency has been to attempt to do theology from the most objective – even neutral – stance, Dionysius could only conceive of theology in erotic terms:

> And the divine Eros also brings rapture, not allowing them that are touched by it to belong to themselves, but only to the objects of their love … And hence the great Paul, constrained by the divine Eros, and having received a share in its ecstatic power, says, with inspired utterance: 'I live, and yet no longer I, but Christ lives in me.' These are the words of a true lover, of one who (as he himself states) was beside himself (out of his senses!) and unto God (2 Cor. 5.13), not possessing a life of his own (2 Cor. 5.15) but the life of his Beloved, a life surrounded on all sides by ardent love … In short, both to possess eros and to love erotically belong to everything Good and Beautiful, and eros has its primal roots in the Beautiful and the Good: eros exists and comes into being only through the Beautiful and Good.[13]

This is an important distinction to keep in mind: in one sense, both the ancients, with their cosmocentric approach, and the moderns, with their anthropocentric approach, will come under the critique of being forgetful of beauty, but in another sense, modernity – the 'metaphysics of the spirit' – will be singled out for its reduction of truth to the 'theoretical'.

One other thing should be clarified before taking a closer look at the program of *Love Alone*. Although Balthasar's aesthetic approach includes within it the Protestant concern for the concrete and the historical, it does not simply stop there. As was said above, Balthasar's theological aesthetics cuts both ways. If one aspect of his strategy is to make more room for the concrete, historical realm, another aspect is his concern for the inseparability of form and matter, 'Spirit and Institution', and the like. One of the weaknesses that Balthasar will find in both Luther and Barth is their persistent tendency to oppose 'spirit' to 'matter'. Here Balthasar's 'narrative' sensibilities are complemented by his 'sacramental' sensibilities, and the above quote brings out both of these aspects at once. For Christianity, there cannot be a merely dialectical understanding of spirit and matter because Christ was raised in the flesh.[14]

It is possible, and perhaps even necessary, to understand Balthasar's theological work as one of the first, and certainly the most sustained, attempts by a Roman Catholic theologian to come to terms with the *origins* of postmodern thought.[15] Certainly Rahner has also attempted to integrate Aquinas' philosophy into the thought-worlds of Kant and Heidegger, but, as Rowan Williams has pointed out,

> Rahner's relation to this hermeneutical development is less easy to assess. Certainly the Heidegger of *Sein und Zeit* is a considerable (if muted) presence in *Spirit in the World*; but whether the later Heidegger has left any serious impression on Rahner's mature work is dubious. In so far as Rahner remains firmly within the limits of a transcendentalist analysis of subjectivity, he belongs in that world of 'onto-theology' and Cartesian introspection on which Heidegger so firmly turned his back. Attempts have been made to present Rahner as the author of a historical hermeneutics comparable to Gadamer's, chiefly on the ground of Rahner's repeated insistence upon the historical mediation of all consciousness; but the question remains of whether, if this historical mediation is taken with complete seriousness, the whole transcendentalist apparatus will not need radical revision, such as Rahner has not in fact chosen to undertake.[16]

In any case, Balthasar's insistence upon the indispensable role of the concrete in our apprehension of the transcendental is surely in keeping with his concern to do justice not only to Luther's and Barth's concerns, but also Heidegger's critique of onto-theology. If, in fact, postmodernism finds its origins in Kierkegaard's critique of Hegel, then the very thing which makes Balthasar's thought amicable to Protestantism is the very thing which enables him to sustain a positive dialogue with postmodern philosophy.

This willingness to engage the thought of postmodernity is something which is evident from Balthasar's earliest work – *Apokalypse der deutschen Seele* – wherein he engages thinkers from Lessing to Goethe to Kierkegaard to Nietzsche to Heidegger, among others! And *Love Alone* already illustrates the degree to which Balthasar is ready to question the legitimacy of the project of Modernity in a critique which echoes those of Kierkegaard and Heidegger. The main question asked is this: What role does love have in humanity's access to the transcendent? And, does the universe still bear any traces of this transcendence? What Balthasar suggests is that the original metaphysical question – Why is there anything at all rather than nothing? – cannot be simply ignored; neither is it answerable apart from the context of love, which is really the context of the aesthetic.

It would be misleading, however, if we were to highlight this philosophical aspect of Balthasar's thought – which is really a critique of Enlightenment rationalism – at the expense of the theological emphasis to which it is giving voice. Repeatedly Balthasar has pointed out that the realm of aesthetics is simply a way of highlighting the fact that we do not have access to reality apart from its mediation in concrete forms, and that these concrete forms, whether a beautiful object in nature, a beautiful work of art, or even a beautiful person, such as a saint, give us a unique and unsurpassable access to this transcendental reality. Of course this presupposes a 'theological a priori', it presupposes, that is, that the place where Christianity stands apart from all other philosophical and religious approaches – in its christological marriage of matter and spirit, the concrete and the universal – is the very place where it is most 'relevant' to humanity in its movement towards God. So, Balthasar's concern is not primarily a philosophical one, but a theological one. Balthasar insists, at one and the same time, *both* that theology necessarily presupposes some philosophy – implicitly or otherwise – *and* that philosophy is never hermetically sealed from the influence of theology. In short, theology always needs philosophy in order to do its work, but not just any philosophy will do.

> The thesis, laid out at the beginning of *Love Alone*, is this:
> The framework of God's message to man in Christ cannot be tied to the world in general, nor to man in particular; God's message is theological, or better theo-pragmatic. It is an act of God on man; an act done for and on behalf of man – and only then to man.[17]

This thesis alludes to the place which aesthetics will play in Balthasar's thought, while exposing the weaknesses of what he calls the 'cosmological' and 'anthropological' methods. What sets Christianity apart for Balthasar is the fact that in this religion the way to God, which is certainly of benefit to humanity, is presented to us in a person; in fact, this person *is* the way.

This reversal of orders, from humanity's search for God to God's search for humanity, is best understood, according to Balthasar, in aesthetic terms, or, in the terms of love.[18] The interpersonal realm of love is enlightening because in this realm the universality of scope is coextensive with the 'categorial' aspect of manifestation. The universal experience of love is only available to human beings in their concrete dealings with other persons. It is also revealing because the realm of love places a much-needed check on the hubris of human reason, especially in its tendency to objectify the other: there is no sense in which I can demand the love of another, nor is it possible for me to know the other apart from the other's willing surrender to me.

This approach is aesthetic in the sense that it emphasizes the aspect of receptivity, just mentioned, over that of striving. In contrast to Descartes' search for truth from within the *cogito*, the aesthetic approach places itself at the mercy of that which is not itself. One stands before a beautiful painting primarily as a receiver, ready to receive something new, something not already possessed by the subject. Think of the submission of a good listener before a symphony of Mozart. There is a confidence that everything is just as it should be, that not one note could be otherwise: the listener is forgetful of herself and is enraptured by the world of the music. In what is a fitting pointer to the appropriate attitude towards God's self-revelation in Christ, the subject here is in no way the measure of the truth of the work of art, rather, the work of art measures the subject.[19] This intentional reversal of the Enlightenment's obsession with subjectivity is the main purpose of Balthasar's theological aesthetics, and,

> this theological approach, far from being a dispensable theological by-road, is in fact the one possible approach to the heart of theology – the cosmic world-historical approach, and the path of anthropological verification, being secondary aspects, complementary aspects to it.[20]

This reminder of Balthasar's theological aesthetics is intended to serve as the necessary backdrop to Balthasar's critique of the cosmological and transcendental approaches. Let it be said again: Balthasar will allow for a certain degree of complementarity between these approaches, as the just-mentioned quote makes explicit, but this cannot be in an extrinsic manner. In other words, it cannot be that the cosmological or anthropological approach serves as one's Fundamental Theology, while a more aesthetic, dramatic approach serves for one's theology proper. Rather, one's Fundamental Theology, and even one's philosophy itself, must bear the marks of the 'way of love', for all natural approaches are already marked by the fact that they might not have existed, that they are, quite simply, already gift. And a gift will always bear the marks of its giver: nature will always, already bear the traces of love, even before the gift of grace, and apart from any 'supernatural existential'.[21] All of the questions put to these contrasting approaches must be understood in this context.

IV. The Cosmological Approach

One of the most striking things about Balthasar's critique of the cosmological approach, the definition of which will emerge in what follows, is the degree to which he is indebted to this very approach. Indeed, often, when Balthasar is discussing one of the Church Fathers, one cannot help but discern a certain hint of self-description. One of the most appealing aspects of this approach for Balthasar is the fact that it arose at a time when the boundaries between theology and philosophy were not yet clearly demarcated. According to the Church Fathers, the philosophical quest, that is, the quest for truth, proceeded from the same set of questions as did the theological quest; the two were inseparable because both the philosopher and the theologian were interested in the question of the *reality* of the world and in the pursuit of the 'good life'. The Christian theologian at this time simply insisted that the revelation of God in Jesus Christ gave a center to the philosophical quest which had been previously lacking. Far from declaring the philosophical quest for the ultimate meaning of the 'cosmos' an illegitimate one, the Fathers saw it as a precursor to the message of Christ, as a '*praeparatio evangelica*'.[22] What attracts Balthasar to this standpoint is the manner in which it betrays a certain youthful confidence – it is not simply a literary flourish when Balthasar refers to the early Church as the Church's adolescent years[23] – that all of the truth that it finds is already Christian. The entire neo-Platonic schema of the eternal procession from and return to the One is taken over almost uncritically by the Fathers to describe Christ as the origin and goal of all things. Along with this theme of 'egress' and 'regress' came the entire ancient notion of exemplars, eternally existing in the eternal realm of the One, and providing the foundation for the unchanging 'forms' of the world. These 'forms' or 'ideas' were spiritual, not material, and were therefore pure, above the world of decaying matter. If there is a marked tendency in the early Fathers to degrade the bodily realm, this neo-Platonic framework is certainly partly responsible.[24]

Although Balthasar cannot hide his admiration for the bold attempt of the early Church to confront its culture with the truth of the gospel, their attempt, that is, to bring the distinctively Christian to bear upon the prevailing worldview of the day in the fullest confidence that the Christian view of things could withstand and survive the confrontation, he is also aware that in this very strength lurks an inherent danger.

> For ironically enough, it was precisely the very certainty of victory with which the Fathers contemplated all the truths that they encountered, it was their very confidence that these truths were already Christian and which they therefore claimed for their own, using them to pour the truth of the Gospel into the language of their time, the thought forms of late Hellenism (above all, of neo-Platonism), that hid the danger of an unconscious alienation of the original deposit of revelation. This danger was all the greater when late Hellenism itself possessed a strongly developed religiosity, thereby threatening, in this hand-to-hand battle of the two forms of religion, to swamp the mutual differences with an apparently supernatural and world-transcendent character.[25]

In a confidence which betrays its youth, the early Church used the language of ancient philosophy to express its message of Christ without realizing the danger inherent in all such attempts, namely, that the differences will fade in the light of the similarities. Only the heretics, for instance Arius and his uncritical use of the neo-Platonist scheme in his Christology, would force the Church to delineate its position more clearly.[26]

This synthesis, however, survived up through the Middle Ages in various forms, perhaps culminating in Nicholas of Cusa's *De Pace Fide* (1453). In this treatise Nicholas presents a 'council' which takes place in heaven in order to deal with the problem of the various religions which have come to populate the earth. In a manner which is strikingly similar to that of the Fathers, Nicholas insists that all of these religious approaches are simply incomplete expressions of the one, true faith. 'Polytheism presupposes one God; a true belief in creation leads naturally to the doctrine of the Trinity; a true prophetical religion hints at the fulfillment of the Incarnation, etc.'[27] Of course Nicholas could presuppose a certain belief in God, indeed, in a God who was always above all that could be conceived of him. The multiplicity of religions, in the end, could be attributed to the basic ignorance of the masses. Nicholas was confident that once everyone was presented with the Catholic faith, all that he had argued in this treatise would be recognized as true. As Balthasar sums up Nicholas's view: 'The wise, whatever their religion, should find little difficulty in reaching that one Catholic position upon which all their fragmentary wisdoms are focused.'[28]

The common emphasis here is upon a natural religiosity which glides smoothly into the Christian view of things, the latter which unites and completes the former. Balthasar also mentions Thomas More's *Utopia* in this regard, and here we are moving into the Renaissance appropriation of the cosmological approach. According to More, whose version of Christianity is reduced to its simplest and most luminous form, when the citizens of Utopia were confronted with the message of Christianity they were easily persuaded of its truth because of its similarities to their own natural religious proclivities. Balthasar is quick to point out at this point that we are not yet dealing with the Deistic instinct to reduce Christianity to its essence in order to mitigate religious intolerance; rather, More is filled with the confidence of a Church Father that the God of Christianity is manifest throughout the entire cosmos, so that when the truths of Christianity are introduced, they will be quickly and easily appropriated. This was not yet, in other words, the elevation of humanity to a position from which it could judge God.

> Yet even the Platonic conception of the world revived at the Renaissance was backward looking; in contrast with the growing natural sciences it was already an anachronism. The removal of the gods from their pedestals was at the same stroke the elevation of man. In place of the world-immanent Logos of the ancient world there slipped in unnoticed 'natural' religion, ethics and philosophy, corresponding to the nature common to all races, peoples and ages; one part of revelation was regarded as belonging to this natural religion (in accordance with Rom. 1:18ff.), while the other part was regarded as belonging to the 'positive' religions (Christian and others), so that these positive religions were more and more insistently called upon to justify themselves before the judgment-seat of the religion of mankind.[29]

In this last paragraph Balthasar charts the gradual transition from a Christian cosmology, in which the cosmic awareness of God is transformed and taken up into the Christian view of the world, to a 'natural' standpoint, in which the Christian worldview is allotted a place alongside of the other 'positive religions'. 'The cosmological background no longer provided a verification for the truths of Christianity; it had absorbed the whole of Christianity into itself.'[30] It is in the light of this final development, where the Christian appropriation of the ancient cosmic worldview turns into the naturalistic appropriation of certain 'general' characteristics of Christianity, that Balthasar places his evaluation of the cosmological approach in general. But, before turning our attention to Balthasar's understanding of this transformation, it is necessary to explain more clearly Balthasar's relationship to the Church Fathers, for this is where the cosmological view arises.

Put briefly, the cosmological viewpoint is based on the ubiquitous presence of the unchanging and transcendent in the world of matter and change. We have already discussed this above in terms of the analogy of being. A further characteristic of this viewpoint, then, is its elevation of the world of spirit over the world of matter, which issues forth in an entire ethic. While Balthasar is one of the chief defenders of the fact that the Church Fathers were not simply Platonists who used Christian language – the sometimes prevailing German assessment of, say, Dionysius – he does acknowledge a certain Platonizing of Christianity at points, which he finds to be misleading. It is in this context that one must understand his repeated assertion that Christianity should have pursued a dialogue with the poets which at least equaled that of its dialogue with the philosophers. It is also here that one finds a certain paradox in Balthasar's view of the Fathers: he is at once insistent on the need for the Church to return to her wellsprings in order to gain new life in her attempt to deal with contemporary problems, and at the same time constantly cautioning the Church against the tendency to assimilate the Christian message too blithely to general philosophical terms. If we look more deeply, however, we see no real contradiction here, for the appropriation of the past is never simply a matter of repetition. It is always a matter of translating certain insights that are perennial and leaving behind certain vistas which are no longer open to the present. Balthasar uses the metaphor of adolescence in order to illuminate a proper attitude to the past.

> We should like to reread a few pages of that intimate journal written by the Church when she was seventeen years old. This we do from the same distance of age but also with the same respectful admiration for the person we once were. It would be a want of taste to desire, when we are forty, to bring laboriously to a conclusion one of those blazing fragments we had carelessly left undone when we were twenty. Youthful fire is not meant to warm up those who are old. We shall not collect the living and sacred documents of our life (and the history of the Church is our life) as a person would collect stamps or butterflies. That would be to demonstrate that we are already dead. Let us read history, our history, as a living account of what we once were, with the double-edged consciousness that all of this has gone on forever and that, in spite of everything, that period of youth and every moment of our lives remain mysteriously present at the wellsprings of our soul in a kind of delectable eternity.[31]

As we have already pointed out, Balthasar admired the daring and confidence which he found in the early Church's willingness to confront every this-worldly thought-form with its Christian message. The question which Balthasar raises is the degree to which the patterns of thought at this time were allowed to distort certain distinctively Christian elements. There are essentially two chief areas in which Balthasar finds evidence of this latter: the first of these is the habit of looking at the world in terms of its graded emanation from a purely spiritual God, and the second is the tendency to construe salvation in terms of a return to this original, spiritual state of affairs.

> In neo-Platonism the relationship of God and world is most fundamentally conceived according to the schema of 'participation'. The world is essentially *what* participates, while God is what is partaken *of*. Seen from God, God is the One who gives a portion, the One who, as it were, holds his own being from himself but who also externalizes himself; and this *egressio* of God from himself *is* itself the world. A series of steps in the potencies of Being characterizes this progressive egression of God from himself. In Plotinus they are called, in descending order: spirit–soul–matter ... To God's egression there corresponds, as the second phase, a

're-uniting' in God, in which the movement of descent reverses itself, the potencies are reabsorbed into one another, each one into the next higher, until they finally all return to God.[32]

The chief difficulty in the attempt to assimilate this structure to that of Christianity is the latter's emphasis on the essential goodness of creation – which includes its essential contingency – and on the fact that in a concrete existent 'the fullness of the Godhead dwelt in bodily form'. Deirdre Carabine has identified two 'themes' which stem from this neo-Platonic framework which Balthasar finds problematic: first, *katabasis/anabasis* – what we have been referring to as egress and regress – and second, the 'Cappadocian concept of the incomprehensibility of God', the latter stemming from the purely spiritual nature of this God.[33] Both of these 'themes' make it difficult to account fully for the Trinitarian nature of the Christian faith. That is, although the Church Fathers were able to articulate a properly Christian understanding of the Trinity, e.g., in the Councils, they found it hard to find a corresponding trinitarian spirituality.

[D]espite the formally orthodox post-Nicene view of the Trinity, no corresponding trinitarian piety and mysticism seemed inclined to develop. For example, in the mystical writings of Gregory of Nyssa one can almost touch the fact, so palpable is it, that the loveliest trinitarian and dogmatic passages in his work remain almost without influence on the actual mystical parties who were striving to ascend to God – not to the trinitarian God but to the absolutely simple 'essence' of God that stands on the summit of the Platonic pyramid.[34]

The mysticism which flows out of the patristic period, while containing certain highpoints which will never become dispensable, also has a marked tendency to degrade the bodily and this-worldly.

But what is most decisive in the outcome of this strategy is the total effect it has on the tendency of the Christian life, the direction of its ideal, its asceticism and mysticism. In consequence of the movement of the ascending, step-by-step return of the world potencies into God, this movement proceeds unambiguously away from the material to the spiritual. Spiritualization, presented in a thousand different colorations, is the basic tendency of the patristic epoch. Early monasticism – with its extremely ascetical experiments, its training in denial of the body, its Encratite traits, its individualism – shows this most clearly: Along with its extraordinarily splendid sides, this brand of monasticism clearly shows the peril of this movement.[35]

In fact, Balthasar is not fully comfortable with the Eastern notion that God became man so that man might become God. 'Balthasar's understanding of the concept of deification is closer to that of Maximus Confessor: it is the reaffirmation and restoration of created humanity in its proper and God-established integrity.'[36] This difference centers around Balthasar's concerns that the patristic writers, under the influence of Plotinus's emanationist theme, sometimes forgot the proper distinction between God and the world established in the doctrine of creation, and thereby lost a sense for the dignity of the particular. We are again back to the proper relationship between God and the world which is articulated in the analogy of being, which finds its concrete expression in the incarnation. Since God became a human being, the essential goodness of the human is affirmed; since Jesus is not only fully God, but also fully human, humanity is not something that has to be diminished in order for divinity to flourish.

> The man Christ is, at one and the same time, a genuine human being and a human being who has been assumed into God. As genuine man he is not a super man [*Übermensch*], but rather the perfection of creatureliness in its proper ontological and cognitive distance from the Creator, the perfection of the Old Testament covenant-relationship between the chosen people, the chosen individual, and the God of the Covenant. In this sense Christ possesses archetypal faith and the hiddenness of the relation to God which it implies. But ... he is man *only* as assumed man, he understands even his genuinely human experience of God as an expression and function of his divine person ... [37]

For Balthasar, one need not cease to be human in order to become an instrument for God; indeed, it is precisely in our humanness that we become God's servants. On the other hand, our humanity, far from being threatened by being taken into God's service, finds its proper expression only there. There is a reversal, then, of the patristic emphasis on *ascent* to God; now the emphasis is on our being, like Christ, *sent* by God.[38]

The second problem which Balthasar addresses is the patristic stress on the ineffability of God. Here, an extreme negative theology, stemming from Plotinus' insistence that the One is beyond all categories of human knowing, is not always sufficiently and integrally related to a positive theology, stemming from the incarnation.

> According to Gregory of Nyssa, even the Incarnation does not reveal God's nature, it simply manifests his goodness to humanity. For Balthasar, on the other hand, the fact that the Incarnation guarantees ever open access to the Father, means that we cannot, as some of the Fathers have intimated, understand the Son to be a sign pointing beyond himself to the groundlessness of the Father. Christ is not a means to an end, but a 'legible' form: the content is within the form not behind it.[39]

This latter phrase, 'the content is within the form not behind it', is a key aspect of Balthasar's theological aesthetics and will often serve as a point of departure between his work and that of the patristics which he admires so much. A distinction must be kept in mind at this point between Balthasar's discussion of general patristic tendencies, which admittedly he finds throughout the work of specific patristic thinkers, and his discussions of individual patristic thinkers, such as Maximus, Origen, Gregory of Nyssa, and the like, which is always more nuanced and generally more positive. In fact, Balthasar will often find, in one and the same thinker, a model of his theological aesthetics *and* tendencies toward Platonist spiritualism.[40]

It is in keeping with Balthasar's concerns regarding the dangerous tendency in patristic thought to overemphasize the 'egress–regress' schemata over that of the descending God, and the tendency to sever *theologia* from *economia* that he exalts Maximus the Confessor as *the* theologian of the patristic period. All of the dangerous inclinations toward Platonism which Balthasar finds in Dionysius – and this goes even for the very positive assessment of Dionysius laid out in the second volume of GL – are avoided in Maximus' consistent grounding of theology in Christology. Maximus is the aesthetic theologian par excellence because he applies the unity of spirit and matter, which occurs in Christ, to his entire worldview. In this christological outlook the Platonist tendency to degrade the material and creaturely is overcome so that the creaturely now finds its true end in unification with Christ, and this without being totally absorbed into the divine.

> It is only in the coming of Christ that it became indisputably clear that the creature is not the pure negative of God, and that it thus cannot be redeemed onesidedly by mystical dissolution in God, but – even with its elevation to divine participation and its dying to this world – only in the explicit preservation and perfection of its nature. The great deed of Maximus remains the choice of the christological formula as the axial point of his world view.[41]

The centrality in Maximus's thought of this unification of opposites in Christ also militates against the tendency to downplay the *economia* in favor of the *theologia*, for if God chose to manifest himself in what is sensible, that which is sensible receives a newfound value. So, Balthasar can quote Maximus approvingly in the following vein:

> [O]nce Christ had finished his work for us in the history of salvation and together with the assumed body had ascended, he unified through himself heaven and earth, and joined the sensible things with the spiritual and so showed forth the unity of creation in the polarity of its parts.[42]

By way of summary then, Balthasar's critique of the 'cosmological' approach centers around its tendency to make an overly hasty synthesis of Greek and Christian thought in such a way that the distinctively Christian emphasis on the centrality of the visible Christ for our knowledge of God, and the radical incomprehensibility of God's agapaic descent to us – over and against any erotic ascent to God – is in danger of being lost.

This means, especially, that Balthasar will want to insist on a consistent theology of the cross in order to counter such tendencies. Although he will defend many of the individual Church Fathers against the accusations of Hellenization from a Harnack, he will acknowledge that a greater emphasis on the importance of the historical-contingent would have benefited this glorious age of the Church. This helps to explain Balthasar's repeated conjecture that the Church should have focused at least as much of its energies to the dialogue with tragedy as it did with philosophy. But let us give Balthasar the last word on such concerns:

> None of these three themes – procession–return, *eros–desiderium*, the beauty of the soul–eschatological marriage feast – can be spared the critical question: in what relation they stand to 'philosophical' beauty and 'biblical' glory. Wherever the monstrance has referred to itself instead of to the bread and has drawn men's gaze to itself, it has awakened Christian mistrust and finally called down upon itself Christian iconoclasm. And yet such iconoclasm was never a solution, because it is negative and contradicts the universality of Christian truth. In the end there remains the critical balance which demands, ever again, Christian watchfulness about what is distinctive.[43]

That Balthasar has defined his own theological task as striking such a balance, between philosophical reductionism and iconoclastic sectarianism, should by now have become obvious. Having examined Balthasar's engagement with the 'cosmocentric' approach of the Fathers, we can now proceed to his engagement with the 'anthropocentric' turn of modern theology.

V. The Anthropological Alternative: Balthasar's Critique of Rahner

Before proceeding to Balthasar's critique of Rahner, the following should be made clear. The intent of this section is not to present Balthasar's entire critique of Rahner and then offer an evaluation thereof. This has been done often enough, although without a real resolution. Instead, we are interested in Balthasar's critique insofar as it highlights two aspects of the present study: first, as it serves to highlight Balthasar's desire to do justice to certain aspects of the Protestant critique of Catholic theological method, especially as this stems from Luther and Barth; second, as this critique serves to highlight Balthasar's own approach to theology, which he identifies as 'theological aesthetics'. The first of these, that Balthasar's critique of Rahner stems from his ecumenical concerns, is too often overlooked in the secondary literature, and, even when it is acknowledged, it is given too little weight. Also, it is not our intention to offer a presentation of Rahner's thought, which we could then compare to Balthasar's; this would require a book in itself. We are interested only in Balthasar's understanding of Rahner and his critique of this understanding, in as much as this will help us to better understand Balthasar's ecumenical theological style. It is admitted, then, at the outset that there are places in Balthasar where he exaggerates Rahner's position, where he takes thoughts out of their original context, and where he overlooks places in Rahner's thought where certain dangerous tendencies are nuanced. Balthasar acknowledges as much when he repeatedly insists that he is merely taking certain 'formal tendencies' in Rahner to their logical conclusions.[44]

It would not surprise Balthasar, therefore, that many of Rahner's interpreters find a properly theological foundation in his work coupled with a sufficient emphasis on the categorial and historical. It is not Balthasar's intention to suggest that Rahner ostensibly subverts the Christian message to an Idealist one. His concern is rather that the use of Idealist terminology such as 'categorial' and 'transcendental' – the terminology is really Kant's, but Balthasar also discerns a Fichtean influence – is inadequate to the fullness of the Christian mystery.[45] In this he is proceeding from the Thomistic dictum that a small mistake in the beginning will result in a large one in the end. Some may respond that if it was acceptable for Aquinas to use the philosophy of Aristotle, including Aristotle's terminology, then why should Rahner not borrow the language of modern philosophy, provided that he uses it to articulate the Christian message. After all, there are no 'historical-cultural periods which are intrinsically evil'.[46] Responses such as these are problematic, however, in their insinuation that there are no thought-forms which are intrinsically better than any others, and that the Christian theologian has no means of determining which ones might be of more use than others. With such a view Balthasar is in complete disagreement:

> It is clear now that it is not every *Weltanschauung* or philosophy that can provide the foundation for rational reflection on divine revelation (of the Old and New Covenants). Rather *it is God, in his freedom to determine himself and his revelation, who, in the act of revelation itself, judges between the philosophies.* A philosophy can only be used as a vehicle for the (decidedly indispensable) preunderstanding of revelation provided it is already open, or can be made open by theology, to the primacy of God's sovereign freedom. In revelation itself, man is challenged to acquire a particular view of existence.[47]

In order to fully understand the differences between Balthasar and Rahner, then, we have to look beyond the rather more superficial difference over the 'anonymous Christian', and to the more substantial difference over the relationship between Dogmatic and Fundamental Theology. Here we will be back with those issues which were raised in the Barth chapter regarding the relationship between nature and grace, reason and faith, philosophy and theology. Before we look at Balthasar's criticisms in any detail this much should be said: Balthasar believes that great care must be taken by any theologian in the modern period so as not to give credence to the Enlightenment prejudice that matters of truth can and should be separated from matters of ethical commitment. This is known, classically, as the fact–value distinction; it has its origin in Kant and was widely disseminated through Max Weber's social science. This is the place to recall the quote from *Theo-Logik* given above (pp. 105–6) to the effect that modern rationalism has tried to limit the field of truth to that which is purely theoretical, thereby isolating it from the good and the beautiful. As Balthasar puts it, '[w]hen truth is without decision, then decision, the personal decision that determines one's view of the world, is without truth'. He follows this up with a crucial warning to Christian philosophers: 'And so Christian philosophy must be careful not to give any encouragement, even unconsciously and unintentionally, to this kind of rationalism.'[48]

Such an approach to the matter of truth goes against the grain of the entire modern way of thinking, but this 'modern way' has already been decried to some degree from the side of philosophy by Kierkegaard and his 'existentialist' heirs. The entire purpose of Gadamer's monumental *Truth and Method* is to expose the error of the Enlightenment's insistence that truth be measured by the standard of the exact sciences, and to expose the 'prejudice against prejudice' which flows from this error. Along with this critique Balthasar offers a distinctively Christian one stemming from his view of the relationship between revelation and reason.

> First of all, the world, as it really exists, is a world that stands, positively or negatively, in a relationship with the God of grace and supernatural revelation. In this relationship there are no neutral points or aspects. The world, as an object of knowledge, is always embedded in this supernatural sphere, which is why the knowing power of man is always marked with the positive sign of faith or the negative sign of unbelief.[49]

The differences between Rahner's and Balthasar's approach, then, must be sought in the subtle origins of their respective theological methods, and in the necessary implications which these early decisions make in their subsequent theological developments. This, as we will see, is precisely how Balthasar undertakes to articulate their differences: he begins with Rahner's Fundamental Theology in order to illustrate how these issues affect subsequent matters of theological substance.

As Manfred Lochbrunner has pointed out, at the origin of Balthasar's critique of Rahner – and here he is referring to the early review of *Geist in Welt* – stands Rahner's concept of *Vorgriff* (i.e., pre-apprehension).[50] Lochbrunner is also right to note that Balthasar's study of Barth lies in the background of his critique of Rahner.[51] According to Balthasar, Rahner's understanding of *Vorgriff* comes about as a strange mixture of Aquinas and German Idealism from Kant to Fichte (elsewhere he adds Heidegger to this mix). Building upon Thomas's notion of '*potentia oboedientialis*', Rahner speaks of the dynamic potential of the subject, always bound to the sensual world, to intuit the mystery which transcends all sensual knowledge. Intuit, here, is my word; in its place Rahner speaks of a preapprehension, preconception, or *Vorgriff* of transcendental being.[52] In an affirmation of the particular existent one is, implicitly, affirming existence itself (being as a whole, God) which distances itself from the particular existent as such. Metaphysics exists for Rahner, therefore, in the dynamic and implicit desire of the subjective spirit for the infinite.[53]

We should note that Balthasar knows full well that this *Vorgriff* on the part of the subject is not a purely human striving after grace, so that Rahner could be accused of Pelagianism.[54] No, God's gracious decision to seek out humanity from the very outset stands at the beginning of Rahner's entire thought-world. The questions which Balthasar raises in this context are rather these: Has grace been pushed back so far in Rahner's view of things, that is, all the way back to humanity's natural openness to transcendence, that it becomes difficult to speak still of nature at all, but only of a 'supernatural existential'? Is what was originally only given to theology now given to philosophy? In other words, prior to the concrete revelation of God in Jesus Christ, have we not already encountered the gracious, saving God of redemption in the very structures of human nature? Finally, does Rahner's *Vorgriff* do justice to Aquinas's fundamental distinction between *esse* and *essentia*?[55]

According to Balthasar, one's anthropology must already bear the marks of the central role which love plays in the Christian revelation. Aquinas's metaphysics is not intended primarily to establish a 'natural' relationship between God and humanity, in Balthasar's view, but is intended, rather, to show the 'ever greater dissimilarity' between the One who is his own being and one who has been given being. This chasm not only makes the self-revelation of God a possibility, it makes it a necessity for any sufficient knowledge on the part of the subject. Already, in the natural structure of things, and not on the basis of a further 'supernatural existential', this need for revelation becomes apparent as a deficiency on the part of the creature. This is Balthasar's 'take' on Aquinas, and he will later say that this is the view which Gustav Siewerth establishes against Maréchal.[56] What Balthasar feels is lacking in the approach of Maréchal and Rahner is a sufficient appreciation for the intersubjective, that one only comes to an experience of being as it is mediated to me by one who is other than me, who is not reducible to my pre-apprehension. It is only through the use of such inter-personal categories that one can do justice to the central roles played by love and freedom in the Christian story. Indeed, it is here that Balthasar will allude to the opposition of the sexes. My apprehension of being is never possible apart from the free self-revelation of the one who is not me, upon whom I can never make a claim, but who must freely open him/herself to me. Such intersubjective categories are intended to point to that dimension of theology which distinguishes it most sharply from modern, subjectivist philosophies.[57]

This critique, which contains the seeds of Balthasar's entire subsequent critique of Rahner, and this already in 1939(!), is stated less abstractly in Balthasar's subsequent works. In 'Analogie und Natur', Balthasar sums it up accordingly:

> The qualitative distance between the revelation of the 'principium et finis' and the revelation of the now really personal, speaking God is not sufficiently paid attention to here. The content of this religious-philosophy can only be established from the already issued speech of God himself, it is therefore unconsciously theology. And when at last the *potentia oboedientialis*, determined through the ethical self-decision of man, is placed in the hands of man, when he thus asserts that the word of God possesses the possibility to be heard, he can also give it this possibility, so now the '*Vorgriff*' threatens to become an *Übergriff* into theology.[58]

Even if Rahner is constantly insisting that the very possibility of such a hearing of the word is based upon the prior act of the gracious God, such an assertion is a theological one, and this should be made explicit.

> The creature does not 'hear' a silence of God, but with the 'supernatural' ears of belief (or unbelief) confronts the gracious (or wrathful) God. If one does not observe this barrier, Barth's critique of the starting point becomes justified.[59]

Balthasar's critique here concerns the implication which is given when Rahner does not distinguish clearly enough between the 'being' which is implicitly known in every finite act of knowing and the God who speaks. With regard to the former one can be 'neutral', but with regard to the latter, knowledge is inseparable from decision and love (the good and the beautiful). In short, the realm of metaphysics is incapable of itself to provide an adequate *Vorgriff* for the object of theology.

This criticism, from 'Analogie und Natur', is further explored in *The Theology of Karl Barth*. Balthasar begins with a discussion of the revolution initiated into theology with Maréchal's renewed interpretation of Aquinas, an interpretation directed against the dualism of neo-Scholasticism. Balthasar's interpretation of Maréchal is much more subtle than those who would wish simply to accuse the latter of 'ontologism', that is, a possession of the absolute by the finite spirit. This was the error of German Idealism, and Balthasar knows that Maréchal intends to overcome Idealism with its own categories. Like Rahner, Maréchal attempts to move beyond the extrinsicism of neo-Scholasticism by emphasizing the finite spirit's openness to transcendence in each of its acts of knowing. Maréchal: 'The absolute end of the intelligent subject enters, as a constitutive element, in all acts of judgment.'[60] In order to pull off this 'immanentism' without infringing upon the grace of God – Balthasar keeps insisting that there is a tension between Maréchal's mysticism and his metaphysics – Maréchal must keep resorting back to the neo-Scholastic doctrine that 'the *desiderium naturale visionis Dei* in nature as such (*natura pura*) is a *desiderium inefficax et conditionale*, and mere *velleitas sei* ...'[61] Yet such a distinction hardly seems to do justice to Maréchal's ultimate dynamism. There is thus an unresolved tension in Maréchal's work which Balthasar locates in his refusal to admit a 'theological a priori'.

> Although we see, here and in other places, how Maréchal kept going back with such scrupulosity to the statements of the Scholastic tradition, we should not forget that a great *reversal of perspective* lies at the root of his thinking. But, if the point from which Maréchal basically *thinks back to* the point of mysticism, the Schleiermachian point of 'resting in the Absolute' beyond all discursive potentialities of the intellect and will, if this point of convergence of mysticism and metaphysics is 'the true unifying point in the work of Maréchal', then this unifying moment in his philosophizing is in truth a hidden theology. He is therefore a thinker who tried to probe in his philosophy the conditions for the possibility of the supernatural vision of God as the ultimate goal of man in his human nature. If this is so, then the question naturally arises whether or not the object of Maréchal's investigations – human nature – is not already in a hidden way a 'theological object'.[62]

We are once again at the problem of nature and grace and it would appear as if Balthasar is returning to the old, Scholastic separation of realms, the realm of nature on the one hand, which provides natural knowledge of the world and God, and the realm of grace/revelation, which provides additional and supernatural knowledge of God. But Balthasar is not a dualist: the distinction between his thought and Rahner's goes back to Balthasar's mentor, Henri de Lubac, whom Balthasar follows closely in these matters. And the difference between Maréchal-Rahner and de Lubac on these issues is too often overlooked in the secondary literature. One reason is that modern theologians seem unable to make any but a pre- and post-Vatican II distinction. Both Rahner and de Lubac propelled the Church beyond the old neo-Scholastic dualism, thus, the reasoning goes, they must be doing the same thing. This reasoning is supported by de Lubac's refusal to challenge publicly Rahner's solution to this problem. It is also supported by the fact that both thinkers were heavily influenced by Maréchal's interpretation of Aquinas. But Balthasar insists, and the case he makes is a strong one, that there is a difference in the approach of the two, a difference which proves to be decisive in Balthasar's critique of Rahner.

The question which concerns us at present is how one can get beyond the old nature–grace dualism of neo-Scholasticism without thereby giving to philosophy and natural reason what properly belongs to theology and the free revelation of God. Like Maréchal, de Lubac will insist that human beings are open to the infinite, but de Lubac went even one step farther than Maréchal, insisting that this openness is based upon the concrete understanding of nature as this was articulated in the theology of the Fathers and medieval Scholastics. This 'concrete understanding of nature' prevented these earlier theologians from prescinding from the one true realm of revelation and grace: human nature, both according to its origin and its goal, is ordered according to the single plan which God has always had in salvation-history.

> De Lubac thus was able to throw a powerful spotlight on the hidden theological a priori in Maréchal's thought: in creation as it actually exists concretely, the 'point of identity' on which Maréchal based his thought is not a *purely* philosophical one at all. It is actually a theological identity-point: namely, the one and only goal that God has set for human nature, the beatific vision. In the face of this irreducible uniqueness of our concrete goal – which is the only reason the work of creation was undertaken at all – it was otiose and pointless, says de Lubac, to ask about some other world order that might possibly have some other 'purely natural' goal.[63]

The paradox, discussed in Chapter 3 above, that human beings are ordered to the beatific vision, but are incapable of and not entitled to such a vision on the basis of their created natures, stands at the center of all of de Lubac's theological writings. Because creation is already a gift, a gift which endows created humanity with a longing for their creator, they will only find completion in the reception of a second gift, the gift of grace.[64] De Lubac does not need, and, indeed, does not permit, a 'supernatural existential' beyond one's created nature.[65] But this means that we must be careful with the very use of the word 'nature' when we speak of human beings, and 'recognize that man's spirit is a paradoxical creation that straddles the threshold between natural and supernatural and belongs to both orders in the concrete creation we know'.[66] In this way he can distinguish between the realms of nature and grace, philosophy and theology, without sealing them off from one another. Furthermore, his thought is really faith seeking understanding, for his starting-point is in faith, the only state in which one can comprehend the working of God in history. And this means an absolute reversal of order with regard to typical modern ways of thought:

> The goal is what determines in all things the ontological ground for the properties of an entity ... The major objection is based on an ingrained habit of proceeding

> from the creature (it does not matter whether that creature is understood as nature or as person who can raise a rightful claim) in order to think toward the goal that is either hidden or denied (to the creature). But that is the order of realization, and, if we keep that in mind, then we will not lose sight of the intentional order that moves *from the goal to nature.*[67]

It is after this brief examination of de Lubac's thought vis-à-vis that from Maréchal, and after pointing out the similarities between the movement from Schleiermacher to Barth and that from Maréchal to de Lubac – i.e., from 'philosophical and natural thinking to theological and historical thought' – that Balthasar turns to Rahner's place in this history. This is made somewhat easier by Rahner's direct treatment of de Lubac's 'revolution' in an essay on the relationship between nature and grace, an essay which impressed Balthasar as 'the only one to subject [de Lubac's] thought to a competent, careful, informed critique'.[68] Although Rahner agrees with de Lubac that we must move beyond the old extrinsicist approach of neo-Scholasticism – certainly his doctrine of the 'supernatural existential' is nothing less than such a move – his critique of de Lubac sounds strangely similar to the neo-Scholastic critique. He asks if de Lubac does not make the order of grace so constitutive of the order of nature that the latter becomes owed to the former:

> Is man's inner orientation to grace so constitutive of his 'nature' that the latter (as pure nature) cannot be conceived apart from grace, and thus that the concept of pure nature is unusable? … Can grace then still be seen as undeserved?[69]

Rahner's solution to this dilemma is not exactly neo-Scholastic in nature, not even to the degree which Maréchal's was, for Rahner simply asserts that in order to avoid the problem in de Lubac, that God has ordered us to something which he may or may not grant us, we should simply insist that God has given us the means to attain his grace; that is, he has given us a 'supernatural existential'.

> It follows from the innermost essence of grace that man cannot have a capacity for grace (*Anlage für die Gnade*) that belongs to his nature. *Or, if it is necessary to his nature, it must itself already belong to the order of the supernatural* … Naturally the concrete goal of man is the first thing that God wills and for which he designed the concrete essence of man in the first place. But this only means: if God wills a supernatural and undeserved goal for man, and if God so wills it that the created essence has a capacity for this goal either of a positive or unconditioned type, *then God must give to man along with this a capacity for this goal.* But *it does not follow that this capacity must then belong to his nature.*[70]

'Pure nature' remains, then, a purely abstract notion for Rahner, one which simply serves to accentuate the gratuity of grace, even if such a nature does not in fact exist.

> In Rahner's opinion, God cannot place an unconditional dynamism in nature and then leave it unfulfilled. And so he proposes that we distinguish between a twofold dynamism in our nature – an abstract one that we never see, but a necessary one nonetheless. The first makes our spirit-nature what it is; but we cannot simply equate it with the second dynamism that 'we experience in the adventure of our concrete spiritual existence within the one real order'.[71]

This 'residual concept' (*Restbegriff*) is therefore only intended to safeguard the gratuity of grace, and Rahner admits that in speaking of it we are prescinding from that which is most intimate and unique in humanity.

Balthasar's response to this is crucial to his overall critique of Rahner's approach. In it he elaborates on his previous assertion that Rahner gives to philosophy things which belong properly to theology, and that in abstracting from the realm of revelation in order to construct an anthropology, Rahner sets himself up for difficulties in giving full weight to the *necessity* of the concrete revelation of God in Christ, scripture, and church.[72] Part of the difficulty, and here even de Lubac, in his earlier writings, is partly guilty, is starting with the abstract categories of nature and grace, rather than the more concrete categories of creation and redemption. Once we agree to speak in these more concrete terms, can we still justify 'abstracting from the deepest core of things'? This is the first question. Secondly, how does one avoid equating the residual concept of 'pure nature' with humanity's spirit nature? As de Lubac soon realized, and here he came very close to Barth, the real distinction is between the biblical terms, creation and covenant. Such an apparently small issue of semantics makes it much easier to situate humanity *within* the context of God's plan in salvation-history.[73]

Abstract ideas such as those of 'pure nature', and here Balthasar is willing to concede the helpfulness of this concept as a 'residual' concept, are only helpful if they illuminate the way things really are.

> So Rahner is quite right not simply to drop the formal concept of pure nature *when looked at from the point of view of a 'creaturely' theology*. But what happens when we look at it from God's point of view? 'Pure nature' hardly keeps the same meaning in this context. From all eternity God has willed one and only one thing: to open up his love to the human race. For that he created the world. Thus from God's standpoint it is an utterly idle question whether there might have been a world even without this grace. And what has no weight in God's eyes should carry no weight with us either, especially considering our humble estate.[74]

Now of course Balthasar knows that we cannot pursue a simply divine theology; we need always put the language of revelation into human language. But he is insistent that this language must do full justice to its subject matter, and this means that it must proceed from the standpoint of faith before it begins to deal with the problems of human nature, culture, and the like. He also admits, however, that the tendency to which he, Barth, and de Lubac gravitate must always be careful not to swallow up the realm of nature into that of grace.

> We are stuck with the tension that comes from asserting that nature has on its own no access to the world of grace, even though it has finally been created only because of grace and for grace and cannot be understood apart from grace.[75]

It is on this level that we can acknowledge, even from Balthasar's perspective, a certain complementarity between his and Rahner's approach. For the philosopher will always tend to push to the outer limit the degree to which human nature opens out into the realm of grace, and the theologian will always want to proceed *from* the fact of God's self-revelation in Christ *to* humanity's deep-seated longing for this revelation.

> In other words, we have moved from a 'natural desire' to that answer to grace that must bear the name of grace. At this point a dialogue on the theme of nature and grace is feasible without either side of the dialogue having to give up its own most deeply held position.[76]

The dialogue, here, is between a Maréchalian–Rahnerian approach – and we must also include here the cosmological approach insofar as it too wishes to emphasize the continuity between humanity's erotic search for the eternal and Christianity's answer found in Christ – and that of de Lubac, Barth and Balthasar. As Balthasar points out, confessional differences (i.e., those between Catholics and Protestants) often pale in the face of such a dialogue. This is true provided that neither side gives credence to the Idealist tendency to subsume the Christian revelation into a larger world-historical vision, and this is a tendency that, as we shall see, Balthasar is not completely sure that Rahner always successfully avoids.[77]

> If both sides agree that the order of grace takes absolute priority over the order of nature in the order of intention (in *ordine intentionis*) and the created order takes relative priority over the order of grace in the order of executing the divine plan (in *ordine executionis*), then we are permitted – even obligated – to look at the order of nature from Adam to Christ and from created reason to covenant faith, *within* the prevailing order of revelation and faith.[78]

This is the essence of Balthasar's critique of Rahner, that is, that he sometimes allows an abstract residual concept of nature to displace a proper emphasis on the actual order of things. He removes 'human nature' farther from the realm of explicit revelation than did de Lubac, only then to give this 'nature' more than is warranted without an explicit, categorical/historical act from God's side. This 'foundational' critique will not be changed in the later, more polemical critiques, such as that in *The Moment of Christian Witness*, it will only be sharpened. We will be able to deal with this critique, then, rather briefly, but first we should point out the importance, mentioned above, of the role of the intersubjective realm in this critique.

Here, Balthasar's critique of Barth must be kept in mind: because God has chosen to couch his address to humanity in the form of a human word, the realm of human reason will necessarily have a defining influence in the articulation of this word. In short, 'God speaks as man.' This means that the precise relationship between faith and reason which we have been wrestling with in these last several pages can only be articulated, to borrow the words of Robert Sokolowski, at the intersection of faith and reason.[79] It is not, then, that Balthasar does not appreciate the need for a philosophical contribution to our articulation of the faith, indeed he insists upon it; it is simply that he insists upon a reciprocal relationship between theological content and philosophical foundations. Because all of our thought takes place in the context of a decision for or against God, it will always be marked either positively or negatively by this decision. And this means that the philosophy that the Christian makes use of will always already bear the influence of the concrete, self-revelation of God in history. Put simply, not just any philosophy will do. In the end, it will only be a philosophy that does justice to the personal-dramatic dimension of human existence that will facilitate our attempt to articulate a distinctively Christian message.

In the review of *Spirit in the World* discussed above, it was mentioned that Balthasar complained of the insufficient attention given to human intersubjectivity in Rahner's anthropology. This remained an abiding component of Balthasar's critique right up to the important 'Afterword' (1987) to the third edition of *The Moment of Christian Witness*. We will here quote liberally from this section:

> I have never made a secret of my admiration for the speculative power and the courage of Rahner, and in difficult moment [*sic*] I have done my best to defend him, but even early on I did not suppress certain doubts [Balthasar here refers to the previously discussed review of *Geist in Welt*], inasmuch as his choice of German Idealism as a point of departure seemed to me not without danger. But to develop these reservations would mean reviving the whole debate about the legitimacy of Maréchal's interpretation of Thomas – the transposition back and forth between Thomas and a reading of Kant in the direction of Fichte – a dispute whose interest has faded today before the challenge to confront what remains valid in Thomas with that Hegel whom Feuerbach and Marx interpreted as the key to the contemporary technological world. Even J. B. Metz, Rahner's most authoritative disciple …, has resolutely gone beyond his master here; and, among others, Gustav

> Siewerth in particular has stigmatized the entire interpretation of Thomas advanced by Maréchal's school as an erroneous path, in his passionate work *Das Schicksal der Metaphysik von Thomas zu Heidegger* ... We shall not enter into this whole complex of problems here; it suffices to point out that the Maréchalian and Rahnerian interpretation of Thomas' 'excessus' as the dynamism of the *affirmation ontologique* hardly does justice to the texts and above all considerably fails to capture the Thomistic understanding of *esse*. In contrast, intersubjectivity – newly discovered by Feuerbach (in the wake of Hegel) and fully exploited by Metz – the encounter between the I and Thou, or personal love, plays a decisive role in the 'precomprehension' of Christian revelation.[80]

It would be hard to overestimate the importance of this quote for an understanding of Balthasar's critique of Rahner. We have already mentioned Balthasar's misgivings about Maréchal's reading of Thomas, that Balthasar saw the crucial point as being the Thomistic distinction between *esse* and *essentia*, for it is here that the real difference between God and the world is preserved.[81] But the second thing to be noted is the central role which Balthasar thinks that intersubjectivity must be given in any adequate philosophy. This is why he insists that the polemical and dogmatic critique of *Moment of Christian Witness* be kept together with the more foundational critique of *Love Alone*.[82]

Briefly, given the central role in Christian theology of the gracious self-communication of God, primacy can neither be given to the general manifestation of God in the cosmos – as in the cosmological approach – nor to the subject's openness to transcendence – as in the anthropological approach – but must be given to the fact that being is opened up to the human person in the encounter between the I and Thou. As Balthasar will repeatedly insist, our experience of the transcendent is not to be located, first, in the introspective musings of a Descartes, but in the love-encounter between the child and its mother. It is only in the realm of inter-subjectivity that one can avoid the 'Scylla of extrinsicism and the Charybdis of immanentism':

> Two approaches present themselves, but they converge into one. The first is the personalist approach we have just described. No I has the possibility or the right to master intellectually the Thou who encounters him in his freedom, nor can he understand or deduce his attitude prior to their meeting ... The second approach is that of aesthetics. This forms a third area, apart from that of thought or action, and is independent of these. When one experiences startling beauty (in nature or in art) then phenomena normally veiled are perceived in their uniqueness. What confronts us is overpowering, like a miracle, and only as a miracle can it be understood; it can never be tied down by the person having the experience. The appearance of its inner necessity is both binding and freeing, for it is seen clearly in the appearance of freedom itself ... Such a union of the undiscoverable and the highest plausibility is only to be found in the realm of disinterested beauty.[83]

And finally, '[t]he two approaches converge: even in nature eros is the chosen place of beauty'.[84]

The crucial point is this, far from diminishing the need for a personal self-revelation from God, the analogy of being, properly understood, actually highlights it. In the light of the paradoxical nature of the human person, that she exists but may not have existed, that is, in the light of the Thomistic distinction between *esse* and *essentia*, it becomes clear that only the interpersonal realm – the realm in which the child becomes conscious, in the smile of its mother, of the fact that its existence has been *granted* – provides the appropriate philosophical grounding for a sufficiently Christian theology. And, as Balthasar points out, this realm of the interpersonal overflows into the realm of the aesthetic, for the latter is also the place in which one encounters another which cannot be overtaken (i.e., comprehended) apart from its self-gift. This is the proper realm, not of 'pure reason', but of 'love alone', and it is this realm which provides a fitting 'pre-understanding' for the distinctively theological.

Balthasar's critique of Rahner is not that Rahner intentionally wants to forfeit the contents of Christianity to an overall philosophical-religious viewpoint. This was the move of Protestant Liberalism, not of Rahner. It is rather that Rahner's philosophical starting-point – the openness of humanity to infinitude in every concrete act of knowing – makes it difficult for him to account for the *necessity* of the historical mediation of our knowledge of God. And, even if Rahner does insist on the categorial completion of this transcendent starting-point, how can he account for the fact that this categorial mediation proved to be such a scandal to the most religiously astute – the Jews – and the most philosophically astute – the Greeks.[85] It is in order to demonstrate the fundamental assertion that a transcendentalist approach cannot give sufficient weight to the categorical – especially considering the centrality which the categorical is given in the Christian scriptures – that Balthasar writes *The Moment of Christian Witness*. As we have said, this book should not be understood as the fullness of Balthasar's critique of Rahner, but only as the 'fleshing out' of these fundamental concerns.

Since we have now dealt at sufficient length with these fundamental issues, the specifics of Balthasar's critique in his shorter, polemical works can be dealt with quite briefly. In essence, the critique found in *The Moment of Christian Witness* is intended to highlight the dangerous tendency of modern philosophy and its 'system' to swallow up Christian content, reducing it to the highest aspirations of humanity. By simply identifying love of neighbor and love of God, Rahner plays into modernity's tendency towards hegemony, its tendency, in short, to see Christianity as nothing more than humanitarianism. In such a view, the supernatural dimension of Christianity is seen as little more than a teaching device to highlight what are really natural truths knowable to reason alone and achievable through *Realpolitik*. For Balthasar – and his differences from Rahner here are really quite strategic in nature – the threat of modernity is not so much its atheism as its idolatry, its tendency to treat that which is merely human as that which is divine. The modern philosophical system which dominates from Kant to Marx is, according to Balthasar, not so much a set of natural ideas to which Christianity can add certain supernatural truths as it is an alternative worldview which can really allow for nothing 'from above' at all. Whether religion is now to be treated within the bounds of reason alone or the kingdom of God is equated with the transformation of this world through human genius (and the redistribution of wealth), the result is the same: Christianity has been absorbed, incorporated and reduced. It is not that Rahner's theology accepts such a reduction, it is that it is not delineated enough to withstand it. As Russell Reno puts it:

> Rahner tends to view the spiritlessness of our technological age and a consequent skepticism about religious matters as the greatest challenge to Christianity. As a result, he views any gain for 'transcendence' and 'mystery' as a gain for Christianity – we may worry later about reforming the experience of the Other with the normative *symbolis* of Christianity. This assumption is, I think, both wrong and naive. The twentieth century has shocked Enlightenment culture precisely by its powerful (and seemingly ever more destructive) attachments to the 'mysteries' of party, wealth, nation, and leader. Contrary to the assumption that Rahner makes over and over again in his apologetic writing, unbelief is far less of a problem than 'mythological credulities' of all different and distinctively modern sorts. As a result, the relationship between the mystery of man and the mystery of God is absolutely crucial from the very outset. The modern self does not so much need to be convinced of the possibility of mystery as to be directed toward the *saving* Mystery.[86]

The sharpness of Balthasar's polemic against Rahner in *The Moment of Christian Witness* should not, then, be taken as a personal assault upon Rahner, nor as a calling into question of his theological genius, but as a significantly different assessment of Christianity's relationship to modern culture. Balthasar did not see modern philosophy as a natural set of ideas to which Christianity could add theological specifics, but as a rival theology.

VI. Summary and Conclusion

We will examine Balthasar's theology of the cross more closely in the next, and final, chapter, and will distinguish it to some degree from a more Rahnerian approach, but for the moment we are concerned only with Balthasar's suggestion that Rahner's theological *method* does not adequately reflect the central role which the cross plays in the Christian story. Methodologically speaking, for Balthasar the cross highlights the utter unpredictability and incomprehensibility of God's way of responding to the human religious quest. The utter newness of this event must be accounted for in the very manner in which one relates humanity's quest for God, including the human attempt to construe the true, the good, and the beautiful, to the explicit answer which this quest receives in God's self-revelation to humanity. Yes, revelation assumes this religious quest, and therefore, in a sense, theology presupposes a certain philosophical grounding – a *praeparatio evangelica*; but this quest, this human *Vorgriff*, can never be allowed to predetermine the content of this revelation, nor may it posture itself in such a way as to preempt the freedom, uniqueness, and strangeness that all self-revelations of an 'other' necessarily imply.

In Balthasar's confrontation with modernity we have witnessed a mixed response that will only become fully clear in what follows. By way of summary, however, this much can be said. In response to the attempt of the ancients to subsume humanity into a general cosmological order, or, into the order of nature, modernity has insisted on the basic autonomy of the human subject in the face of the impersonal laws of nature. This became necessary in part as a result of the transformation of the concept of nature which came about through Newtonian physics, but the increased value placed on the individual person was already under way as a result of the influence of Christianity. Modernity is inextricably bound up with Christianity, making the solution of the Renaissance a false one. But the links are even deeper than this. There is also the linear concept of history introduced into the West as a result of the collision between Judaeo-Christian and Classical cultures.[87] Any simple return to the ancients is therefore blocked in Balthasar's view. The question which remains is the manner in which Christianity can confront the changes of modernity without sacrificing its own distinctive voice. The responses of Luther and the early Barth, that Christian theology should concern itself with the content of revelation and allow reason to reign in the affairs of this world is to ignore the necessary link between creation and covenant, nature and grace. This-worldly reason is already marked by the image of the Triune God. Protestant dualism is not a viable solution to the problem of the relationship between revelation and reason.

The cosmological and anthropological responses, on the other hand, take up the challenge to relate the God of revelation to that which is human. Balthasar is sympathetic to the boldness of these approaches, but, with regard to the former, he perceives a couple of dangers. In the first place, there is the tendency in practice to treat the Christian God in terms of Plotinus's One, so that a Christian spirituality which reflected the inherent dynamism of the Trinitarian God and which reflected the essential goodness of the bodily was never fully developed. The spirituality of the early Church was too bound up with the ascetic spirituality of neo-Platonism, and therefore sometimes neglected the inextricable connection between contemplation and action. Secondly, because of a typically Greek understanding of the incomprehensibility of God, there was a tendency to downplay the full implications of the revelation of God which occurred in the person of Jesus Christ. This realization would have prevented the Church Fathers from sometimes severing *theologia* and *economia* in a way that is not warranted by the centrality of the historical, concrete in the biblical narrative. For Balthasar, it was Maximus who best overcame this tendency and allowed his theology to be permeated by the centrality of the revelation of God in Jesus Christ. In his theology *theologia* and *economia*, and therefore theology and sanctity, were inextricably connected.

Once the cosmos became emptied of its mystery, once, that is, it ceased to be able to manifest the glory of God, philosophy began to search for this glory in the human subject. Modern theology followed suit to some degree in its attempt to assimilate the biblical revelation to the realm of anthropology. If human beings are by nature opened to the infinite in their untiring desire to answer the ultimate questions, then the Christian God, who is claimed to be the pinnacle of this search, should not appear to modern human beings as an untenable hypothesis. Even if modern science refuses to see any manifestation of God in the cosmos, it cannot deny this infinite questioning at the heart of the human enterprise. So far so good. The problem arises when one wishes to relate the specific God of Christianity – including the ultimate revelation of the Trinity in the Son's willingness to take upon himself the sins of the world – to this search. According to Balthasar the anthropological starting-point, not flawed in itself, must be articulated in such a way as to be able to account for the incomprehensible love which is manifest to us in the cross of Christ. This means that greater attention must be given, than is given by Maréchal and his disciples, to the interpersonal nature of all human knowing, to the fact that human knowing is always dependent upon the free self-gift of the other, and that its primary posture before the mystery of existence is not, therefore, one of human striving, but one of receptivity before the gracious mystery of the gift of human existence. This means that human knowing and human loving are always, already inextricably linked, and that the true, the good, and the beautiful always interpenetrate one another.

In the final chapter we will look at Balthasar's treatment of a series of issues which should illustrate his unique capacity to mediate between the two tendencies just outlined: the dialectical position, which tends to reduce the theological enterprise to the level of a private, incommensurable discourse (a 'language game') reserved for the initiated few, and the cosmological/anthropological position, which tends to allow a prior understanding of the world, either intentionally or unintentionally, to stand as the measure of the self-revelation of God in Jesus Christ. It will hopefully become clear as that chapter unfolds that Balthasar's ecumenical contribution does not merely consist in its ability to bridge the gap between a certain style of Protestant theology and a certain style of Catholic theology, but that it also contributes to the even greater gap in our times between revelational positivism and anthropological reductionism.

5

Applications and Conclusion

I. Introduction

In order to complete the circle which we began in the first chapter with Balthasar's treatment of the ecumenical question in general, we will now look at how these principles play out with regard to some central, specific issues of fundamental and dogmatic theology, issues which have been dealt with but simply require a more direct treatment. Our purpose throughout has been to make explicit the ecumenical implications of Balthasar's particular manner of theologizing, and we have sought to do so in two 'movements'. In the first movement, we sought to highlight Balthasar's careful attention to the concerns of the Reformation, but, secondly, because it was impossible to draw the full implications of this engagement on its own terms, we had to examine the manner in which this first engagement affected Balthasar's reaction to his own theological tradition: that of Catholicism in its cosmocentric and anthropocentric forms.

Balthasar refuses to take his eyes off of either of these alternatives when engaging the other. Because many interpreters have lost sight of this, it has become somewhat common to interpret Balthasar in a one-sided fashion. In any case, in his dialogue with Barth, especially in the two essays, 'God Speaks as Man', and 'The Implications of the Word', Balthasar may appear to some as overly foundationalist. This is also true of his aesthetic approach in general, for Balthasar insists that the one who has lost the ability to see inner-worldly beauty will have little hope of recognizing the glory of the Lord when it appears. In his dialogue with Rahner, on the other hand, he will appear to many as fideistic, anti-intellectual, or as a revelational positivist. My thesis has thus been twofold: first, Balthasar's entire theological method, which can be characterized in general as a theological aesthetics, has a thoroughly ecumenical intention; and second, if either side of the dialogue just mentioned is forgotten, Balthasar will be misunderstood in a one-sided fashion.

What is left for this final chapter, then, is to draw out the explicit ecumenical ramifications of Balthasar's theology with respect to some contested issues, both in the history of theology and in the current debate. It should be noted at this point that although this study has primarily focused on Balthasar's dialogue with Protestantism, and the effect that this dialogue has on his understanding of certain Catholic approaches, the ecumenical implications of his work are more far-reaching than the dialogue between Catholics and Protestants. In fact, within the dialogue which we have examined so far lies the seeds of a dialogue that transcends it. This is true because the basic tendencies found in the extreme dialectical approach, and in the extreme correlationist[1] approach, do not always coincide with the Protestant and Catholic views per se. Indeed, in the current academic and ecclesial setting, that which divides Protestants and Catholics is often less important than that which divides the revelocentric approach to theology from its correlationist counterpart.[2] As I hope to illustrate, Balthasar's aesthetic approach can also serve as a resource for overcoming the often extreme division in the Church along these latter lines.

The issues which will maintain the focus of this chapter will include: the nature of our knowledge of God in the light of the cross ('Cross and Trinity'), the relationship between finite and infinite freedom, and the possibility of Christian philosophy in the light of Balthasar's treatment of faith and reason. Since these issues have already at least been glimpsed in the midst of the various engagements of the previous chapters, these excurses will simply serve better to bring into relief Balthasar's peculiar treatment of the matters at hand. All of these issues have become crucial ones in the current theological landscape, and they are ones that are all too often overlooked in the specific ecumenical dialogues. These dialogues, for reasons which are often understandable, often move directly into specific theological disputes without examining sufficiently the basic presuppositions of the various interlocutors. It is Balthasar's gift that his fundamental theology is already suited to the nature of the theological object. In short, although the issues which will be examined in this chapter may seem overly formal to some, it should be clear that for Balthasar, *theologia* must always be rooted in *economia*, so that there simply are no purely 'pre-theological' points of view.

Finally, this chapter will conclude with some general remarks, drawing special attention to areas where Balthasar's work might be appropriated, complemented, or corrected by the next theological generation.

II. The Cross and the Trinity

The role of the cross in Luther's theology was discussed above in terms of its implications for soteriology and for theological method. It was noted that these two aspects are inseparable in Luther's thought, as they are for Paul. If God's self-revelation to humanity finds unique expression in the life and work of Jesus Christ, and if the cross is the culmination of God's dealings with human sinfulness, then all theological speculation must pass through the way of the cross. For Luther, the cross symbolizes the utter incomprehensibility of God's manner of overcoming sin and death, and therefore serves the purpose of radically humiliating the human quest for self-understanding and self-redemption. Human beings tried to find God through wisdom and through striving (power), and God came to them in folly and weakness. The God whom one would expect to find on the basis of abstracting from all human imperfections and limitations – through 'negative theology' – a God, that is, who is all-knowing and all-powerful, comes to us in the form of a baby in a manger and as a criminal dying on a cross. This is the God we should wish to encounter, warns Luther, not the majestic God who can be known through his creation. God's plan serves the purpose of humiliating the proud philosopher and of comforting the terrified, humble sinner.

Balthasar does not object to Luther's focus on the cross, but to Luther's unwillingness to make a clearer connection between the 'hidden God' and the God revealed in the cross. There is a sense in which Luther's theology is still under the constraints of the *de Deo Uno/de Deo Trino* approach of Scholasticism. Yes, the cross does hide God under the form of what seems opposite of God, but in this veiled form – and here is the paradox – God is revealed for who he most truly is. A modern outgrowth of Luther's approach can be seen in the move, beginning with Hegel but found more recently in Moltmann, to suggest a change in God himself as a result of his involvement in history. Certainly this is not explicitly present in Luther's theology itself, but Luther's theology of the cross is construed in such a dialectical fashion that the entire emphasis is placed upon the 'admirable exchange' which occurs between Christ and the sinner. In such a view it is too easy to lose the connecting purpose between the cross and the totality of God's plan of creation in Christ. As Balthasar summarizes this:

> The high drama of Luther's reduction in fact suppresses that *other* drama, which presupposes the existence of persons, with their proper being and constitution. We can no longer tell whether man, who is both a sinner and righteous, is one or two; we can no longer tell whether he is a subject enjoying continuity. Formally Luther holds fast to Christ's two natures, but he makes no connection between Christ's Incarnation and his 'becoming sin' (which does not begin, in Luther's view, until he accepts his baptism). Thus the entire traditional view of Christ as the Head of

> mankind falls to the ground. It is only faith that lays hold of justification; love is only involved in the works of 'second righteousness.' Consequently, there is no place for the primary love of the redeemed for the person of the Redeemer. Artificially, but very deliberately, the unity of grace – which justifies *and* sanctifies – is torn asunder. Finally, in reducing theology to the *pro nobis* between Christ and sinners, Luther obscures the entire horizon of God's self-disclosure in Christ, everything that the Fathers understood by *oikonomia* and the 'divinization' of man through the grace of participation.[3]

What Balthasar is trying to articulate in this critique is that, in Luther, the metaphysical implications of the re-creation of humanity in the second Adam are all but lost in favor of a one-sided emphasis on the dialectical relationship between sin and righteousness, law and gospel, works and faith, and the like. In spite of sin, one must be able to account, that is, for the unity of God's plan in creation and redemption, and for the fact that Christ truly is the second Adam, who has become for us a 'life-giving Spirit'. In Moltmann, this tendency towards mythologization is taken even farther. Here, also, the focus is not on the analogy between the love of God and inner-worldly love, instead the love of God is revealed to humanity *sub contrario*, in the contradiction of the cross. Following Rahner, in his equation of the immanent and economic Trinity, Moltmann suggests that the authentication of the Trinity actually occurs in the event of the cross. The patristic concern over the immutability of God was, therefore, mistaken: God is known only according to his activity, indeed, is himself determined by such activity. Behind such a conclusion Balthasar sees the influence of Hegel and even Whitehead, with his evolving God.[4] He concludes that:

> Interpretations of this kind, like all talk of God's suffering, become inevitable wherever the internal divine process, 'procession', is lumped together with the process of salvation history.[5]

At the other end of the theological spectrum from Luther's and Moltmann's tendency toward mythologization stands the patristic and Rahnerian tendency to define God in terms of the philosophical category being. In spite of the fact that both Rahner and Moltmann begin with the identification of the economic and immanent Trinity, they come to quite different conclusions. In fact, Rahner has always located his suspicion of Balthasar's theology precisely in the latter's theology of the cross, which he basically equates with Moltmann's.[6] In keeping with his chief concern to preserve the absolute mystery of God, Rahner does not like to speak of relationality in God as he is in himself, but rather understands all such talk in terms of the economy of salvation. It is only as a man, in other words, that Christ refers to God as Father. This is redolent of our previous discussion of the patristic unwillingness to understand the Incarnation as the true revelation of who God is, an unwillingness that is corrected, according to Balthasar, in the neo-Chalcedonian theology of Maximus the Confessor. Rahner, with his usual perception, notices that this is precisely where the differences between his approach and Balthasar's is to be located, and therefore identifies Balthasar's theology as 'neo-Chalcedonian'.[7]

In keeping with his conservative desire to protect the eternal God from the vicissitudes of history, Rahner develops a theology of the cross which finds its highest purpose in putting an end to any mythic notions about an angry God needing the death of his Son in order to restore himself to a position of love vis-à-vis his creation. This leads him to either downplay or dismiss entirely the biblical, patristic, and Anselmian notion that Christ vicariously represents sinful humanity on the cross. He attributes such a representational formulation to the later Christologies of the New Testament.[8] Balthasar points out that Rahner fails to acknowledge that this 'for us' formula has been shown to have pre-Pauline origins, but then concludes that Rahner's exegetical considerations are really only secondary to his speculative considerations. As we have already pointed out, these considerations are articulated according to the principle that God is 'he-who-is-always-reconciled' to the world, and that to suggest that God can only become reconciled to the world through the violent death of his Son is inconceivable.[9] This is coupled with Rahner's concern to protect the subject's freedom for self-actualization, which is threatened if we concede that another can stand in the subject's place.

The purpose of this discussion is not to present Rahner's doctrine of reconciliation, which is complex to say the least; it is rather to highlight the alternative approach which Balthasar wishes to set forth. In order to understand this, it must be understood that it lies somewhere between the Lutheran-Moltmannian position on the one hand and the Rahnerian position on the other. For Balthasar, missing from Rahner's view is the notion that Christ, as fully God and fully human, is uniquely capable of representing both God and humanity on the cross. In other words, Rahner focuses almost exclusive attention on the fact that Jesus *dies* as a result of his ultimate willingness to obey God to the end, to the almost total neglect of the notion that Jesus became *sin*, and here, paradoxically, he follows the Anselm whom he is usually so quick to condemn. The connection between Christ and his followers, then, is to be located in the fact that they too must die with Christ. For it is in death that one faces the ultimate case of handing oneself over to God. Since Christ, according to Rahner's 'evolutionary Christology', is the highest instance of creaturely openness to transcendence, his manner of facing his death, of willingly handing himself over to the Father, becomes both exemplary and inclusive. This latter is true because of the solidarity between all of humanity and this exceptional human. In light of this emphasis, Balthasar raises the following objections:

> On the other hand, it remains unclear in what sense – if Christ is to be more than an example – Rahner wishes to speak of 'sharing' in the death of Christ… [W]e cannot avoid this question: Why is Jesus' self-surrender to death on the Cross regarded as absolutely unique? … Furthermore, we would have to ask why the death of Mary (and her life, which was a preparation for it) did not lead to the same hypostatic union. Was she not free, according to Catholic teaching, from all inherited and personal guilt?[10]

At the bottom of Rahner's concern is his notion that a God who is able to be so affected by the history of human rebellion is not much comfort to the one who is in the midst of such history. As he puts it, it does not help the one who is in a predicament much if the one who is supposed to help that one is in the same predicament.[11] But Balthasar thinks that this misses the point. For Balthasar, because God is in his very essence self-giving love, his decision to allow himself to be affected by the sin of the world is fully in keeping with his nature. It is not so much that God turns from an angry God into a reconciled God as a result of the sacrifice of his Son; it is rather that God decides to take an active role in the history of humanity's rebellion against him, a role that will mean taking that rebellion into himself, so as to overcome it with pure love.

Between the Lutheran tendency to mythologize the Godhead in the light of the cross – and this stems from an inordinate focus on the *pro nobis* character of this event[12] – and this Rahnerian (and sometimes patristic) tendency to shy away from the full implications of the notion that 'One of the Trinity' took on human sinfulness, Balthasar wishes to present a thoroughly Trinitarian theology of the cross. What we would like to suggest is that, in doing so, Balthasar is able to assuage the fears of a Luther or a Barth that Catholic theology is based on a concept of God that has more to do with philosophical speculation than with God's self-revelation in Jesus Christ, and this without falling into the Protestant tendency toward mythologization. In the process Balthasar parts company with both of these approaches insofar as they misconstrue the relationship between the economic and immanent Trinity: Protestantism does this to the degree that it reduces theology to the 'pro nobis' of the cross, thereby making any discussion of the immanent Trinity irrelevant at best, speculative at worst; Rahner does this in his equation of the two, in which he is not totally consistent. Balthasar, on the other hand, in good neo-Chalcedonian fashion, insists that we can only learn about God as he really is in the light of how God has acted on our behalf, and that the basis for God's activity on our behalf is already to be located in God as he is in himself.

In Balthasar's theology the immanent and economic aspects of the Trinity are allowed to penetrate each other, shedding light on each other, without being simply equated with each other. Balthasar's musings on God as he is in himself are always preserved from gnostic speculation by a constant reference to God's revelation of himself in history, and this culminates on the cross. It is here that we first encounter the immensity of God's love, not as something which occurs for God for the first time, but as something which demonstrates to the world what God has always been.[13] It is only a God who is already a *circumincessio* of loving persons who could get involved, not only in the otherness of his creation, but, even more radically, in the otherness of sin. The infinite prodigality of God's love which we encounter in the cross stems – the point seems almost too obvious – from the fact that God is already love: the fact that each person of the Trinity finds his – we are speaking analogically here – truest 'place' in the other persons provides the necessary backdrop for one of these persons' taking *our* place. This is the expression of God's love us-ward.

Yet for love to be love, there must be a mutuality. Obviously this mutuality is found in the Trinity in the Son's love for the Father through the Holy Spirit, but now that God so loves the world and makes a covenant with that world, there must also be a mutuality of love between God and his creation. The refusal of God's love on the part of creation is, quite simply, sin, and God's No to this No – God's wrath – is the flipside of God's love. This is where the cross becomes a necessity. God so loves the world that he is willing to experience the world's No in order to heal that No from within, so to speak. Contrary to Rahner, Balthasar insists that God's embrace of the world's No, in the person of Jesus Christ, really does effect the reconciliation of the world to God.

> The Son's obedient embracing of Godforsakeness is a work of substitution. He endures desolation for us, as our Head and in our place. He enters into solidarity with all who feel abandoned and forgotten by God. In what the Greek Fathers boldly called his 'foolish' love of mankind, God wants to experience the absence of God. He suffers an abandonment infinitely more wounding than that of sinners, one that somehow embraces theirs, bringing light into the midnight of their anguish, placing pierced hands of love beneath their fall. There are no uncharted territories. Even in the most hellish deserts of this life, no man need despair. Godforsakeness, too, can be a holy place, for it has been hallowed and made hopeful by the person and presence of God incarnate himself.[14]

But his 'for us' is not only one-sided: Christ is God but he is also man. Indeed it is this christological fact that makes Christ's sacrifice both possible and efficacious. Only God could give himself up for the whole of humanity, but only a human being could represent 'us' before the Father.

> This love *must* be twofold: the love of God the Father permitting God the Son to go, in absolute obedience, poverty, and self-abandonment, to where he can be no more than pure receptivity to the divine 'wrath'; and the love of God the Son who, out of love, identifies himself with us sinners (Heb. 2.13), and thereby, through his free obedience, accomplishes the will of the Father (Heb. 10.7). Only this double love provides the key to understand this mystery.[15]

And because Christ is truly human – the second Adam – it becomes possible for the rest of humanity to include themselves in this self-offering to the Father, as the Spirit sheds the inner-Trinitarian love in the hearts of all who believe.

What is important for our purposes is Balthasar's willingness to allow the *economia* to shed a direct light upon the *theologia*, without abandoning the latter to the philosophers. In the conclusion to a very helpful article on the Trinity, Ralph Del Colle sounds very much like Balthasar, when he raises some questions regarding Rahner's trinitarian thought:

> First, the soteriological principle essentially means that what God is in his saving activity is what God is in the divine being itself. Anything less would compromise the nature of the divine revelation and the communion of grace that is constitutive of Christian life and community. Second, in the revelatory events of the sending of Jesus Christ and the outpouring of the Holy Spirit there clearly exist dialogical relations of Christ and the Spirit to the Father and to each other. The presumption in favor of such relations in the immanent being of God is strong if we are not to violate our first principle. Third, the nature of relation and personhood so important for a Christian understanding of the human person and of ecclesial life would then be grounded in the very nature of the divine being, both revealed in the economy of salvation and implanted in human being by virtue of God's creative act culminating in the image of God.[16]

It is not necessary to go into the full details of Balthasar's soteriology, then, to illustrate the importance of his theology of the cross for our present purposes. First, there is a genuine revelation of the Trinity in the cross, in such a way that something which we could never have anticipated about the nature of God outside of this event becomes for us an object of contemplation and adoration. In the light of this event, which is ultimately beyond words – and this is where Balthasar wants to do justice to Rahner's insistence that the mystery of God be preserved – we discover that God is not *primarily* omnipotent, omniscient, immutable, and the like, but that God is, according to his very nature, *primarily* self-giving love.[17] Or, as Balthasar says elsewhere, in God, terms such as 'immutable' must be understood in the light of the 'ever greater dissimilarity' of all language of God. Second,

Balthasar takes Rahner's concerns, that a mythological understanding of the cross would imply a whimsical, all-too-human deity, seriously, and therefore insists that the reason that such an event could occur in the first place is that God is self-giving love in his very 'immutable' nature. He therefore inverts Moltmann's insinuation that the cross somehow changes what God was by insisting that 'what God was' is what makes the cross a possibility in the first place.

> In the Passion, the Father's loving countenance can disappear behind the hard facts of what must be: now, more than ever, this is very much a part of the Trinity's eternal salvific plan laid before him by the Spirit, the witness of the mutual will of Father and Son. It is as if the Spirit, now embodied in the form of a rule, says to them both: This is what you have wanted from all eternity; this is what, from all eternity, we have determined![18]

Finally, the fact that God is always, already self-giving love makes it possible and permissible to say that God has allowed the world's sin to have an effect upon him: the risen Christ still bears the wounds which he took upon himself for the sins of the world, and will bear them for eternity.

Balthasar does not, therefore, have to soften the fact that Christ really did become sin on our behalf, in order to preserve the transcendence of God. But this means that the old Thomist–Scotist debate concerning the task of the cross, upon which Luther and Moltmann take a radically Thomistic stance and Rahner takes a more Scotistic one, is overcome in Balthasar's solution. Concerning this John Saward can say:

> In *Mysterium Paschale*, Balthasar argues that the best insights of both Thomist and Scotist schools can be reconciled, without facile harmonization, when we acknowledge that by serving his creatures and washing their feet, God reveals himself at his most truly divine and shows his supreme glory. We do not have to choose between the 'Scotist' emphasis on the Son coming to glorify the Father and crown creation, and the 'Thomist' emphasis on the Son coming to redeem mankind by his Passion. With St. John the Evangelist, Balthasar sees that it is precisely in the hour of his humiliation and obedience unto death that the Redeemer-Son draws all creation to himself (cf. John 12.32) and glorifies his Father (cf. 17.1ff.).[19]

And perhaps this means that Balthasar need not choose between Rahner's theology of glory, with its proper emphasis on the fact that what God does in history really does fulfill what he began in creation, and Luther's theology of the cross, which draws proper attention to the fact that what God does in history is so unheard-of as to reduce human wisdom to foolishness; no, for Balthasar, both sides of this equation can be true, but only if it be acknowledged that it is precisely the eternally triune God of glory who is revealed to us in the foolishness of the cross.

III. Finite and Infinite Freedom

When we venture into the area of divine and human freedom in Balthasar's work, we enter into one of the most difficult but also one of the most important aspects of his theology. Balthasar's thought here is heavily indebted, in this as in other matters, to the christocentric revolution in theology initiated, on the Protestant side, by Barth and, on the Catholic side, by de Lubac and others. Both of these revolutions are based on a return to a more patristic, communal approach to theology, which gets lost, especially, in the late medieval debates. It is unfortunate that Luther, for instance, is heir to these debates, his return to Augustine offering little help, because Augustine's writings against Pelagius are marked by their own inordinate obsession with *individual* salvation and election. In fact, Balthasar states repeatedly that Augustine marks the beginning of an unhealthy obsession with individual predestination in the West that is not truly challenged until Barth and de Lubac. Of course Barth deals with this question extensively in his *Church Dogmatics*, but it is de Lubac's *Catholicism* that signaled a way out for so many young Catholic thinkers in the late 1930s.[20] Barth's and de Lubac's treatment of the problem of election benefits from two fundamental decisions: first, both thinkers refuse to deal with the question of predestination in any other than the corporate level which predominates both the Old and New Testaments; second, both thinkers treat soteriology *within* the context of Christology, rather than vice versa. It is Balthasar's view that when both Augustine and Luther, for polemical reasons, have to treat soteriology as a separate or primary issue vis-à-vis Christology, they cannot help but offer a one-sided solution to the problem of divine and human freedom. In this, as in the other areas we have discussed in this chapter, Balthasar's theological reflections begin and end with Christ.[21]

Since the final outcome of the first seven ecumenical councils is a Christology that is deeply paradoxical, we should only expect that the Christian treatment of the question of freedom will be equally paradoxical. Since paradoxes are, unfortunately, difficult to maintain, the history of Christian thought on this matter has often vacillated between one extreme and another, often beginning with a false either–or alternative. For instance, if God is omnipotent, infinite and free, then creatures must be powerless, finite and bound. If a space is to be carved out for finite freedom, then something must be taken from God. The famous Calvinist–Arminian debate within Protestant theology has been playing out this hand for centuries now. It seems that one must either insist upon the sovereignty of God and therefore deny human freedom, at least with regard to the 'things above', or one must limit God in order to allow for human freedom. Indeed, there is quite a controversy at present within American Evangelicalism between those who are traditionally Reformed in their theology and the new 'open theists' who limit God's knowledge of the future in order to make room for human freedom.[22] It is unfortunate that the Erasmus and Luther debate in the late Middle Ages was fated from the outset on account of accepting a similarly false alternative. Needless to say, Balthasar has little to offer on either side of these debates.

Balthasar's view of human freedom is rooted, then, in his paradoxical understanding of the human being as, at once, ordered to a supernatural end and yet, at the same time, incapable of attaining this end without assistance. This paradoxical view of human nature dominates the writings of the Church Fathers and is echoed in Pascal's famous assertion that human beings are to be understood as vacillating between greatness and misery, or, better, as grand in their misery and miserable in their very grandness. One is reminded, more recently, of the end of Luigi Giussani's *Religious Sense* wherein the human person is taken to dizzying heights by her natural desire for immortality, only to look down and become faint, realizing that she is incapable of surviving at such heights.[23] Can we really say, in other words, that the human person is free to attain a destiny that is super-human? This is not a question, of course, which is unique to Christianity; it is, perhaps, *the* anthropological question par excellence. And Balthasar frames his entire discussion in terms of the two, predominate ways of construing freedom: freedom as 'consent to the good' or freedom as 'autonomous motion'.[24] It was the ancients who tended to treat human freedom exclusively in terms of consent to the good, a tendency which came to the brink of swallowing up the individual person into an impersonal cosmic process. It was due to this – and, of course, various distortions of the Christian understanding of freedom – that the modern philosophers began to think of freedom in terms of autonomy. If Descartes, for instance, had already facilitated a certain alienation of the spiritual subject from the external world of (mechanically ordered) objects, it was Kant who put the nail in the perennial coffin. To the new, sovereign person, Christ, for instance, could only serve as an example. Any external law or help could only be conceived of as heteronomous to human freedom.

Once Christianity enters into the discussion, things only become more complicated. 'The Good' of ancient philosophy to which all freedom in Plato, for instance, is ordered, has now become personalized in the God of the Old and New Testaments. Christianity, in short, only heightens the stakes as it tries to answer the problem of how finite freedom can survive in the face of a very personal, very interfering infinite freedom. Interestingly enough, however, it is only with the God of Jesus Christ, according to Balthasar, that the two notions of freedom mentioned above can be brought into harmony. The answer lies, not in robbing divine freedom in order to pay human freedom – Balthasar sees the modern tendency as a move towards the divinization of the Self – nor in swallowing up the individual into an impersonal cosmic process, but in conceiving finite freedom as a *gift* from or a *participation in* infinite freedom. In the background of this discussion is the more primal one of the relationship between God and the world.[25] Because the Platonic tradition tended to treat the existence of anything outside of the One in terms of emanation and return, 'God' could neither be rightfully transcendent nor immanent. The individual is conceived, in such a framework, as simply a part of a divine whole. True otherness and individuality are sacrificed at the feet of cosmic wholeness. Modern philosophy, on the other hand, and we are admittedly, with Balthasar, painting in rather broad strokes at this point, tends to drive an immense wedge between the world of matter and that of spirit, such that God is situated off in some distant corner of the cosmos, never interfering with the watch he long ago constructed. Only the human soul can have a sort of immediate experience of God, in Kant, for example, in its awareness of a transcendent moral code. God becomes at once too transcendent and too immanent: too transcendent vis-à-vis a mechanistic and self-sufficient universe; too immanent vis-à-vis a spiritual and quasi-infinite self, who seems to be *naturally* immortal.

To return to Luther, this loss of a rightful understanding of God's transcendence and immanence begins with the nominalists and their juxtaposition, in God, of freedom and nature. God becomes utterly, unfathomably and even nonsensically free. If nominalists, such as Biel, were to preserve human freedom in the face of such divine freedom, they could do so only in rather convoluted and inconsistent ways. We can attribute it to Luther's brilliance that he refused to allow human beings freedom in the face of such a God. As Balthasar puts it:

> Luther's voluntarism, which – whether meant seriously or in jest – is based on Ockham, is of quite a different kind [Balthasar has been speaking of Descartes]. Christologically centered, at an early stage he moves away from the Scotist–Ockhamist speculations; the absoluteness of the divine will appears in the paradoxical justification of the sinner – which transcends all the philosophizing of human reason. But Luther so concentrates on this one, solely significant plane of action that created freedom is limited to purely intramundane operations; it operates downward, as it were, but not upward, toward God. Ultimately only God is free, and as the Grace-giver his is such only if, in the face of his gift, all our gifts become as nothing.[26]

Again, we are back to the notion that if God is free, then nobody else can be, or, if human beings are free, God must either willingly or unwillingly be limited.

If we recall the fact that Balthasar's criticisms of Luther are based on what he perceives as a tendency towards monophysitism, we can guess the solution which Balthasar has in mind. First, Balthasar rejects as overly speculative too many of the discussions of the relationship between divine foreknowledge and human freedom. In speaking of the Calvinist approach to predestination, for instance, Balthasar says,

> The point at which the lightning struck, the New Testament, is unacquainted with the problems that arose later. It does not speak of predestination as some (as it were) neutral factor to be taken into account but as a form of proclamation of the Good News, with all the seriousness this implies. Nor, as yet, does the rising sun of infinite freedom outshine and so obliterate the landscape of finite freedom: it simply illuminates it, so that the 'interrelationship' that was our starting point at the beginning of this chapter may come about. Now that infinite freedom has become accessible to finite freedom, the latter has the opportunity – for the first time – to fulfill itself ... In concrete terms, infinite freedom appears on the stage in the form of Jesus Christ's 'lowliness' and 'obedience unto death'. Thus he can call to himself the 'weary and heavy-laden' and summon even the clumsy and hesitant to be his disciples.[27]

With Luther and against the nominalists, then, Balthasar agrees that the human person is in no position to 'do what is in him' in order freely to attain God's first grace. No one, simply, has a claim on God's forgiveness or aid. On the other hand, God's grace is not the enemy of human freedom, so that some would be destined for Heaven and others for Hell, as it were, against their wills! Rather, as Herbert McCabe has put it, the person who is on her way to Hell needs no divine assistance, for Hell is precisely the absence of freedom and goodness. In other words, to 'choose' Hell, is to choose, precisely nothing, and, so, is not a free choice at all. One is in Hell, even now, in a sense, insofar as one has precisely rejected freedom. God's grace, on the other hand, is the only path to liberty, as we know from Jesus Christ. Christ's lowliness, obedience and even, in some sense, slavery, were in no way opposed to his freedom.[28] Christ did not have to forfeit freedom in order that the will of the Father could reign supreme. Just the opposite: Christ found true freedom precisely in his complete obedience to the will of the Father.[29]

To return to the two kinds of freedom mentioned above, Balthasar will wish to do justice, then, both to freedom as freedom to do the good *and* freedom as autonomous motion. And to say that these two notions of freedom come together only in Christ is not to say that they are not already presaged in philosophical anthropology. In other words, it has been one of the constant concerns of philosophy to try to solve the various antinomies that arise in considerations of human freedom. To repeat, philosophy has tended either to subsume human freedom into a vast cosmic process or to establish human freedom only by alienating the individual both from being as a whole and from other individuals. In short, if I become aware of myself as simply another instance of 'human being' among countless others, in what sense can I be said to be individual or free? Am I not simply another case of a general phenomenon? On the other hand, if I establish my uniqueness as a spiritual subject, what has happened to my relationship with being or nature as a whole? That this was a key problem for modern philosophy should be obvious from even a cursory reading of Kant. We thus return to old cosmocentric/anthropocentric alternatives. For Balthasar, it is Christianity that really mediates between this older cosmocentric approach and the more recent anthropocentric approach. In fact, it is Christianity that gave birth to modernity's recognition of the value of the individual person in the face of all impersonal forces, be they the cosmos as a whole, the Church, or even the State. However, when modern philosophy tries to carry on without its Christian underpinnings, it is bound to run ashore on such insurmountable antimonies as: the individual and the community; the relationship between male and female; and, the body and the soul. That these antinomies are dealt with, even now, in terms of alternative extremes should be enough to prove Balthasar's point.

As such, Balthasar insists that we must allow Christian doctrine to shed its light on our anthropology. If, for the ancients, infinite freedom threatened to swallow finite freedom, and for the moderns, finite freedom seems only able to etch out a space by forfeiting humanity's relationship with being as a whole, in Jesus Christ infinite freedom and finite freedom come together in a harmony which allows both to flourish. And it is here that both notions of freedom come together, even if 'freedom as autonomous motion' must ultimately find its place within 'freedom as consent'. In the *Theo-Drama* the person only finds his true personhood in Christ, because Christ is what God destined humankind to be. Ancient teleology becomes, in *Theo-Drama*, vocation. And it is in this notion of vocation that teleology makes a space for authentic individual freedom. The traditional Christian understanding of mission or vocation gives to the human person what the ancient *telos* could not, true personhood, true individuality. And Balthasar is not afraid to root all of this in the doctrine of the Trinity. It is the vocation of the Son to proceed from the Father; it is the vocation of the Father to eternally beget the Son. Christ's mission on earth is, according to Balthasar, following Thomas, simply an extension of his *processio* from the Father.[30] But notice how the problem of finite and infinite freedom comes together at this point. It is precisely as he fulfills his mission that Christ finds his unique personhood vis-à-vis the Father; the very obedience that unites the will of the Son with the will of the

Father is the very obedience that makes of Christ a unique person who is truly free. This is not the place to go into all of the antinomies mentioned above, but notice how the problem, for instance, of the individual and the community is here resolved. The very mission in which I find my true and unique personhood weds me to a community for which my mission was given in the first place. It is only in the Church, where the very bond which unites the persons of the Trinity is poured out upon all members in the Eucharist, that the perennial problem of individual freedom and common good can be resolved.

While this is in no way an adequate summary of Balthasar's *Theo-Drama*, it should be sufficient to illustrate the manner in which Balthasar's theology can serve as an aid in the dialogue between the perennial Reformation emphasis on the sovereignty of God and the Catholic–Orthodox defense of human freedom. In order to counter the tendency towards Pelagianism in his nominalist contemporaries, Luther reiterated, rightly, the fact that God alone is God, that God is sovereign. Unfortunately, Luther could only conceive such sovereignty, in *The Bondage of the Will*, for instance, as opposed to human freedom. This goes back, as was said before, to Luther's tendency, in the heat of battle, towards a Monophysite or Monothelite Christology. As Balthasar has shown, however, God's infinite freedom is in no way opposed to finite freedom, for the God of Christianity is a God in whom individual personhood and communal identity are never opposed. The Father's sovereignty vis-à-vis the Son is never an annihilating one; rather, the Son, precisely in deferring from his will to the will of his Father, finds his true self, and even his own true will. And so, Balthasar will wish to counter Luther's (and Augustine's) determinism not with an Arminian freedom which grasps after a space of its own in the face of God's omnipotence, but with a freedom which finds everything precisely in its willingness to give everything up. As usual, Balthasar's theology here is deeply Marian. 'He has cast down the mighty from their thrones, and has lifted up the lowly. He has filled the hungry with good things, and the rich he has sent away empty' (Luke 1.52–3).

IV. Christian Philosophy?

A subset of the overarching problem of the relationship between nature and grace is the relationship between faith and reason, or between theology and philosophy. One of the more interesting discussions in modern, academic theology has taken place between the Yale and Chicago schools, the former representing an 'unapologetic', revelation-centered approach to theology, the latter representing a 'correlationist', and more critical approach. While this debate does not break down along Protestant and Catholic lines, it is a further symptom of the problem which Luther addresses in his critique of Scholastic theology. To make matters even more relevant to our current study, Balthasar himself, as was mentioned in the introduction, seems to have been placed in the 'Yale school' by both sides of the debate. What I would like to do in this section, is to clarify some aspects of the relationship between theology and philosophy in Balthasar's work – again it should be mentioned that this will be largely an exercise in summarizing and making explicit what has been argued elsewhere in this study – especially as this relates to the perennial difficulties which various forms of Protestant thought have had concerning the use of philosophy in theology.

What I have been arguing throughout this study should become even clearer in this section: namely, that the questions of Fundamental Theology, such as the relationship between nature and grace, faith and reason, and the like, are at the source of many of the divisions in the Church today. Even if these questions no longer break down along Protestant and Catholic lines, they still remain dividing issues in theology, and are therefore of extreme significance to any ecumenical dialogue, whether it be among Catholics and Protestants, or among the Yale School and the Chicago School. Finally, these questions became especially problematic with the rise of modernity; it therefore seems unlikely that great progress will be made towards unity in terms of specific doctrines, until the deeper issues which have plagued modernity are addressed.

Time and again Balthasar has diagnosed the problem of modern theology in terms of a series of breakdowns: first, there is the central problem of the break between theology and sanctity; then there is the separation of the public and private realm, with religious beliefs being relegated to the latter; at the root of these is the increasing separation of nature from the realm of grace; and, finally, there is the split between philosophy and theology. As for the increased autonomy of the natural sciences, the relative independence of politics from the interference of the Church, and even the relative independence of philosophy from theology, Balthasar has much good to say:

> Catholic philosophy stands today in the same twilight as every other area of the Church's theoretical and practical activity, indeed in the same twilight as the Church as a whole vis-à-vis the modern world. Increasing secularization has forced the Church out of her undisputed position as the crowning of all worldly domains and has brought her ever more strongly into another situation which is juxtaposed, or even subordinated, to worldly structures; seen from the outside and from the perspective of the world, she is permitted to remain in this situation as something perhaps still tolerated, but in any case thoroughly obsolete and questionable. This frequently brutal dismissal of the Church's authority also in worldly matters of politics, of the planning of the world, and above all in matters of the spirit and

> science, does indeed correspond in part to an increasing falling away of the educated and of the masses from the Christian faith, but in part also to a process (acknowledged and justified by the church herself) in which the natural orders and areas of knowledge assume autonomy, as was demanded by the Vatican Council itself in its clear distinction between natural and supernatural orders: *duplex ordo objecto, propria methodo* (Denzinger 1795, 1799). This makes a kind of subordination between Christianity and the worldly domains unavoidable, no matter how much the rank of the two spheres remains different for the believer.[31]

To tie these comments more closely to what has been presented already in this particular study, we will remind the reader that Luther stood as an heir to the nominalist rejection of 'radical Aristotelianism', or, that movement in the Middle Ages which claimed a newfound autonomy for philosophical investigation, only to grant to that investigation an unprecedented access to the very being of God. When this movement identified inner-worldly being with the being of God himself – a move which has been called 'ontologism' – the nominalists made a countermove in order to protect the freedom of God from the control of human reason. Stuck right in the middle of a similar debate in his day was a thinker who was called upon by his church to try to mediate between the radical Augustinians, who adhered to something akin to Luther's *sola scriptura*, and the radical Aristotelians, who, as we have just said, tended to speak of the being of God and the being of the world univocally. We bring up Thomas Aquinas at this juncture because he stands not only at the middle of this debate, but also at the center of Balthasar's attempt to relate the philosophical and theological orders. Understanding the centrality of Aquinas to Balthasar's own 'Christian philosophy' will bring us a long way in overcoming some of the misunderstandings of Balthasar's work which have been mentioned throughout this study: that he is not interested in philosophy, that he thinks that in a postmodern age we can dispense with metaphysical inquiry, that he is merely an intra-church theologian, that his theological method is narrowly 'biblicist', and the like. Instead, I would like to suggest that just as Aquinas stood between the Augustinian and Aristotelian extremes of his own day, so Balthasar has attempted to stand between the Yale (hyper-Barthian) and Chicago (hyper-Rahnerian) extremes in our day.

If Balthasar is concerned to defend the Catholic use of natural theology against the charges of a Karl Barth, he must find a way to speak of the positive role of human reason in the human attempt to understand God, without thereby bringing God down to the level of a human concept, and thereby depriving him of his personal freedom to disclose himself to the act of faith. Just as nature cannot be given such a claim on the presence of God that it renders the subsequent gift of God's saving grace superfluous, or, what amounts to the same thing, a simple extension of an already given human dynamism, so reason cannot be permitted to reach so far into the realm of God as to render God's self-revelation in Jesus Christ either, again, superfluous, or simply an increase of what reason has already discovered. On the other hand, and here Balthasar is on the side of Karl Rahner, if God's message to us in Jesus Christ is merely discontinuous and contrary to everything that we have thought of God on the basis of our innate religiosity and our innate tendency toward transcendence, then there is absolutely no explaining why God created humanity in his image in the first place, or why God chose to reveal himself precisely *in* this human nature. 'God speaks as man': and this means precisely that God addresses us in the very place where our movement toward him has already begun. God does not destroy our yearning for him, he appropriates it.

In order to define this relationship in a manner which avoids the various extremes of modern theology, Balthasar begins his reflections with Thomas's 'real distinction' between *esse* and *essentia*. For Balthasar, Thomas represents a 'kairos' in intellectual history between the ancient tendency to collapse philosophy and theology into one indiscriminate search – and one can easily infer the relationship that this implied for church–state relations – and the modern tendency to isolate the two into radically isolated fields. The key to Thomas's thought lies in his notion of the mutual interdependence within a fundamental distinction between things which actually exist and the being from which they exist. Just as running does not run, Thomas reminds us, but only runners run, so *esse* does not exist outside of the natures in which it inheres. This means that, in spite of the real distinction between *esse* and *essentia*, and the relative priority that Thomas gives to *esse*, *esse* has no existence apart from essences. But if this is the case, if *esse* has no existence outside of actually existing things, then how are we to account for the existence of anything at all. If all we are left with is the mutual interdependence of being and beings, we are left with Heidegger, and the question arises as to how we can avoid nihilism.

Aquinas's solution to Augustinian biblicism and Aristotelian philosophism[32] was to state that philosophy of its own dynamism pointed beyond itself to the biblical solution of creation by a free God, so that, without God's self-revelation, we could never truly know God, but also that without the philosophical search such revelation would be of no concern to us. And this is only possible because 'nature' already contains the traces of the glory of God, metaphysics is already infiltrated by the influence of love. And it is in finding a solution to this very medieval problem that Thomas was able to carve his unique niche in the history of philosophy, overcoming the ancient tendency to treat the cosmos as a necessary emanation from the being of the One.

> Allowing natures to participate in reality – God's most proper prerogative – is not to be understood as the disintegration or diminution (on the part of the creature) of God's being and unicity (which is how it is invariably seen outside the Christian tradition) and the essences of things must not appear as simply the fragmentation of reality, in a negative sense, but must be seen positively as posited and determined by God's omnipotent freedom and therefore grounded in the unique love of God.[33]

Balthasar can even say, in the same vein, that:

> The deessentialising of reality, as demanded by Heidegger and *as achieved by Thomas*, is an extension within philosophy of the illumination by biblical revelation of the idea of God as creative principle. When God, in his knowing and omnipotent love, is seen as freely choosing to create, there can be no question of a restrictive fragmentation of being into finite essences. *Esse* can be suspended without confusion or limitation, in creaturely, free infinity and perfection, before the free God and only thus become the allusive likeness of the divine goodness: *ipsum esse est similitudo divinae bonitatis*.[34]

Enter Martin Luther. Although Luther is not directly concerned with the question of 'being,' and this means that we cannot expect to find the kind of careful treatment of the relationship between theology and philosophy in his work as the one we just outlined, he does bring an insight into the problem of natural theology that seems to have been lost on the theological tradition which preceded him. By focusing so heavily on the activity of God in our behalf, Luther was unable to treat any question as if the cross, and all that this implies, were not at the heart of the matter. Although Aquinas certainly allows the Christian doctrine of creation to shed light on his treatment of the question of being – this is why Gilson can call his philosophy 'Christian philosophy' – his approach tends to slight the personal and historical dimensions of God's activity in our behalf, that is, until he deals with these directly in the *Summa*. Luther's lack of systematization is precisely the thing which works to his advantage when he addresses these problems in his early disputations, for it enables him to think of the problem of natural theology in the light of the event of the cross. What does it imply for the human search for God, asks Luther, that God reveals himself *sub contrario*, in weakness, folly, defeat, death, and, yes, sin? Luther takes at face value Paul's statement that Christ became sin, and he focuses on the affront that this implies to human reason. Although Balthasar is not willing to follow Luther's logic (or, dialectic) all the way to the end – his criticism of Luther can be found in Chapter 2 above – he is prepared to take this central insight to heart.

When Balthasar says that 'one must wait for Luther' to cut across all attempts to trace a smooth transition from the cosmic or the human to the divine, we must take him at his word. This means that, while Balthasar is prepared to follow Aquinas in his treatment of the real distinction between *esse* and *essentia*, in his own treatment of the problem Balthasar is going to want to add a more 'personal' and 'dramatic' dimension to Aquinas's treatment. This is why Balthasar chooses to identify his approach as 'meta-anthropological', rather than strictly metaphysical.[35] It is not too bold to say that, for Balthasar, Christianity achieves the marriage of myth and philosophy in its adherence to the fact that God became a man, that God entered the human drama. To recall our previous discussion about the division in theology today between the Chicago and Yale schools, between a correlation approach and a narrative approach, we might say that, for Balthasar, correlation is impossible without the narrative, and that the narrative is directed precisely at correlating: Christ is the recapitulation of all things![36]

Let us try to summarize briefly what this somewhat cryptic and abstract investigation implies for the relationship between philosophy and theology. As we have stated, Balthasar begins his own musings with the Thomistic distinction between *esse* and *essentia*, insisting that this distinction is not intended to emphasize the continuity between God and his creation, but rather to highlight the ever greater dissimilarity between the one who is his own essence and those of us who only participate in our essences. Yet Balthasar wants to highlight the radically personal nature of this distinction, wants to highlight the fact, that is, that all true philosophy is really rooted in love. If the first thing that we say about God is not that he is being but that he is love, it becomes much easier to account for the continuity of God's single plan of creation and redemption (even redemption on the cross). Our first encounter with being is not, as one might conclude from Descartes, based on the reflection of the self upon the self, but is based on the originary encounter between the child and her mother. My first awareness of my existence consists of the fact that I have lovingly been permitted entry. But this original awareness, this first encounter with existence, will eventually be complemented by another, similar awareness, namely, that my mother was also permitted entry. Not only I, but also all that surrounds me, has been granted existence, has been *given* being. There is a context, an horizon, if you will, which encompasses myself and all that surrounds me, and we can call this horizon existence, or, being. But this leads to yet another question: what would this horizon of being be if it were not for the fact that there were individually existing things through which such Being could manifest itself? Surely we do not intend here that being is merely the totality of existing things, but it is true that being has no existence of its own, that it is dependent upon individually existing things which do exist for its manifestation. Here Balthasar sounds very much like Heidegger who reminds us that being is no-thing, but also like Aquinas who insists that just as running does not exist but only runners, so being is not self-subsisting.[37]

So far, Balthasar tells us, our questioning has been philosophical in nature. But even this philosophical investigation has led us to a very perplexing problem: if being is dependent for its existence upon the beings in the world, how are we to account for the fact that anything exists at all rather than nothing? Heidegger's failure consists in the fact that he refused to push the question all the way back to this originary point; resting content with the mutual interdependence of being and beings he could not avoid the nihilism of postmodernity. Nobody lays down his life, retorts Balthasar, for the sake of being. The threefold distinction which we have just outlined must be allowed, out of its own dynamism, to open up to yet another, ultimate distinction:

> But how can this double dependence, and so mutual conditionedness, produce an Absolute? And so gingerly, almost against our will, we must posit the fourth opening of distinction: beyond the still conditioned, mutually dependent freedom of the existent with regard to Being and the freedom of Being to shine unconstrainedly as a light within the existent: an unconditioned freedom, or one which is at most one which is conditioned through itself, and which is untouched by nothingness, an *actus purus*, which is posited in the first instance only in order to preserve the light of openness between Being and the existent as a free and unconstrained light so that the individual entity is not submerged within the exigencies of a process of explication and Being does not lose its freedom in the same 'Odyssey' of its cosmic evolution towards itself.[38]

The implications of this fourth distinction for the relationship between philosophy and theology are striking indeed. First, philosophy is already rooted in love, in the unmerited, incalculable encountered with the other.[39] If the entirety of being itself has been granted existence by a free act of love, if being, that is, is not a necessary emanation from a One who is even above love – and this has been implied in various ways by the entire Western metaphysical tradition – then it makes sense to say that love is prior to being and even that love is the guardian of being. The fourth distinction, and Balthasar is quick to acknowledge that it is based on Christian revelation, includes and supports the other three distinctions: the order of nature is embedded in the order of redemption. But we must be careful to point out here that Balthasar is not devaluing the natural or philosophical realm: the fact that the natural realm is given an existence of its own, distinct from that of God, gives it an abiding worth which the Christian must be the first to acknowledge. This is why Balthasar can say that Christians have become the guardians of metaphysics in the modern age. The person who is no longer able to feel a certain awe in the face of being, the one who no longer asks the primal question as to why there is anything at all rather than nothing, will be the last person to recognize the explicit glory of God when he or she sees it. Of course this is just another way of saying that the order of redemption presupposes the order of creation, but this means that the order of revelation presupposes the philosophical, mythical, religious quest of the creature created in God's image. As Balthasar puts it:

> We are following the right path when we genuinely locate the metaphysical act within the Ontological Difference – even if it naturally points to God at its depths – and understand the Christian act as a new response to the new word of God which, of course, contains the metaphysical act within itself and beyond that, contributes also to its fulfillment.[40]

I offer this outline of Balthasar's 'Christian philosophy' in order to draw attention to the care with which he approaches the problem of being so as to avoid the kinds of criticisms which have been launched at the Catholic philosophical tradition from the likes of Luther and Barth. If it is true that through the concept of being we have somehow gained a point of access to the divine mystery, so that God must now behave in accordance with what we have discovered about him on the basis of our metaphysical reflections, then Luther's and Barth's misgivings about the legitimacy of natural theology are legitimate. But what if the human investigation into being leads, not directly to the knowledge of God, but rather, first, to the awareness of our own neediness, to the fleeting nature of our own existence and the existence of all that is around us, and only then, *indirectly* (*via negativa*), to a positing of the existence of an Absolute, and what if, furthermore, this search is itself part of the gift of this Absolute to us? Is it still legitimate to call all 'natural' theology the product of whore reason or the invention of the Antichrist? By rooting the philosophical quest itself, not in impulse of the human person to climb to the heavens, but in the gift of being opened up to us in the smile of our mothers, Balthasar attempts once more to heal the modern rift between philosophy and theology. He does this not by bringing the theological search down from its heights, something which a great deal of modern correlating theology has done, but by instilling the philosophical *eros* with some of the *agape* that is proper to God alone. Having said this we can let Balthasar have the last words:

> Believing in the absolute love of God for the world, [the Christian] is obliged to understand Being in its ontological difference as pointing to love, and to live in accordance with this indication ... The Christian remains the guardian of that metaphysical wonderment which is that point of origin for philosophy and the continuation of which is the basis of its further existence ... The metaphysical eros prevails at a higher and earlier level, and it is ordered not to beauty but to glory.[41]

V. Conclusion

A. Summary

We have now come to a place in our study where it is appropriate to retrace our steps and assess Balthasar's contribution to ecumenical dialogue. At the very beginning of this study we mentioned a division which occurred at the origins of modernity between the radical Aristotelians and the radical Augustinians. This division led to two radically different ways of configuring the theological task. The former emphasized the correspondence between human reason and the being of God, while the latter emphasized the radical incommensurability between the human conception of God and God as he is revealed in history. This division occurred in the wake of a series of 'breakdowns' in late medieval theology which Balthasar identifies in terms of theology and sanctity, nature and grace, faith and reason, theology and philosophy, and the like.

At the beginning of this century, two theologians, significantly different in temperament and theological vision, and basically independently of each other, moved toward a reintegration of nature and grace in terms of a theological a priori. These theologians were Henri de Lubac and Karl Barth. That Balthasar saw a connection between these two thinkers was made evident in the letter to de Lubac mentioned at the beginning of the Barth chapter above. That these two thinkers are considered chief representatives of Catholic and Protestant theology in the twentieth century is not without significance for Balthasar's attempt to bring them together. Before we could deal with this unexpected correspondence of viewpoints from two seemingly quite different thinkers, we had first to address the origins of the break between Catholic and Protestant theology as this arose in the work of Martin Luther.

Luther's theology can be seen as an exasperated attempt to overcome the nature/grace, theology/sanctity breakdown which marked the late Middle Ages. Luther wished to reform the decadent theology of late Scholasticism by bringing it into a stark confrontation with the naked word of God. Luther's writings are directed against the misuse of reason in two main areas. First, reason was being allowed to press so far towards a knowledge of God on the basis of metaphysical speculation, that revelation's proper prerogative to correct all prior conceptions of God was being short-circuited. And second, *within* the theological enterprise, reason was being used to harmonize those attributes of God which are learned solely on the basis of the Christ-event – and here we must highlight particularly the 'folly' of the cross – with those attributes of God discoverable on the basis of metaphysical speculation, such that the former were not allowed to influence the latter. Yet, as we have tried to demonstrate, Luther's tirade was not directed at the natural knowability of God; of such knowledge he was thoroughly convinced. What Luther wanted to emphasize was the utter novelty of the God whom we encounter in the event of the cross. This is a God whom we could never have imagined. This is the only God whom the contrite sinner should wish to encounter.

Luther's emphasis on the utter novelty and gratuity of God's self-revelation, culminating in the death and resurrection of Christ, is something which strikes a powerful chord with Balthasar. Balthasar was especially sensitive to the human tendency to tie God to a concept which can be easily manipulated and comprehended. For Balthasar, too, what God reveals about himself in the Christ-event is something which could never have been predicted from the side of the creature, and is something which must stand as the measure of all creaturely constructions. But as we also showed, Balthasar was not willing to rest content with Luther's dialectical configuration of theological knowledge. By accepting a certain nominalist dualism between knowledge of God derived from reason and knowledge of God derived from revelation, Luther unwittingly contributed to the modern separation of nature and grace. As we have mentioned, Luther was right to critique the exaggerations of the Aristotelians regarding unaided reason's ability to know God, but he was wrong to accept their formulation of the problem. In other words, the question – 'How far can unaided reason go towards knowledge of God?' – is wrongly put in the first place, for there is no purely 'unaided' search for God. Of course this does not totally discredit Luther's theological approach, because even if the 'natural' quest for God is already a result of the fact that God instills a natural desire for himself in each of us, the precise answer which he gives to this desire is utterly incommensurate with our expectations! This is where a proper emphasis on the folly of the cross is to be located.

If there is a tendency in Luther to treat the realms of nature and grace as two distinct realms existing, in a manner of speaking, side by side, Balthasar finds in the later Barth a Protestant who is willing to examine this problem *within* the context of grace. In fact, Barth's theology evolves, in Balthasar's view, from a creation-rejecting dialectical approach to creation-embracing christocentrism. In short, if God saw fit to unite himself with human nature in order to redeem that nature, then created nature must be something good from the outset. Instead of viewing creation as a realm fallen from the heights of heaven, Barth came to see creation as the already gratuitous presupposition for the Incarnation. If Balthasar has a question for Barth, it will be addressed to the latter's unwillingness to follow through with the full implications of God's willingness to take what he began in creation into the work of redemption. Once God decides to make use of his creation in order to achieve his work of redemption, vistas open up to this creation which were previously unimaginable. Here Balthasar will remind the reader of Paul's willingness to hold himself up as an icon of Christ to his churches, or even his insistence that all Christians are being transformed by the Spirit in varying degrees into such icons of Christ (cf. 2 Cor. 3.18).

Here we should pause to remind the reader of our central thesis. Balthasar's theological aesthetics demands that adequate attention be paid both to the fact that God has chosen to manifest himself in that which is finite and visible, and that such self-manifestation is the result of a radically new and unpredictable act of God on behalf of sinful creatures. The fact that the *act* of God presupposes and makes use of the *being* of creation should guard against any tendency simply to juxtapose being and act. My reason for recalling this basic critique of Barth is to remind the reader that Balthasar should not simply be read as the Catholic Barth. I mentioned earlier that there has been a tendency to focus on Balthasar's critique of Rahner and to isolate this critique from Balthasar's ecumenical concerns, but also to isolate it from his equally penetrating critique of the Luther–Barth position. In the first half of this study I presented Balthasar's engagement with Luther and Barth in order to highlight the similarities and dissimilarities between their work and his. But, because this engagement was ultimately inseparable from Balthasar's treatment of the cosmological and anthropological approaches within Catholic theology, I spent the next chapter summarizing Balthasar's appropriation and criticism of these two approaches as well.

With regard to the first of these theological styles, the cosmological, Balthasar's view is not one-dimensional. On the one hand, Balthasar respects the willingness of the Church Fathers to challenge the most impressive worldviews of the time with the 'philosophy of Christ'. Neither does Balthasar view the use of certain ancient philosophical categories as the 'Hellenization of Christianity'. On the other hand, Balthasar will critique the Church Fathers primarily on two accounts. First, there was a tendency to adapt the Christian message, especially in the area of spirituality, to the 'egress/regress' metaphysics of the ancient philosophers. Balthasar insists that this needs to be complemented by a Trinitarian-based understanding of mission: just as Christ proceeded from the Father and was sent by the Father into the world, so the disciple has been sent by Christ into the world. Furthermore, the patristic notion of divinization needs to be made more sensitive to the proper ontological and cognitive distinction between the creature and God. The human being does not become less human the more he or she becomes like God; rather, the more the human person becomes expropriated by God for his purposes, the more he or she becomes authentically human. Christ, whose mission is equated with his very person, is the highest instance of what it means to be human.

The second negative tendency in the theology of the Fathers stems from an overemphasis on the ineffability of God, to such a degree that there can even be a reluctance to see the Incarnation as a revelation of the nature of God. As Deirdre Carabine puts it, for Balthasar, 'Christ is not a means to an end, but a "legible" form: the content is within the form not behind it.'[42] In both of these cases Balthasar sees an occasional tendency in the Church Fathers to allow a neo-Platonic metaphysic to eclipse a distinctively Christian, Trinitarian vision of God. It should also be remembered that Balthasar held up Maximus Confessor as an example of a Church Father who, while making use of ancient Greek metaphysics, had thoroughly reconfigured the ancient dualism of form and matter in the light of Jesus Christ, the concrete universal.

After examining Balthasar's treatment of the Church Fathers and their 'cosmological approach', we turned our attention to Balthasar's engagement with the anthropological approach stemming from the work of Blondel and Maréchal. Both Henri de Lubac and Karl Rahner developed this new stress on the immanence of God, but, according to Balthasar, in slightly different directions. For de Lubac, the difficulty with the neo-Scholastic reading of Thomas Aquinas consisted in its tendency to interpret grace and revelation as extrinsic additions to the spheres of nature and reason. By stressing a duality of ends, one accessible to nature and another accessible through grace alone, the neo-Scholastics had unwittingly contributed to the very secularism which they were trying to overcome. In order to overcome this dualism, de Lubac did a thorough study of the traditional treatment of nature and grace, both in the Church Fathers and in High Scholasticism, and demonstrated that the Fathers and medievals were consistent in their conviction that humanity is ultimately ordained for only one end: the beatific vision.

Rahner, too, saw such dualism as a gross misreading of Aquinas, but his solution to the problem was somewhat different than de Lubac's. While de Lubac had preferred to speak of the human situation in terms of a paradox, such that the human person is intrinsically designated for an end that eludes its natural capacities, Rahner preferred to speak of the 'supernatural existential' orientation of humanity toward the divine. The former pointed towards a fundamental 'lack' at the center of human existence, while the latter implied an implicit or inchoate possession. Even if Rahner insisted that this inchoate possession (transcendental orientation) was possible only on the basis of the actual, concrete, historical activity of God (categorial revelation), Balthasar feared that Rahner was unable to account sufficiently for the utterly strange answer which God gives to this human orientation: namely, the cross.

This brings us to the present chapter. In this chapter three rather tricky theological/philosophical problems were examined in order to illustrate what was argued throughout regarding Balthasar's theological approach. The first of these questions concerned the relationship between the immanent and economic Trinity, but with a view toward the larger question of the relationship between natural and positive theology, or, to borrow the language of the Fathers, between *theologia* and *economia*. Here we saw Balthasar trying to steer a middle course between the patristic and even Rahnerian tendency to conform the God who is revealed in history to a previously conceived, philosophical understanding of God, and a tendency, also found in Luther, to discourage all speculation over God as he is in himself. The question which Balthasar raises against the former is whether it has sufficiently allowed its *theologia* to be educated in the *economia*. But against a more Lutheran approach, Balthasar questions whether Luther has really allowed the God who is revealed in the manger and on the cross to *reveal* to us the God who created the heavens and earth. In order to mediate between these approaches, Balthasar insists, with Luther and Moltmann, that the event of the cross be made central to our conception of God. But, with Rahner, Balthasar refuses to see this event as somehow implying a change in God himself. These two approaches can be brought together if, in the light of the event of the cross, we understand God not primarily in terms of unchanging Being, but in terms of eternally self-giving love. A God who has always been self-giving love need not undergo an essential change in order to give himself out of love to his creation.

Next, we examined the classic problem for both philosophy and theology of human freedom. If the ancient and cosmocentric tendency was to swallow up individual freedom into a sort of cosmic necessity, the opposite tendency in modernity has been to found individual freedom only by creating an alienation between the individual and being as a whole. This philosophical debate finds its way into Christian theology in the twin dangers either, first, of so emphasizing the sovereignty of God that there is no real role for the creature to play in the drama, or, second, by so emphasizing human freedom that Christ is reduced to a mere example to be followed. Balthasar's solution to the problem is found precisely in the neo-Chalcedonian insistence that the humanity of Christ, in terms both of its proper nature and will, is in no way diminished when in unity with the divinity of Christ. Instead, the more the divine shines through, the more, that is, the Son offers himself in complete obedience to the will of the Father, the more his humanity is brought into relief. Jesus is not only God, he is also the first, authentic human person! Balthasar roots this understanding of infinite and finite freedom in the Trinity. In such an approach, it is not necessary to diminish the sovereignty of God in order to make room for human freedom; rather, already in the Trinity, the various persons remain distinct, emerge as persons, that is, precisely in their mutual interdependence and unity. Here individual freedom can never be opposed to mutual love and obedience.

With regard to the relationship between nature and grace, Balthasar sought to overcome the older dualism in a manner similar to that of de Lubac and Rahner. But at a crucial point in Balthasar's treatment we can see the influence of Luther and Barth with their innovative prioritization of Act over Being. Preferring the more concrete categories of creation and covenant to the more abstract categories of nature and grace, Balthasar was able to emphasize the historical foundation of both creation and covenant. Once creation itself is understood primarily in terms of gift, the newness of redemption – the second gift – need not be viewed as such an affront to reason, nor as discontinuous with the work begun in creation. One can begin to get an idea of Balthasar's approach in the light of his comment that only a Trinitarian God could have created. In order to make his comments on this relationship as concrete as possible, Balthasar used the transition from the Old Covenant to the New as an analogy for the relationship between nature and grace: although the latter does not destroy the proper integrity of the former, it does fulfill it in a manner which is wholly unpredictable from the side of nature.

Finally, we looked at the age-old problem of the relationship between philosophy and theology. Balthasar's treatment of this problem centers around his attempt to avoid the fateful separation of spheres which has marked so much modern thought, while at the same time avoiding the uncritical merging of spheres which had marked ancient thought. I thought it would be especially helpful to highlight the importance of Thomas Aquinas as the source for Balthasar's treatment of this problem. In Thomas, Balthasar found a thinker who was willing to grant the philosophical search its proper autonomy, while never closing himself off to the light of faith. Balthasar's reading of Aquinas focuses on the fundamental distinction between *esse* and *essentia*, and the idea that there is a mutual interdependence between existence itself and actually existing things. What is radical in Balthasar's reading is the notion that, for Aquinas, the philosophical search opens out, from its very own impetus, to the answer, given in revelation, of a free act of creation by a loving God. Revelation, in this view, is neither reducible to the philosophical search nor extrinsic to it: the mutual interdependence of Being and beings, discoverable by philosophy itself, calls for an answer as to why there is anything at all, rather than nothing. Balthasar wants to move beyond Aquinas's discussion only insofar as he wishes to place the entire inquiry regarding Being in the context of the originary, inter-personal encounter between the child and its mother. This provides for an even closer connection between the universal experience of Being and the revelation in history of the God who is love. My original experience of Being is not centered so much upon the fact that in every finite act of knowing I am somehow implying the infinite, but in the realization that I have somehow been granted my existence by another.

B. Final Questions

In this study I have tried to open up a new way of understanding Balthasar's theological method which moves beyond the two predominant interpretations in the academy. The first, which is becoming increasingly rare, views Balthasar in terms of a conservative reaction against the *aggiornamento* of Vatican II. The second, which is more subtle and still holds a great deal of currency, views Balthasar as representing the 'revelocentric, anti-apologetic' wing in the current debate over theological method. By looking at Balthasar primarily as an ecumenical theologian – and here I have in mind primarily his concern to give voice to the legitimate warnings of Luther and Barth *within* a Catholic context, and the implied concern to mediate between the dialectical approach and the critical-correlational approach – I have tried to move beyond this older interpretation of his theology. It would be a mistake to look to this study, then, for a comparison between Balthasar's theology and that of Luther, Barth or Rahner. Rather, all of these latter thinkers were examined through Balthasarian lenses, not in order to do a disservice to their thought – which, in each case, is important in its own right – but in order to show how Balthasar's serious engagement with each of these thinkers helped to form his unique theological style.

Until now too many interpreters of Balthasar's have examined his critique of Rahner, for instance, in isolation from his critical appropriation of Barth. It is true that Balthasar wrote some rather negative pieces directed against certain tendencies in Rahner's theology, but none of these in any way detract from the degree to which Balthasar attempts to incorporate Rahner's 'correlating' concerns into his theology. One can see an example of this in Balthasar's treatment of anthropology in *Theo-Drama* prior to his explicit treatments of Jesus Christ or soteriology. Another example, is the fact that Balthasar's treatment of ancient and modern metaphysics, with its corresponding attempt to find a metaphysical analogue to the biblical concept of glory, preceded his study of the New and Old Covenants in *The Glory of the Lord*. In both of these cases, and there are numerous others, Balthasar has taken a more Rahnerian than Barthian approach. I have tried to argue throughout that Balthasar's critique of Rahner must be kept alongside of his critique of Luther and Barth in order to avoid a one-sided interpretation of Balthasar's method.

As I said in the final chapter of this study, the theological aesthetics 'cuts both ways'. Against the transcendentalist tendency to relativize the particular, a theological aesthetics insists that our access to the invisible or universal is always through the visible or particular. It also emphasizes the freedom and initiative of the other to present itself on its own terms. But against the dialectical approach, Balthasar insists that there really is an analogue to the biblical concept of glory in the inner-worldly experience of beauty, that the experience of inner-worldly beauty and love can serve as an indispensable *Vorgriff* for the experience of biblical glory.

For those of us who are interested in pursuing not only the dialogue between Protestants and Catholics but also a dialogue between the revelocentric and correlational approaches, I think that *this* Balthasar can make a real contribution. In terms of the former dialogue, there must be a real engagement between Protestants and Catholics which is genuinely open to the truth of the other, and is willing to take the necessary steps towards full communion. It must be kept in mind, however, that the Catholic is in a unique position in this dialogue because of intrinsic aspects of Catholic ecclesiology which cannot simply be abandoned if the Catholic is going to come to the table as a Catholic. In view of Balthasar's insistence upon the ultimately mysterious nature of Christian doctrine, such a strong ecclesial stance need not mean resistance to genuine dialogue. While Balthasar's engagement with Barth is exemplary in this regard, questions can be raised concerning his treatment of Luther. Although, ultimately, one would have to concede the legitimacy of many of Balthasar's criticisms, it could be pointed out that Balthasar tends to read Luther at his 'worst moments'. In this he does not follow the model which he set in reading the more 'catholic' Barth against the more 'protestant' Barth. Here Balthasar's work could be complemented by the work of Carl Braaten and Robert Jenson, and also the Finnish Luther scholars who were mentioned in the Luther chapter above.[43]

With regard to the more fierce debate between 'traditionalists' and 'progressives' – insofar as these tend to represent the revelocentric and correlational approaches – within the various churches, there seems to be an impasse at present regarding just what theology is. In my view, until this question is addressed, there is little hope that true dialogue can occur. Here again, Balthasar can be seen as a helpful guide, for he has shown that theology can proceed according to a strong revelocentric stance without thereby placing a straitjacket on theological development. In short, theological dialogue cannot be simply equated with the dialogue which is undertaken in other academic disciplines. While the recent rise of hermeneutical approaches to philosophy can be seen as a refreshing step beyond the dogmatism of the Enlightenment, such a hermeneutical approach cannot simply be co-opted by the theologian without further ado. At the beginning of the theological enterprise stands the mystery of God in Jesus Christ, and all theological dialogue must have as its final goal a deeper understanding of this central mystery. The implication is often given that theology proceeds from a neutral stance – as if even philosophy proceeded in this way – in hope that it can dialogue its way to the truth.

On the other hand, and this is equally important, theology cannot be limited to the simple repetition of what has been defined in the Church's tradition. This would be a wrong-headed approach for several reasons, chief of which are the following. First, at no time in history has the Church or the theologian been in a position to contain the mystery of God in a human concept. Balthasar makes mention here, for instance, of the term 'transubstantiation' used at the Council of Trent. '[T]he designation "transubstantiation" is indeed very well suited to point to the mystery without expressing it adequately in words.'[44] Secondly, each period of history gives birth to new philosophical and scientific languages which the Church must utilize in order to make her message comprehensible to the person of that age. This must be given the fullest consideration without allowing these languages to become normative for the Church's theology.

> Theology is not to be equated with any anthropological science, be it psychology, sociology, or religious studies. It therefore receives no normative injunctions from the historically changing forms of such sciences.[45]

That Balthasar himself has understood the need to engage in such creative theological investigation can be seen in his somewhat progressive views on the possibility of an empty Hell and his bold treatment of the cross as a Trinitarian event. It cannot be denied that such investigations were undertaken in the light of modern challenges to the Christian faith and even in the light of modern historical events, such as the Holocaust. But in such cases, Balthasar is insistent that any 'innovations' must finally stem from the heart of the Christian faith, rather than from cultural pressures. In neither case does he reduce the deposit of faith to one voice among many in an ongoing dialogue, nor does he allow human expectations and experiences to become a norm for Christian proclamation. It is in order to highlight this delicate balance that I have placed Balthasar's theology between the dialectical approach of Luther and Barth on the one hand and the cosmological and anthropological approaches on the other. The question as to whether Balthasar always achieves such a balance in his own theological investigations is a question for another study. I have intentionally focused on certain fundamental questions because I think it is here that theology at present is most confused, and it is here that I think Balthasar can make an especially valuable contribution. If I have enticed the reader to take a new look at Balthasar by presenting him in a dialogical light, then I feel this study will have accomplished its purpose.

Notes

Introduction

1 For an extremely helpful interpretation of this transition, one which makes this debate central, see the book of that title by Louis Dupré, *Passage to Modernity: An Essay in the Hermeneutics of Nature and Culture* (New Haven: Yale University Press, 1993).

2 David Tracy, foreword to *God Without Being*, trans. Thomas A. Carson (Chicago: University of Chicago Press, 1991), ix–x.

3 Cornelia Capol, *Hans Urs von Balthasar: Bibliography, 1925–1990* (Einsiedeln: Johannes Verlag, 1990).

4 See the bibliography for available English translations and their dates.

5 Almost all of the English translations of Balthasar's works, prior to 1980, came from Britain (see Capol's bibliography).

6 Jeffrey Kay, 'Balthasar as Post-critical Theologian', in *Neo-conservatism: Social and Religious Phenomenon*, ed. Gregory Baum and Marcus LeFebure (Edinburgh: T&T Clark, 1981). Even if the author of the article understood Balthasar differently, the editors, at least, affiliated him with 'neo-conservatism'.

7 Francis Fiorenza, introduction to *Spirit in the World*, trans. William Dych, SJ (New York: Continuum, 1994), xxxii (emphasis mine). It would be a misnomer to say that Fiorenza misunderstands Balthasar's 'misunderstanding' of Rahner, for he makes no real attempt to understand. A few catchphrases – 'conservative' or 'negative criticism of contemporary tendencies' – are enough to make a serious evaluation unnecessary. Fiorenza bases his two-page evaluation of Balthasar's reading of Rahner on the short polemic, *Cordula*, a work which makes little sense apart from the more foundational critique located in early reviews and articles and then in Balthasar's study of Karl Barth. I will discuss Balthasar's view of Rahner at some length in Chapter 4 below, but this much should be said at this point. It makes no more sense to call Balthasar's critique of Rahner 'conservative' than it does to so call Luther's critique of Erasmus, Pascal's critique of Descartes, or Kierkegaard's critique of Hegel. It is difficult for me to see how the word 'conservative' is helpful in these analogous contexts. Furthermore, Fiorenza reduces Balthasar's critique of Rahner and Maréchal to a total rejection, and this could not be farther from the truth. In an important section of his study of Karl Barth, which we will discuss below, Balthasar makes his appreciation of the Maréchalian/Rahnerian approach very clear. He never reduces their work to 'Idealism', but simply asks if their

alleged anthropological subject is not already a theological subject. Again, this will be addressed more closely in Chapter 5 below.

8 I am borrowing this phrase from Cyril O'Regan, 'Von Balthasar and Thick Retrieval: Post-Chalcedonian Symphonic Theology', *Gregorianum* 77/2 (Spring 1996), 227–60.

9 See especially, Rowan Williams, 'Balthasar and Rahner', in *The Analogy of Beauty: The Theology of Hans Urs von Balthasar*, ed. John Riches (Edinburgh: T&T Clark, 1986), and John Milbank's, *Theology and Social Theory: Beyond Secular Reason* (Cambridge, Mass.: Blackwell, 1990), especially pages 219–23, and also George Lindbeck's critique of Rahner in *The Nature of Doctrine: Religion and Theology in a Postliberal Age* (Philadelphia: Westminster Press, 1984).

10 John R. Kevern, 'Form in Tragedy: Balthasar as Correlational Theologian', *Communio* 21 (Summer 1994), 311. This understanding of Balthasar's work is widespread. See especially: Franz Josef van Beeck, SJ, *God Encountered: A Contemporary Catholic Systematic Theology*, vol. I: *Understanding the Christian Faith* (San Francisco: Harper & Row, 1989): 'While Karl Rahner showed a lifelong interest in, and respect for, positive theology, his leading idea hails from fundamental theology; in many ways, his thought can be interpreted as a consistent effort to settle Roman Catholic arrears with the Enlightenment, which had charged that Christian dogma was an insult to human intelligence and freedom. Hans Urs von Balthasar's literary tastes have spontaneously driven him in the direction of positive, dogmatic theology; his appreciation of Barth is far from incidental to his thought … *It must be said, however, that von Balthasar has not shown the kind of appreciation for fundamental theology that Rahner has shown for dogmatics*' (45, emphasis mine); Robert M. Doran, SJ, 'Lonergan and Balthasar: Methodological Considerations', *Theological Studies* 58 (March 1997), 61–84, where Doran suggests that Lonergan's strength lies in his work on methodology while Balthasar's strength lies in his dogmatics proper; Fergus Kerr, 'Natural Desire for God', in *Immortal Longings: Versions of Transcending Humanity* (Notre Dame, Ind.: University of Notre Dame Press, 1997), 159–84; and Eamonn Conway, *The Anonymous Christian – a Relativized Christianity? An Evaluation of Hans Urs von Balthasar's Criticisms of Karl Rahner's Theory of the Anonymous Christian* (New York: Peter Lang, 1993), to name just a few. I will address these readings in greater detail in Chapters 4 and 5 below.

11 *Theo-Drama: Theological Dramatic Theory*, vol. I: *Prolegomena*, trans. Graham Harrison (San Francisco: Ignatius Press, 1988), 626–7. Hereafter, TD I.

12 As we will see, Balthasar was articulating his earliest critique of Rahner's 'transcendental Thomism' in the context of his dialogue with Karl Barth in the 1940s. Balthasar was afraid that Rahner's *Hearers of the Word* would in fact affirm Barth's worst fears about the 'analogy of being'.

Chapter 1: Balthasar and Dialogue

1 Herbert McCabe, OP, *God Matters* (Springfield, Ill.: Templegate, 1991), 60.

2 Examples of this 'take' on Balthasar's role abound. Eamon Conway, in *The Anonymous Christian*, summarizes Balthasar's thought almost exclusively on the basis of his short, polemical works, giving it an extremely fideistic coloring, only then to show why it needs the more philosophically rigorous approach of Rahner to give it a complementary foundation. It is not without significance

that Conway offers little to no discussion of *Theo-logik* or the volumes on metaphysics in *The Glory of the Lord*. This 'fideistic' interpretation is also present in an article by Robert M. Doran, SJ, 'Lonergan and Balthasar: Methodological Considerations', *Theological Studies* 58 (1997), in which the author locates Balthasar's contribution to modern theology in his treatment of the concrete aspects of Christian revelation, while Lonergan's is to be found in his work on method. It is then suggested that the two should complement each other. As Doran states it, '[A] systematic theology must employ both "general" categories, shared with other disciplines, and "special" categories proper to theology ... [W]hile Lonergan illuminates principally the ground of general categories, Balthasar may in the long run be more helpful in illuminating the ground of special categories' (63). But this is to privilege the transcendental approach from the very outset, only then to concede to Balthasar a voice *within* that approach. Balthasar is not, however, offering Catholic substance to go along with a Lonerganian method; he is challenging the 'transcendental' method from the ground up. In other words, it is not clear from Doran's article what he is asking Lonergan to 'give up' in this confrontation with Balthasar, for Lonergan has always made room for Catholic substance; Balthasar is asked, however, to give up his entire 'theological aesthetics', which is his version of a method in theology. In my view, a more helpful comparison of Balthasar's aesthetic approach and Lonergan's transcendental approach is found in Anthony Kelly's, 'Is Lonergan's Method Adequate to Christian Mystery?', *The Thomist* 39/3 (1975), 437–70. Although we are not interested in pursuing the differences between Balthasar and Lonergan, we will say that they originate in Balthasar's notion that any method should be determined by the nature of its object. As such, a 'general' method which would undergird all human inquiries will not suffice, in Balthasar's view. Another example of this (mis)understanding of the differences between Balthasar and Rahner is presented succinctly by Franz Jozef van Beeck, SJ, *God Encountered: A Contemporary Catholic Systematic Theology*, vol. I: 'While Karl Rahner showed a lifelong interest in, and respect for, positive theology, his leading idea hails from fundamental theology; in many ways, his thought can be interpreted as a consistent effort to settle Roman Catholic theology's arrears with the Enlightenment, which had charged that Christian dogma was an insult to human intelligence and freedom. Hans Urs von Balthasar's literary tastes have spontaneously driven him in the direction of positive, dogmatic theology; his appreciation of Barth is far from incidental to his thought' (45). And then in a footnote to this comment: 'It must be said, however, that von Balthasar has not shown the kind of appreciation for fundamental theology that Rahner has shown for dogmatics' (ibid.).

3 'The Claim to Catholicity', ET IV, 74–5.

4 See, for instance, Hans Urs von Balthasar, *The Office of Peter and the Structure of the Church*, trans. Andrée Emery (San Francisco: Ignatius Press, 1986), 121–30 (hereafter, OP); *A Short Primer for Unsettled Laymen*, trans. Michael Waldstein (San Francisco: Ignatius Press, 1985), 118–21 (hereafter, *Short Primer*); *Convergences: To the Source of the Christian Mystery* (hereafter *Convergences*), trans. E. A. Nelson (San Francisco: Ignatius Press, 1984), 108–10. See also, Christoph Schönborn, OP, 'Hans Urs von Balthasar's Contribution to Ecumenism', in *Hans Urs von Balthasar: His Life and Work*, ed. David L. Schindler (San Francisco: Ignatius Press, 1991), 252–4.

5 Adrian Walker, 'Dialogue, Communion, and Martyrdom: Thoughts on the

Relation Between Intra-ecclesial and Inter-religious Dialogue', *Communio* 27/4 (2000), 816–24.

6 *Explorations in Theology*, vol. IV: *Spirit and Institution* (hereafter, ET IV), trans. Edward T. Oakes, SJ (San Francisco: Ignatius Press, 1995).

7 *The Glory of the Lord: A Theological Aesthetics*, vol. IV: *The Realm of Metaphysics in Antiquity* (hereafter, GL IV), trans. Oliver Davies, Andrew Louth, Brian McNeil, CRV, John Saward and Rowan Williams (San Francisco: Ignatius Press, 1989), 17.

8 Ibid., 75.

9 Ibid., 75, n. 11.

10 Ibid.

11 Ibid., 76.

12 *Theo-Logic*, vol. I: *Truth of the World* (hereafter TL I), trans. Adrian Walker (San Francisco: Ignatius Press, 2000), 29–30.

13 Cited in Josef Pieper, *Living the Truth*, trans. Lothar Krauth (San Francisco: Ignatius Press, 1989), 19 (emphasis mine).

14 GL IV, 29–30.

15 *The Glory of the Lord: A Theological Aesthetics*, vol. I: *Seeing the Form* (hereafter GL I), trans. Erasmo Leiva-Merikakis (San Francisco: Ignatius Press, 1982), 21.

16 GL IV, 30.

17 GL I, 25.

18 GL I, 19–20.

19 For an English translation of this work, which actually contains this essay and two others, see *The Silence of St. Thomas*, trans. John Murray and Daniel O'Connor (South Bend, Ind.: St Augustine's Press, 1999).

20 Ibid., 96.

21 TL I, 17.

22 TL I, 41.

23 Ibid.

24 In the section entitled 'Unveiling and Veiling', Balthasar emphasizes this point accordingly: 'On the other hand, this confession in which things divulge their truth is neither indiscreet not unlimited. It is bounded by the intimate space in being. Things are not only unveiled. They are, in equal measure, essentially veiled, and they remain so from their beginning to end. This veiling naturally entails a limitation of their unveiling but not necessarily a limitation of their truth. For veiling is not simply opposed to unveiling like some barrier confining it within its limits from the outside. Rather, it is more like a form or property that is inherent in the unveiling itself. In fact, things are unveiling as veiled, and it is in this form that they become objects of knowledge' (TL I, 207).

25 TL I, 25.

26 Ibid.

27 TL I, 55.

28 Cf. Thomas Prufer, 'A Pretreptic: What is Philosophy?', *Communio: International Catholic Review* (Summer 2003), 337–58.

29 Josef Pieper puts this accordingly, 'The world in which man today leads his ordinary life is becoming more and more a purely technological one. The things with which he is concerned are artificial; they are artifacts, not creations. The danger inherent in this situation is that man might, erroneously, come to regard the world as a whole and the created things with it – above all, man himself – in the same manner in which he regards, correctly, his own artifacts belonging to

the technological sphere; in other words, man is beginning to consider the whole of creation as completely fathomable, fully accessible to rational comprehension, and, above all, as something which it is permissible to change, transform, or even destroy' (*The Silence of St. Thomas*, trans. John Murray, SJ, and Daniel O'Connor (South Bend, Ind.: St Augustine's Press, 1999), 91–2).

30 TL I, 11–12.

31 TL I, 187.

32 Nobody has told this story as brilliantly as Hans Georg Gadamer in *Truth and Method*, trans. Joel Weinsheimer and Donald G. Marshall (New York: Crossroad, 1991).

33 TL I, 181.

34 TL I, 182.

35 This would be the place to locate the foundation for Balthasar's impatience with the historical-critical method when it is misused. It is not that Balthasar is pre-critically behind the times, it's that he is post-critically ahead of them.

36 TL I, 183–4.

37 TL I, 185.

38 TL I, 186.

39 This is not, of course, to suggest that with supernatural revelation such a bird's-eye perspective does become available; however, revelation does give one an unparalleled participation in God's view of the whole, according, of course, to the mode of the knower.

40 Christoph Schönborn, OP, foreword to *Razing the Bastions* by Hans Urs von Balthasar, trans. Brian McNeil, CRV (San Francisco: Ignatius Press, 1993), 13.

41 Hans Urs von Balthasar, *My Work in Retrospect*, trans. John Saward and Brian McNeil (San Francisco: Ignatius Press, 1993), 96. Hereafter, MW. It is unfortunate that Balthasar never specifically addresses the actual ecumenical dialogues that have taken place especially in the latter half of the twentieth century. His criticism of overhasty ecumenism, however, should not be taken as a rejection of legitimate ecumenical dialogue. Indeed, Balthasar was quite enthusiastic about Hans Küng's ecumenical study of justification. Instead, his occasional and typically generalized criticism of ecumenism should be understood as directed at a style of theology which pretends to proceed from a neutral or pre-confessional stance. As this chapter will hopefully show, a strong faith stance need not preclude an openess to genuine dialogue.

42 Balthasar is not, it should be noted, referring to the evangelicalism which is currently prominent in the United States, but to the German variety stemming from the Lutheran side of the Reformation. This 'evangelicalism' can take on quite 'liberal' forms, as it did in 19th-century Germany.

43 *Convergences*, 108–9.

44 'It should once more be emphasized that we do not intend to detract from the urgency of ecumenical dialogue; nor do we reject this typical sequence of theological negotiations out of hand. It seems to be a psychological necessity, theologically defensible so long as what is presently relegated to the periphery is not treated as a trifle, a thing of no importance' (OP, 125).

45 *Elucidations*, trans. John Riches (San Francisco: Ignatius Press, 1998), 40.

46 This way of putting it comes from a very helpful study of Balthasar's theology of revelation by Larry Chapp, *The God who Speaks: Hans Urs von Balthasar's Theology of Revelation* (Rowman & Littlefield, 1997).

47 *Elucidations*, 36–7; KB, 255–7.

[48] ET I, 11–26.

[49] Balthasar will often quote John 20.30; 21.25, in this context to the effect that scripture could never contain, in an exhaustive way, all that Jesus said and did. See, for instance, ET I, 17. See also TD II for the fullest treatment of what Balthasar calls, 'theodramatic hermeneutics'.

[50] Robert Sokolowski has brilliantly developed this aspect of Balthasar's theology, in *Eucharistic Presence: A Study in the Theology of Disclosure* (Washington, DC: Catholic University of America Press, 1994). In the chapter 'Disclosure in Scripture', Sokolowski has this to say, 'Once we recognize the fact that the written word is a prerequisite for biblical revelation, however, we must be careful to avoid the danger of making the text the primary focus, of making the text and not the things it discloses the center of our attention ... Writing therefore intensifies the temptation to make the text stand on its own and become an object in its own right ... The Bible, both the Old and New Testaments, comes to life in its proper form when read in the liturgy. When it is so read, it does not draw attention to itself as a text – as it does for the scholar – but presents to us the things it is about. It points beyond itself to the things it records and manifests' (141–3).

[51] ET I, 19.

[52] Here we get a glimpse of Balthasar's interpretation of Newman's understanding of doctrinal development. For a treatment of this, see, Aidan Nichols, 'Littlemore from Lucerne: Newman's *Essay on Development* in Balthasarian Perspective', in Ian Ker (ed.), *Newman and Conversion* (Edinburgh: T&T Clark, 1997), 100–16. See also TD II, 130–6.

[53] ET I, 17.

[54] *Elucidations*, 38.

[55] *Elucidations*, 40.

[56] KB, 13.

[57] 'But, on the other hand, we must also be quite clear that precisely those Fathers who helped decisively to formulate the Trinitarian and christological dogmas – Athanasius, the Cappadocians, Hilary – are full of passages in which they expound the transcendence and unintelligibility of the divine nature in the course of their relentless struggle against the Arian and Eunomian rationalism. It is this which makes it clear that the conciliar definitions of the patristic age are to be taken as attempts to protect the mystery against one-sided "rationalization", attempts repeatedly made always in the consciousness of their inadequacy' (*Elucidations*, 41–2).

[58] *Short Primer*, 119.

[59] David Schindler, 'On the Catholic Common Ground Project: The Christological Foundations of Dialogue', *Communio* 23 (Winter 1996), 829.

[60] Ibid., 831.

[61] Of course this is the current self-understanding of the best of what is called science today. The critique of the positivistic view of science from Nietzsche, Husserl, Heidegger and, more recently, Polanyi and Kuhn, is now well known, but is not always sufficiently incorporated into all aspects of modern theology. For attempts to integrate these insights into theological method, see especially Andrew Louth's *Discerning the Mystery: An Essay on the Nature of Theology* (Oxford: Oxford University Press, 1983); William C. Placher, *Unapologetic Theology: A Christian Voice in a Pluralistic Conversation* (Louisville, Ky.: Westminster/John Knox Press, 1989); and Colin Gunton, *Enlightenment and Alienation: An Essay Towards a Trinitarian Theology* (Grand Rapids, Mich.: William B. Eerdmans, 1985).

[62] This is not the place to investigate Balthasar's highly nuanced position on the historical-critical method. For a fuller discussion see especially: GL VII; TD III; *Does Jesus Know Us; Do We Know Him,* trans. Graham Harrison (San Francisco: Ignatius Press, 1983); and 'Exegese und Dogmatik', *Communio: Internationale katholische Zeitschrift* 5 (1976): 385–96; and in the secondary literature see: Aidan Nichols, introduction to *Mysterium Paschale: The Mystery of Easter*, trans. Aidan Nichols (Grand Rapids, Mich.: William B. Eerdmans, 1990), 1–10; Oakes, *Pattern of Redemption*, 183–208; Chantraine, 'Exegesis and Contemplation in the Work of Hans Urs von Balthasar'; and John Riches, 'The Biblical Basis of Glory', in *The Beauty of Christ: An Introduction to the Theology of Hans Urs von Balthasar*, ed. Bede McGregor, OP and Thomas Norris (Edinburgh: T&T Clark, 1994).

[63] *Einfaltungen*, 72.

[64] *Convergences*, 76–7.

[65] Hans Urs von Balthasar, 'Implications of the Word', in *Explorations in Theology*, vol. I, *The Word Made Flesh* (hereafter, ET I), trans. A. V. Littledale and Alexander Dru (San Francisco: Ignatius Press, 1989).

[66] *Convergences*, 84–5; *Einfaltungen*, 78.

[67] *Convergences*, 90–6.

[68] Ibid., 97–8.

[69] This is all spelled out in much more detail in Balthasar's two volumes on the Old and New Covenants (GL VI and VII) and, with regard to method, in GL I, but we must content ourselves at present with this general sketch. De Lubac's work on medieval exegesis is also presupposed here. Balthasar published and wrote an introduction to the German version of this: *Geist aus der Geschichte* (Einsiedeln: Johannes Verlag, 1968). See also, Riches, 'Biblical Basis of Glory'.

[70] Balthasar draws attention, here, to the fact that not only Paul, but even the Synoptic Gospels refuse to treat Jesus in a purely 'historical' manner, but insist that he is always present to their respective communities: 'But all three, in addition, return to the simultaneity of the faithful with the earthly Lord moving toward the Cross ... But for Paul, the Exalted one who encountered him remains essentially the Crucified one with whom he, Paul, wishes to be crucified, but at the same time resurrected; all questions of chronological time ... pale completely in the face of this paradox' (*Convergences*, 99–100).

[71] See, *Truth is Symphonic.*

[72] *Convergences*, 105–10. With regard to Karl Barth's invectives in particular, Balthasar has the following to say, 'Karl Barth's invectives against the "Catholic And" can be important and even indispensable as earnest brotherly exhortation – particularly when they protest against something secondary being put in the place of something primary – but they can also prejudice, too quickly and unnecessarily, a necessary integration' (107–8). Lest anyone think that Balthasar only speaks of these things in the abstract, he makes such an attempt at integration, with a specific view to Protestants, in his short work, *In the Fullness of the Faith: On the Centrality of the Distinctively Catholic*, trans. Graham Harrison (San Francisco: Ignatius Press, 1988).

[73] ET IV.

[74] Hans Urs von Balthasar, *The Theology of Karl Barth*, trans. Edward T. Oakes, SJ (San Francisco: Ignatius Press, 1992), 4. Hereafter, KB.

[75] For what follows see especially, *Theo-Drama: Theological Dramatic Theory,* vol. III: *Dramatis Personae: Persons in Christ*, trans. Graham Harrison (San Francisco: Ignatius Press, 1992), 353–60, hereafter TD III; OP, 183–266; and 'Office in the

Church', in *Explorations in Theology*, vol. II: *Spouse of the Word*, trans. A.V. Littledale and Alexander Dru (San Francisco: Ignatius Press, 1991), 81–142. This volume cited hereafter as ET II.

76 'Office in the Church', 133.

77 Ibid., 132–5.

78 Ibid., 133.

79 Like Balthasar, Bernanos understood obedience to be among the highest of Christian virtues. But, in both cases, this obedience is not of the blind or infantile sort. In, *Bernanos: An Ecclesial Existence*, trans. Erasmo Leiva-Merikakis (San Francisco: Communio Books/Ignatius Press, 1996), Balthasar discusses Bernanos on this matter: 'We here encounter for the first time the *diagnosis of obedience* that is so important in Bernanos, obedience being that noble Christian virtue that nowadays is so easily looked upon as the lowest of vices. Whether addressing civil or ecclesial authorities, Bernanos cannot impress upon them enough the fact that "sabotaging this high and indispensable faculty of the soul called 'judgment' can only lead to great disasters ... People trained to obey blindly are the very ones who will suddenly disobey blindly. To obey without discussion does not at all mean the same thing as to obey without understanding, and total docility is not as far as we think from total revolt. Christian obedience, by its very nature, has a heroic character"' (88).

80 'Office in the Church', 132.

81 For a detailed discussion of this, see Hans Urs von Balthasar, *The Christian State of Life*, trans. Sister Mary Frances McCarthy (San Francisco: Ignatius Press, 1983).

82 Ibid., 106–7. Lest there be any misunderstanding about this treatment of the sexes, Edward Oakes has this to say in his study of Balthasar's theology: 'There is, then, an essential equality of the sexes, mixed also with a symbolic ranking of masculine/feminine as an expression of the God/creature relationship. But since Adam is also a creature, he too is feminine *vis-à-vis* God. In fact, it would be theologically disastrous to equate Adam's role with that of the Creator ...' (*Pattern of Redemption*, 254–5). Or, as Balthasar puts it, 'There is for all the equality of persons and of their sexual functions (Eve is as unambiguously created by God as Adam!) an "order" in the realm of the sexual, a prefiguration of the quite other and yet analogous order between the new Adam and the new Eve' (*Elucidations*, 106).

83 'Office in the Church', 107.

84 TD III, 339–60; cf., OP, 131–82.

85 Ibid., 355 (emphasis mine).

86 Ibid., 355–6.

87 Ibid., 356.

88 Ibid., 357.

89 Ibid., 358. In order to do justice to Balthasar's ecclesiology one would also have to discuss the Johannine aspect of the Church, which mediates between the Petrine and Marian dimensions. See OP, 183–266.

90 Schönborn, 'Hans Urs von Balthasar's Contribution to Ecumenism', 255.

91 *Short Primer*, 118, cited in Schönborn, ibid., 258.

Chapter 2: Balthasar on Luther's *Theologia Crucis*

1 I am referring to the work of Paul Hacker, *Das Ich im Glauben bei Martin Luther* (Cologne: Styria, 1966), and Theobald Beer, *Der fröliche Wechsel und Streit: Grundzüge der Theologie Martin Luthers* (Einsiedeln: Johannes Verlag, 1980).

2 The work of Heiko Oberman and his students can be seen in this light.

3 For an overview of this interpretation see Carl E. Braaten, 'The Finnish Breakthrough in Luther Research', and Risto Saarinen, 'Salvation in the Lutheran–Orthodox Dialogue', *Pro Ecclesia* 5/2 (Spring 1996), 141–3; 202–13.

4 Similar problems arise when one looks at Catholic Luther scholarship which has passed from an era of sharp polemic against Luther to an era of nearly unequivocal recommendation. See Joseph Cardinal Ratzinger, 'Luther and the Unity of the Churches: An Interview with Joseph Cardinal Ratzinger', *Communio* 11 (Fall 1984), 210–26.

5 A quick glance at the title of Heiko Oberman's formidable study of Gabriel Biel, *The Harvest of Medieval Theology* (Cambridge, Mass.: Harvard University Press, 1963), when compared with a chapter of Étienne Gilson's *The Unity of the Philosophical Experience* (New York: Charles Scribner's Sons, 1937), 'The Breakdown of the Medieval Synthesis', illustrates this difference well enough. We might add, at this point, that Balthasar's assessment of nominalism lies somewhere between these two positions. In other words, while he understands that nominalism is motivated by a proper concern to safeguard the truths of faith against 'whore' reason, he thinks that the attempt to do so on the basis of a radical separation of realms of jurisdiction is mistaken.

6 De Lubac's overall thesis, that in the late Middle Ages the relationship between nature and grace is construed in increasingly extrinsic ways, is well known. This theme, along with its role in the birth of modernity, is addressed in the book-length essay by Louis Dupré, *The Passage to Modernity: An Essay in the Hermeneutics of Culture* (New Haven: Yale University Press, 1993). Again, Dupré tends to give a more negative assessment than does Oberman, but part of the reason for this can be derived from their respective enterprises. Oberman is trying to overcome a situation in Luther scholarship in which it is typically assumed that nominalism had lost touch with the Thomistic synthesis, and that Luther's criticisms were, therefore, directed at this aberration and not at the Catholic view per se. Often, this criticism is taken even farther, to say that Luther is only 'orthodox' to a certain point, but that his refusal to speak of 'faith informed by love', for instance, is an example of the remaining nominalist influence on his thought. The degree to which Luther is still subject to nominalist thought, it is maintained, is the degree to which his thought diverges from sound theology. In the face of this, Oberman seems to wish to correct the Catholic prejudice against nominalist thought, in order to facilitate his defense of Luther. Dupré, on the other hand, is concerned with the increasing relegation, in modern times, of the realm of faith to the private and subjective realm, while the realm of reason is left to the secular scientists and technocrats. He traces the beginnings of this 'secularization', at least in part, to late medieval nominalism.

7 Jaroslav Pelikan, *The Christian Tradition: A History of the Development of Doctrine*, vol. IV, *Reformation of Church and Dogma (1300–1700)* (Chicago: University of Chicago Press, 1984).

8 Ibid., 13, 17.

9 Heiko Oberman, *Luther: Man Between God and the Devil*, trans. Eileen Walliser-Schwarzbart (New York: Doubleday/Image Books, 1992), 117.

[10] Ibid., 118.
[11] Attributed to Bartholomaeus Arnoldi von Usingen, cited in ibid., 119.
[12] *Harvest of Medieval Theology*, 30–5.
[13] Ibid., 36–41.
[14] Ibid., 43–6.
[15] Ibid., 44.
[16] Ibid., 46–7.
[17] Ibid., 49.
[18] George Tavard, *Justification: An Ecumenical Study* (New York: Paulist Press, 1983): 'It is Ockham's doctrine, endorsed by Biel, that God could have willed predestination either with or without previous merit, but that the ground for merit does not lie in man's actions, but in man's being accepted by God in view of his future predestination, before any merit of his own. In this case, the Nominalists are not Pelagian, and they deny that one can be saved *ex puris naturalibus*, without grace' (48).
[19] Harry McSorely, *Luther, Right or Wrong?* (London: Newman Press, 1969).
[20] Oberman, *Luther*, 116.
[21] Ibid., 118.
[22] Ibid., 120.
[23] *D. Martin Luthers Werke. Kritische Gesamtausgabe* (Weimar Ausgabe) (Weimar: Hermann Böhlau, 1883–), 6.195.4 (hereafter, WA). Cited in ibid., 120.
[24] *Luther's Works*, ed. Jaroslav Pelikan and Helmut T. Lehmann (Philadelphia: Fortress Press, 1958–72), 31. 9–16 (hereafter, LW).
[25] For a more detailed study of this disputation and its relation to Biel's and Occam's teaching, see Paul Vignaux, 'On Luther and Ockham', trans. James Coleman, in *Reformation in Medieval Perspective*, ed. Steven Ozment (Chicago: Quadrangle Books, 1971), 107–18. One of the key issues addressed by Vignaux's essay is the Catholic scholar Denifle's notion that Luther, in the above disputation, accepts the nominalist distinction between God's absolute and ordained power, and that, accordingly, Luther teaches that God can accept one apart from sanctifying grace. Vignaux refutes this argument by pointing to what Luther means by 'loving God above all things', and insisting that this is possible only in grace. That Luther insists that grace, when present, is always active should assuage any such concerns.
[26] Gerhard O. Forde, *On Being a Theologian of the Cross: Reflections on Luther's Heidelberg Disputation, 1518* (Grand Rapids, Mich.: William B. Eerdmans, 1997), 19.
[27] Heinrich Bornkamm, 'Die theologischen Thesen Luthers bei der Heidelberger Disputation 1518 und seine theologia Crucis', in *Luther, Gestalt und Wirkungen* (Gütersloh: Gütersloher Verlagshaus Gerd Mohn, 1975).
[28] *On Being a Theologian of the Cross*, 21.
[29] Walther von Loewenich, *Luther's Theology of the Cross*, trans. Herbert J. A. Bouman (Minneapolis, Minn.: Augsburg, 1976): 'Luther's theology of the cross is not to be confined to a special period in Luther's theological development; it is a principle of his entire theology' (12–13).
[30] *Heidelberg Disputation* in *Martin Luther's Basic Theological Writings*, ed. Timothy Lull (Minneapolis, Minn.: Augsburg Fortress Press, 1989), 30 (hereafter, HD). This should come as no surprise considering, first, that Luther is holding this disputation before the 'Augustinians' of Heidelberg, and, second, that Luther's opponents also claimed the authority of Augustine in their formulations. In other words, Augustine was somewhat of a theological authority in the context of these debates.

[31] Forde, *On Being a Theologian of the Cross*, 21. Here, Forde is following Bornkamm, *Luther, Gestalt und Wirkungen*.

[32] HD, 34, 37.

[33] This disputation, with its emphasis on the sin of pride and the necessity of humility in accompanying every good work, has been singled out as evidence for the influence of mysticism in Luther's theology. The earlier Luther scholars of the nineteenth and early twentieth centuries relegated this to an early phase in Luther's development, which, they alleged, he eventually outgrew. More recently, however, Luther's relationship to mysticism has been reassessed. Heiko Oberman, in 'Simil Gemitus et Raptus: Luther and Mysticism', in *The Reformation in Medieval Perspective*, ed. Steven Ozment (Chicago, Quadrangle Books, 1971), 219–51, has maintained that certain aspects of mystical thought, especially German mysticism, continue to have a strong influence on Luther's theology throughout his career. For a more detailed study, see Bengt Hoffman, *Luther and the Mystics: A Re-examination of Luther's Spiritual Experience and His Relationship to the Mystics* (Minneapolis, Minn.: Augsburg, 1976). If anything, Hoffman goes even farther than Oberman in stressing Luther's affinities for mystical theology.

[34] HD, 41.

[35] Following the thought of such medieval thinkers as Robert Holcot (d. 1349), even the young Luther maintained that one could not be rewarded with knowledge of God by *thinking* one's best, yet he still accepted the notion that one could be rewarded with God's grace by *doing* one's best. This distinction is still maintained in his commentary on Lombard's *Sentences* (1509–16). The turning-point comes, apparently, some time in late 1516 or early 1517. For more on this turning-point, see, Heiko Oberman, '*Facientibus Quod in se est Deus non Denegat Gratiam:* Robert Holcot O.P. and the Beginnings of Luther's Theology', *Harvard Theological Review* 55 (1962), 317–42.

[36] *Luther's Theology of the Cross*, 76.

[37] The reference is implicit in this disputation but becomes more explicit in Luther's *Bondage of the Will* and his *Lectures of Genesis*. For a more detailed discussion of this, see, von Loewenich, *Luther's Theology of the Cross*, 25–49. In this text Luther simply refers to the Genesis text involving Moses and the 'back parts' of God in his explanation of thesis 20: 'The "back" and visible things of God are placed in opposition to the invisible, namely his human nature, weakness, foolishness' (HD, 43–4).

[38] David Steinmetz, *Luther in Context* (Bloomington, Ind.: Indiana University Press, 1986), 24.

[39] Ibid.

[40] In his debate with Erasmus, Luther makes explicit reference to the difference between the God who is revealed and preached and the God who is hidden, whose will is secret. In reference to the passage in Ezekiel which states, 'I do not desire the death of the sinner,' Luther responds: 'For he is here speaking of the preached and offered mercy of God, not of that hidden and awful will of God whereby he ordains by his own counsel which and what sort of persons he wills to be recipients and partakers of his preached and offered mercy. This will is not to be inquired into, but reverently adored, as by far the most awe-inspiring secret of the Divine Majesty, reserved for him alone and forbidden to us much more religiously than any number of Corysian caverns' (LW, 33, 138–9). As to the discomfort this might cause the tortured soul, Paul Althaus says the following: 'This means that the Christian should not stare into the abyss of predestination

of the hidden God with the tortured question whether or not he is chosen; but he should hold to that predestination which is revealed in Christ and to his calling as he has revealed it in his baptism and through the proclamation of the word' (Paul Althaus, *The Theology of Martin Luther*, trans. Robert C. Schultz (Philadelphia: Fortress Press, 1966), 281). All of this talk of the will of God beyond the revealed will of God has led Ritschl and others to speak of a lapse, on Luther's part, to the nominalist idea of the arbitrary God of the *potentia absoluta*, but both von Loewenich and Althaus deny such a charge. In this regard, Althaus says, 'He himself is his own law. He does not will and act arbitrarily but according to the norm of his holy nature. Since this is the essence of all goodness, whatever he wills must be good, for he wills it out of his own being' (ibid., 282).

41 *The Freedom of a Christian*, in *Martin Luther's Basic Theological Writings*, 596.

42 See the interesting treatment of this 'breakthrough' and the scholarly discussion surrounding it in Gordon Rupp, *The Righteousness of God: Luther Studies* (London: Hodder & Stoughton, 1953).

43 *The Freedom of a Christian*, 601.

44 Ibid.

45 Althaus, *Theology of Martin Luther*, 232.

46 *The Freedom of a Christian*, 603.

47 Ibid., 610.

48 *Theology of Martin Luther*, 249.

49 Peter Manns, 'Absolute and Incarnate Faith – Luther on Justification in the Galatians' Commentary of 1531–1535', in *Catholic Scholars Dialogue with Luther*, ed. Joseph Lortz (Chicago: Loyola University Press, 1970).

50 LW 26, 10.

51 LW 26, 266–7: 'Everything that is attributed to works belongs to faith. For works must not be looked at in a moral sense; they must be looked at in a theological and faithful sense. Therefore in theology let faith always be the divinity of works diffused throughout the works in the same way that the divinity is throughout the humanity of Christ ... Thus faith is universally the divinity in the work, the person, and the members of the body as the one and only cause of justification; afterwards this is attributed to the matter on account of the form, to the work on account of the faith. The kingly authority of the divinity is given to Christ the man, not because of His humanity but because of His divinity. For the divinity alone created all things, without the cooperation of the humanity. Nor did the humanity conquer sin and death; but the hook that was concealed under the worm, at which the devil struck, conquered and devoured the devil, who was attempting to devour the worm.'

52 This use of Christology was soundly criticized by Yves Congar, who thinks that the problems with Luther's doctrine of justification can be traced to problems with his Christology. For instance, Luther seems to be saying here that the humanity of Christ has no real role in our redemption, other than, in a strange passage on Christ's descent into Hell, fooling the devil into thinking that he was merely human. Congar finds support for his accusation in quotes such as the following: 'Thus a theological man is a man of faith. In like manner, a right reason and a good will are a reason and will in faith. Thus faith is universally the divinity in the work, the person, and the members of the body, as the one and only cause of justification; afterwards this is attributed to the matter on account of the form, to the work on account of the faith. The kingly authority of the divinity is given to Christ the man, not because of His divinity. For the divinity alone created all

things, without the cooperation of the humanity. Nor did the humanity conquer sin and death; but the hook that was concealed under the worm, at which the devil struck, conquered and devoured the devil, who was attempting to devour the worm' (LW 26, 266f., cited in Manns, 'Absolute and Incarnate Faith', 127). Congar's discussion of this problem is found in, Yves Congar, 'Considerations and Reflections on the Christology of Luther', in *Dialogue Between Christians*, trans. P. Loretz (Westminster: Newman Press, 1966).

53 Manns, 'Absolute and Incarnate Faith', 210, n. 54.

54 Ibid., 130. Manns notes that elsewhere Luther is more ready to point out the incarnate aspect of faith. As the following makes clear: 'Therefore faith always justifies and makes alive; and yet it does not remain alone, that is, idle. Not that it does not remain alone on its own level and in its own function, for it always justifies alone. But it is incarnate and becomes man; that is, it neither is nor remains idle or without love' (LW 26, 272).

55 Adrienne von Speyr, *Erde und Himmel. Ein Tagebuch. Zweiter Teil II: Die Zeit der großen Diktate*, ed. with an introduction by Hans Urs von Balthasar (Einsiedeln: Johannes Verlag, 1975), 195ff. Cited in Schindler, *Hans Urs von Balthasar*, 13.

56 MW, 74.

57 Balthasar, 'Movement Toward God', in ET III, 23.

58 Ibid., 25.

59 Ibid.

60 GL I, 45.

61 Ibid., 46–7.

62 *The Glory of the Lord*, vol. V: *The Realm of Metaphysics in the Modern Age*, trans. Oliver Davies, Andrew Louth, John Saward and Martin Simon, ed. Brian McNeil, CRV and John Riches (San Francisco: Ignatius Press, 1991), 99. (Hereafter, GL V).

63 See especially 'Theology and Sanctity', in ET I.

64 GL V, 12–13.

65 Ibid., 13.

66 For further discussion of these issues see Oberman's, 'Simul Gemitus et Raptus: Luther and Mysticism', and Hoffman's, *Luther and the Mystics.*

67 GL V, 102.

68 *Theo-Drama: Theological-Dramatic Theory*, vol. IV: *The Action*, trans. Graham Harrison (San Francisco: Ignatius Press, 1994), 240–3 (hereafter, TD IV).

69 Ibid., 243–4.

70 Between the section on the medievals and Luther, Balthasar inserted a discussion of Rahner's treatment of these issues. It is almost certain that Balthasar breaks with the historical sequence in order to draw attention to the contrast between Luther's and Rahner's positions.

71 Balthasar relies fairly heavily in this section on the provocative study of Luther by Theobald Beer, *Der froeliche Wechsel und Streit. Grundzuege der Theologie Martin Luthers* (Einsiedeln: Johannes Verlag, 1980).

72 TD IV, 284.

73 Ibid., 285–6.

74 Ibid., 286. See also the discussion in *Theologik*, II: *Wahrheit Gottes* (Einsiedeln: Johannes Verlag, 1985), 305ff. (hereafter, TL II). Balthasar's discussion in this volume focuses primarily on the metaphysical implications of Luther's focus on this 'central *commercium*' as the following should make clear: 'Luther hätte schon gegen unsern Titel "Theologik" protestiert. Gott hat mit Logik nichts zu tun. Mit ihr hat die Rede von Gott ebensowenig zu tun wie mit

Metaphysik oder Grammatik. "Spiritus Sanctus habet suam grammaticam," in der der Begriff der Analogie nichts verloren hat. So kann Luther teils nach der überkommenen Logik, aber auch teils ohne und gegen sie sprechen. Dann kann auch sich Widersprechendes als gleich wahr ausgesagt werden. Vom Christen wird immer wieder sagen, er sei "zugleich Sünder und Heileger, Feind und Sohn Gottes": "Reim das, wer reimen kann. Zwei entgegengesetzte Dinge in demselben Subjekt und zum gleichen Zeitpunkt." Althaus spricht hier von einer Paradox-Christologie, die sich als metaphysische Theorie aufhebe. Es geht aber, nüchterner gesagt, um die Aufhebung des Nichtwiderspruchsatzes. Wie kommt es zu dieser Aufhebung?' (305–7).

75 TD IV, 287. As we will see below, this understanding is linked to Luther's understanding of the two kinds of righteousness. Just as it is Christ's divinity which wins out over sin and the devil, so it is the Christ present to the believer through faith alone who is responsible for Luther's first kind of righteousness: 'passive righteousness'. The works which flow out of this righteousness, the second kind of righteousness which is the evidence of the indwelling Spirit of Christ, have no bearing on this first, passive righteousness. In TL II Balthasar states this accordingly: 'Die Gleichsetzung der beiden Widerspruchsidentitäten aber ist nur möglich, weil in und zwischen beiden jeder vermittelnde Übergang negiert wird: um die "Werkheiligkeit zu vermeiden, muß aus dem reinen Glauben jedes Moment aktiven Kämpfens (um fortschreitende Sündelosigkeit) absolut ferngehalten werden, und entsprechend muß die Menscheit Christi rein passiv von der Gottheit dem Teufel als Köder hingehalten werden", den dieser verschlingt, während sie dank der Idiomenkommunikation mit der Gottheit als tote lebendig ist und deshalb den teuflischen Tod von innen her überwindet' (309–10).

76 TD IV, 290.

77 *Unbekannte Fragmente aus Luthers zweiter Psalmenvorlesung 1518*, ed. E. Vogelsang (Berlin, 1840), 45. Cited in TD IV, 287.

78 TD IV, 290.

79 'Summa Summarum', in ET III, 375.

80 'Two Modes of Faith', in ET III, 90–1.

81 'Immediacy to God', in ET III, 347–8.

82 TD IV, 147. In this section (137–48) Balthasar gives an encapsulated discussion of the lengthy treatment of freedom contained in *Theo-Drama: Theological Dramatic Theory*, vol. II: *Dramatis Personae: Man in God*, trans. Graham Harrison (San Francisco: Ignatius Press, 1990) (hereafter, TD II).

83 See ibid.: 'De Lubac is right, therefore, to emphasize that there does not need to be a supernatural element of any kind in the natural *desiderium visionis*, in the longing to know God *as he is in himself*' (TD IV, 142, emphasis in original).

84 It is here that the relationship between Luther and Staupitz is of particular importance. Oberman and Hoffman have rightly emphasized the importance of Staupitz's thought for Luther. See Oberman, 'Simul Gemitus et Raptus: Luther and Mysticism', and Hoffman, *Luther and the Mystics.*

85 'Immediacy to God', ET III, 348.

86 'Two Modes of Faith', ET III, 96.

87 Make no mistake, we are in no way intending that Luther believed that the natural knowledge of God that can be had outside of Jesus Christ has been abrogated by the fall, or any other such assertion. In fact, Luther believed that the natural knowledge of God which human beings have comes from God himself (see, LW 26, 399–400, and the discussion thereof, in Althaus, *Theology of Martin Luther*,

15–19). It is only that the God that is encountered outside of his word is always an enemy to humanity in its current, fallen state: 'Some through their speculations ascend into heaven and speculate about God the creator, etc. Do not get mixed up with this God. Whoever wishes to be saved should leave the majestic God alone – for He and the human creature are enemies. Rather grasp that God whom David [Psalm 51] also grasps. He is the God who is clothed in his promises – God as he is present in Christ ... This is the God you need. May you as you are yourself never be confronted by the unclothed God ... ' (LW 12, 312–13, cited in Althaus, *Theology of Martin Luther*, 20).

88 *Theology of Martin Luther*, 34.

89 *Mysterium Paschale*, trans. Aidan Nichols, OP (Grand Rapids, Mich.: William B. Eerdmans, 1990) (hereafter, MP).

90 'One can only regret that scholastic theology has so little understood the full significance of Holy Saturday, and that it let itself be absorbed by the futile question as to if and how Christ, during the time of his death, remained the God-Man: a vigorously contested question in the twelfth century' (MP, 83).

91 MP, 49.

92 Ibid., 52.

93 Ibid.

94 Ibid., 61–2.

95 Ibid., 53.

96 Karl Rahner, for instance, has been very resistant to any notion that the event of the cross *effected* a change in the relationship between God and humanity. We will address Balthasar's response to this in Chapter 5. It is enough to note at this point that Balthasar is trying to steer a middle course between Luther and Rahner on this issue.

97 It is in this context that we are to understand Balthasar's regret that Christianity spent so much time dialoging with the philosophers that it failed to engage on a similar level with the tragedians.

98 MP, 59.

99 MP, 69, citing Luke 24.6–7.

100 MP, 80. From, Karl Barth, *Kirchliche Dogmatik* IV/I (Zollikon, 1953), 145–7.

101 MP, 82.

102 Thus Oakes, *Pattern of Redemption*: 'But it all comes together here: trinitarian and christological themes all play essential roles in clarifying the Great Event of the Triduum and its saving significance. But if that were not challenge enough, in Balthasar's thought, these themes all get transposed into dramatic terms, because, according to his interpretation, in the Triduum of Good Friday, Holy Saturday, and Easter Sunday, *something happens to God*, and this is why this part of the trilogy deserves the title *Theo-Drama* in every sense of the word, being both a subjective as well as objective prefix' (230–1). While this is not the place to address Balthasar's full-blown doctrine of the Trinity, we can say that the reason that this does not result in a mythological or 'process' view of God, is because Balthasar insists that this event is perfectly in keeping with God's nature as eternal, self-giving love. Gerald O'Hanlon can say, accordingly, 'What is distinctive among theologians like Balthasar is precisely the explicit attempt to combine the static with the dynamic, to preserve the category of state while being open to that of event, to avoid the rationalism of an essentialist ontology, not by giving priority to the notion of "process" but rather by retaining the ontological, without denying the abiding truth of the notion of "becoming."

In Balthasar himself, then, the *Theodramatik* can never be separated from the *Theologik*: goodness and truth, with the other transcendentals of unity and beauty, must together help us to form our notion in which the philosophical elements are quite explicitly inspired by (while being able to contribute to) the theological, in that symbiosis between theology and philosophy in which Balthasar insists on the priority of the former' (Gerald O'Hanlon, SJ, *The Immutability of God in the Theology of Hans Urs von Balthasar* (Cambridge: Cambridge University Press, 1990), 112), cited in Oakes, *Pattern of Redemption*, 283.

103 Jared Wicks, review of *Der fröhliche Wechsel und Streit. Grundzüge der Theologie Martin Luthers*, in *Gregorianum* 63 (1982), 163.

104 See Hans-Georg Gadamer, *Truth and Method*, trans. Joel Weinsheimer and Donald G. Marshall (New York: Crossroad, 1991): 'Historical interest is directed not only toward the historical phenomenon and the traditionary work but also, secondarily, toward their effect in history . . .' (300). The operative German word here is *Wirkungsgeschichte*.

105 Helpful here is J. Christian Beker's distinction between 'contingency' and 'coherence'. He applies these categories to Paul's thought in order to sort out those aspects of Paul's thought which are strictly limited to a non repeatable historical circumstance, such as, for instance, the problem of Jews and Gentiles in the one Church of Christ, from those principles which have a timeless significance. Although those issues are no longer ours ('contingency'), they have implications for our current understanding of the nature of salvation ('coherence'). See, J. Christian Beker, *The Triumph of God: The Essence of Paul's Thought*, trans. Loren T. Stuckenbruck (Minneapolis, Minn.: Fortress Press, 1990), especially 15–19.

106 'Two Modes of Faith', ET III, 91–2.

107 See especially, E. P. Sanders, *Paul and Palestinian Judaism* (Philadelphia: Fortress Press, 1977); and *Paul, the Law, and the Jewish People* (Philadelphia: Fortress Press, 1983).

108 See the helpful study by John Reumann, Joseph Fitzmyer and Jerome Quinn, *'Righteousness' in the New Testament* (Philadelphia: Fortress Press, 1982).

Chapter 3: Balthasar on Barth and the *Analogia Entis*

1 After a brief discussion of Luther in his study of the rise of modernity, Louis Dupré concludes with a statement that nicely captures the point we are trying to make: 'Luther was among the first fully to perceive the magnitude of the problem created by the split between nature and grace. His entire theology addresses it. Did he actually succeed in closing the breach? It seems not. Precisely the dialectical nature of his thought that makes him so modern prevented him from doing so. Uncompromising in his refusal to present as one what in the theology of his time appeared inherently divided, Luther converted the religious tension into the very essence of a new Christian piety. His appears the most religiously authentic of all attempts toward a reintegration. But a theology that fails to overcome the dialectical opposition between a totally corrupt nature and a divine justification must fall short of solving the particular problem afflicting the religious consciousness of the modern age, namely, the separation of nature from grace. The one-sidedness of the concept of a definitively corrupt nature parallels the naturalism of the late Renaissance. How much substance does such a totally negative concept of nature preserve? The unresolved tension between Luther's mysticism and his

nominalist dualism leaves the answer ambiguous' *Passage to Modernity: An Essay in the Hermeneutics of Nature and Culture* (New Haven and London: Yale University Press, 1993), 208–9. In other words, although Luther answered the question, 'What can unassisted human nature do toward obtaining divine grace?' in a more orthodox way than his Nominalist forebears, he still presupposed the legitimacy of this framing of the question when he answered, 'Nothing!'

2 Hans Urs von Balthasar to Henri de Lubac (July 1950), from the Appendix to Henri de Lubac, *Theology in History*, trans. Anne Englund Nash (San Francisco: Ignatius Press, 1996), 597.

3 Hans Urs von Balthasar, *The Theology of Karl Barth: Exposition and Interpretation*, trans. Edward T. Oakes, SJ (San Francisco: Ignatius Press, 1992) (hereafter, KB).

4 See, *Letters of Étienne Gilson to Henri de Lubac*, trans. Mary Emily Hamilton (San Francisco: Ignatius Press, 1988). On 8 July, 1956, Gilson wrote: 'People conjure up a Thomism after the manner of the Schools, a sort of dull rationalism which panders to the kind of deism that most of them, deep down, really prefer to teach. Our only salvation lies in a return to Saint Thomas himself, before the Thomism of John of Saint Thomas, before that of Cajetan as well – Cajetan, whose famous commentary is in every respect the consummate example of a *corruptorium Thomae*. … Let us say rather to emasculate his doctrine and to make of his theology a brew of watered-down philosophia *aristotelico-thomistica* concocted to give off a vague deism fit only for the use of right-thinking candidates for high-school diplomas and Arts degrees. Salvation lies in returning to the real Saint Thomas, rightly called the Universal Doctor of the Church; accept no substitutes!' (23–5).

5 Cited in Jonathan Barnes, ed., *Early Greek Philosophy* (New York: Penguin Books, 1987), 120.

6 See Edward T. Oakes's careful discussion of analogy, in *Pattern of Redemption: The Theology of Hans Urs von Balthasar* (New York: Continuum, 1994), 15–44.

7 Étienne Gilson, *Being and Some Philosophers* (Toronto, Canada: Pontifical Institute of Mediaeval Studies, 1949), 154: 'The better to recapture his message, we must first consider the essential transformation which the Aristotelian notion of metaphysics underwent in Thomas Aquinas' own doctrine.'

8 See, Gilson, *Being and Some Philosophers*, 154–89, and the discussion of analogy in Oakes, *Pattern of Redemption*, 15–44.

9 Balthasar will make a similar point in his study of Gregory of Nyssa. *Presence and Thought: An Essay on the Religious Philosophy of Gregory of Nyssa*, trans. Mark Sebanc (San Francisco: Ignatius Press, 1995), 18, 21: 'What distinguishes Gregory at once from Philo and Plotinus is the radical opposition between the triune God and the creature, an opposition that is not mitigated by any intermediary zone. … For Plotinus, Ideas are objects, "things," above which, by a supreme "separation" or chorismos, there rises the One, the en. For Gregory, ideal knowledge has no other object than the Supreme Being himself.'

10 Oakes, *Patterns of Redemption*, 34–5.

11 *Letters of Étienne Gilson to Henri de Lubac*, '*Le Mystère du surnaturel*, which I have just thoroughly enjoyed reading from cover to cover, is absolutely perfect. I really have the impression, not that the question is closed, because people always have to muddle things up, but that it ought to be' (91).

12 *Being and Some Philosophers*, 156.

13 Ibid., 157 (emphasis mine).

[14] Hans Urs von Balthasar, *The Theology of Henri de Lubac: An Overview*, trans. Joseph Fessio and Michael Waldstein (San Francisco: Ignatius Press, 1991), 61.

[15] See especially, *Summa Theologica* I-II q 5, a 5, ad 2. Cited in Balthasar, *Theology of Henri de Lubac*, 67.

[16] Gilson had already insisted that this was, indeed, the case with Aquinas: 'What deeply alters the Aristotelian notion of metaphysics in the doctrine of Thomas Aquinas is the presence, above natural theology, of a higher theology, which is the science of God known through revelation' (Gilson, *Being and Some Philosophies*, 157).

[17] Hans Urs von Balthasar, *The Theology of Karl Barth*, trans. Edward T. Oakes (San Francisco: Ignatius Press, 1992), 295 (hereafter KB).

[18] For a fuller discussion of this encounter, see Busch, *Karl Barth*, 184–5, 215–16.

[19] Both McCormack (*Karl Barth's Critically Realistic Dialectical Theology*) and Barth objected to the fact that Balthasar remained too long on formal issues, but neither seems to consider sufficiently the purpose for which Balthasar was writing the book. When asked to write a foreword to Balthasar's study of him, Barth replied: 'My difference with Balthasar has nothing whatever to do with the ecumenical question. It is simply that, like many Protestants, he is interested in certain philosophical structures of my theology instead of in the theology itself. But I do not want to criticize him publicly for this and therefore I would rather not write the foreword' (17 July, 1963): *Karl Barth: Letters, 1961–1968*, ed. Jürgen Fangmeier and Heinrich Stoevesandt, trans. Geoffrey Bromiley (Grand Rapids, Mich.: William B. Eerdmans, 1981), 112.

[20] For Barth's later assessment of this theological program, see his 'Evangelical Theology in the 19th Century', in *The Humanity of God*, trans. Thomas Weiser and John Newton Thomas (Richmond, Va.: John Knox Press, 1960). According to Barth, this 'theology retreated to the epistemology and ethics of Kant rediscovered, and to an interpretation of Luther rediscovered in the light of Kant' (13).

[21] Busch, *Karl Barth*, 45.

[22] Ibid., 46.

[23] Ibid., 54.

[24] 'Man in the nineteenth century might have taken the theologians more seriously if they themselves had not taken him so seriously' (Barth, 'Evangelical Theology in the 19th Century', in *The Humanity of God*, 21).

[25] I intend by 'subjectivist' and 'subjectivism' to refer to the style of theology which arose in the wake of Kant's critique of knowledge. This theology, following the lead of Schleiermacher, felt that the 'objective' truths of theology had to be tested in the light of the experience of the subject. Schleiermacher's theology begins, accordingly, with humanity's feeling of absolute dependence and only then proceeds to the dogmas of the Christian faith, salvaging only those dogmas which seem to correspond to this subjective starting-point.

[26] Busch, *Karl Barth*, 97.

[27] Ibid., 99.

[28] Karl Barth, *The Word of God and the Word of Man*, trans. Douglas Horton (New York: Harper & Row, 1956).

[29] McCormack, *Karl Barth's Critically Realistic Dialectical Theology*, 134.

[30] KB, 26.

[31] Mention has already been made of Bruce McCormack's recent study of Barth's early theology (see *Karl Barth's Critically Realistic Dialectical Theology*) in which he

directly takes on the thesis of Balthasar just mentioned. Because McCormack had access to more of Barth's publications, because he had the advantage of historical distance, and, finally, because he was free of the polemical context in which Balthasar was writing, it should be said that McCormack's study adds valuable nuance to Balthasar's evolutionary thesis. Because of the importance of McCormack's study, and because it directly challenges Balthasar's view, a few comments regarding it are in order. In McCormack's view, Balthasar really has two working theses in his study of Barth. The first is overly simplistic and basically asserts that Barth's theology was 'dialectical' in style from 1918 to 1931, and that, after the writing of the Anselm book, it became 'analogical' in approach (from 1931 on). The other thesis, which is stated in Balthasar's study, and the one which is actually operative in the contents of the study, is more subtle. It states that there were really two 'conversions' in Barth's theology. First, there was the dialectical phase (1918–27). This was followed – and this time the transition is located, not with the Anselm study, but with the writing of the *Christliche Dogmatik im Entwurf* – by a 'conversion to analogy' phase (1927–38). The final phase is, then, the analogical phase which does not fully begin until 1938 and marks the remainder of Barth's theology. According to McCormack, 'If a guess were to be hazarded as to which of these two models lay closest to von Balthasar's intentions, it would have to be that the second more closely approximated what he wanted to say. Unfortunately, it is the first model which has exercised the greater influence, especially in the English-speaking world. This influence was unfortunate because (as will be demonstrated in this book) the second model actually lay closer to the truth' (4).

In short, McCormack isolates four problems with Balthasar's thesis. First, there is a vagueness to Balthasar's use of the word 'dialectic'; Balthasar seems to use it to refer to a hard-and-fast method. Second, and more substantive, Balthasar fails to realize that the *analogia fidei* is already 'an inherently dialectical concept'. It refers, not to an analogy between the being of God and the being of creation, but to an analogy between the act of God's self-knowledge and the human act of knowing God. This can occur *objectively* only in revelation and *subjectively* only in faith. Third, to imply a simple transition from the dialectical method to the analogical method is to imply that the latter is a method too, that it is a human means to knowing God. And, finally, McCormack asserts that Balthasar downplays the 'material shift' in Barth's theology which gives rise to the methodological shift (16–19). Thus McCormack: 'It was as Barth concentrated his attention on the material problems of Trinity and Christology in 1924 that solutions to methodological questions also began to emerge – something which Barth himself was only gradually aware of' (20).

In McCormack's final analysis then, there are really four phases in Barth's theological development: (1) 'dialectical – process eschatology'; (2) 'dialectical – consistent eschatology'; (3) 'dialectical – anhypostatic-enhypostatic Christology' (Spirit-centered); and (4) 'dialectical – anhypostatic-enhypostatic Christology' (Christ-centered). It is not necessary to go into the specifics of McCormack's argument to draw some general conclusions. First, McCormack's criticism of Balthasar's thesis does not amount to a wholesale rejection, but is, rather, a matter of nuance. Regarding the central criticism, that Balthasar should have placed more emphasis upon the actual doctrinal changes behind the methodological changes, McCormack is, no doubt, correct. However, it should be noted that Balthasar was writing in a particular context, for a particular audience, and with a particular goal in mind, all of which made the focus on 'formal matters' prudent. In other words, in a theological context which was still very committed to neo-Scholastic dualism, Balthasar wished to present Barth's christocentric construal of the nature–grace problem without getting into specific theological debates, which would only have obscured his central intention. Furthermore, Balthasar *does* make note of the dogmatic shift from 'Word of God' versus 'Word of man' to 'Jesus Christ, God and man'. As McCormack admits: 'Thus there is a truth contained in von Balthasar's talk of a shift from concentration on "the Word" to a concentration on "Jesus Christ" – though his way of describing it was hardly satisfactory' (22). Second, with regard to the 'analogy of faith' versus the 'analogy of being', there does seem to be a legitimate theological difference which will become clear in the remainder of this chapter. Both McCormack and Barth fail to understand that the Przywara/Balthasar way of speaking of the analogy of being – and this stems directly from St Thomas – already presupposes the context of God's redemptive activity, but wishes to grant creation a rightful autonomy *within* God's activity in history. This occurs at that intersection between faith and reason which gives rise to what Przywara, de Lubac, Gilson, Balthasar and others call 'Christian philosophy'. Such philosophy need not involve the reduction of God to the level of a purely human concept.

32 KB, 64.

33 Ibid., 70.

34 Ibid., 73–7.

35 Ibid., 71.

36 Ibid., 80–4.

37 Karl Barth, *Anselm: Fides quaerens intellectum* (London: SCM Press, 1960).

38 KB, 96.

39 Ibid., 105.

40 Ibid., 108.

41 Ibid., 111.

42 KB, 114.

43 Quoted in KB, 121. Barth unpacks the first half of this quote in III.1, pp. 94–228, and the second half in pp. 228–330 of *Church Dogmatics*, ed. Geoffrey Bromiley and Thomas F. Torrance (Edinburgh: T&T Clark, 1936–69, 1975) (hereafter, CD).

44 CD III/1, 573.

45 The above quote also explains the possibility of philosophy and even atheism, the latter which Barth sometimes calls the 'impossible possibility'. Because he is allowing 'creation' or 'nature' a legitimate autonomy at this stage, he can account for the possibility of pagan philosophy. In the last analysis, however, without wishing to get ahead of ourselves, Balthasar thinks that Barth is not consistently this generous, and therefore still tends to collapse everything into God (to such a degree that he cannot adequately account for the fundamental distinction between God and the world). In a discussion of similar issues Robert Sokolowski says that the Transcendental Thomists fail at this point also: i.e., they cannot sufficiently account for a realm relatively independent of the order of grace/revelation/covenant, and therefore cannot adequately account for a 'pagan' outlook. See Robert Sokolowski, *The God of Faith and Reason: Foundations of Christian Theology* (Notre Dame: University of Notre Dame Press, 1982), where he, certainly under Balthasar's influence, tries to steer a middle course between Barth and Rahner with regard to the relationship between God and the world. For the comparison of Barth and the Transcendental Thomists, see pages 104–18.

46 CD III/1, 574.

47 I choose these two because they are more in keeping with the issues of 'fundamental' theology which are the subject of this study. The other two certainly bear upon these issues, especially because Barth refuses to separate fundamental and positive theology, but in order to limit repetition, I will deal with the two which are more pertinent to my topic.

48 KB, 136.

49 KB, 151.

50 KB, 152.

51 KB, 137–53.

52 KB, 162.

53 KB, 163.

54 KB, 163.

55 Ibid., 163–6. These are Balthasar's words, but he insists that it is implicit in Barth's thought. The differences between Balthasar's *analogia entis* and Barth's *analogia fidei* are so subtle that even Balthasar, in the foreword to the second edition of his Barth study, felt that there was basic agreement. This, he hoped, pointed to the possibility of pursuing more substantive theological issues with a greater hope of rapprochement. Yet, the differences between Barth and he on such issues as the sacraments, the Church, the saints, and, especially, Mary, are telling symptoms of a more significant difference than Balthasar seemed willing to acknowledge. In a helpful article, John Thompson has summarized their differences accordingly: 'The question between Balthasar and Barth is a complex one but I can put it only in brief outline. Is there a correspondence, an *analogia entis*, in the very being of our creatureliness between humanity and God however dissimilar the creation and Creator may be? Balthasar answers yes and this is due to the prevenient grace of God in creation which enables a certain human aptitude or capacity for God. Barth denies this *analogia entis* and sees all correspondences or analogies grounded only in God's revelation in Christ and perceived through faith …' (John Thompson, 'Barth and Balthasar: An Ecumenical Dialogue', in *The Beauty of Christ: A* [*sic*] *Introduction to the Theology of Hans Urs von Balthasar*, ed. Bede McGregor, OP, and Thomas Norris (Edinburgh: T&T Clark, 1994)), 177.

56 The word which Balthasar uses throughout his study to express this – *Engführung* – has a musical usage, referring to the practice of highlighting one instrument in the orchestra over the rest. See the 'author's note' in the afterword to Balthasar, *The Theology of Karl Barth*, 393. Balthasar's discussion of Barth's 'idealism' begins in KB chapter 8 'The Roots of Barth's Thought', and culminates in chapter 9, 'Idealism and Revelation'.

57 KB, 242.

58 KB, 242.

59 KB, 241–3. Elsewhere Balthasar summarizes his critique accordingly, 'To summarize my objection once more, I have criticized Barth because to me his rejection of a philosophical reflection concomitant to theology is self-destructive: to reject philosophy because it works only with material drawn from within this world (and thus is only "positivistic") means that all the truths about man and the world have to be derived from the Christology that presupposes them. But while this sounds like it preserves the integrity of a dynamic Christology, it has the ironic effect of forcing us, at the very place where we must discuss a historical *event* between God and man, to construct a *doctrine* about God, man and the world from the ground up' (ibid., 393).

60 KB, 244–5.
61 KB, 245–7.
62 They are, in order of their appearance, 'The Implications of the Word' and 'God Speaks as Man', in *Explorations in Theology*, vol. I: *The Word Made Flesh*, trans. A. V. Littledale and Alexander Dru (San Francisco: Ignatius Press, 1989).
63 Enlightening in this regard are Joseph Ratzinger's comments on *Gaudium et Spes*: '[T]he chapter on the dignity of man culminates in Christ who is now presented as the true answer to the question of being human, and therefore to the question of true humanism and of atheism. Article 22 thus returns to the starting-point, Article 12, and presents Christ as the eschatological Adam to whom the first Adam already pointed; as the true image of God which transforms man once more into the likeness to God. … We are probably justified in saying that here for the first time in an official document of the magisterium, a new type of completely christocentric theology appears. On the basis of Christ this dares to present theology as anthropology and only thus becomes radically theological by including man in discourse about God by way of Christ, thus manifesting the deepest unity of theology' (cited in David Schindler, 'Christology and the *Imago Dei*: Interpreting *Gaudium et Spes*', *Communio* 23 (1996), 168).
64 Balthasar, 'Implications of the Word', in ET I, 57.
65 Ibid., 61.
66 Ibid., 62.
67 Ibid., 66–70.
68 Ibid., 72.
69 Ibid., 75: 'This character however does not consist in a platonist longing after grace and the vision of God, a longing that includes a latent claim to these.' Here we have a subtle response to the danger of Maréchal's approach. Balthasar also writes: 'This means that God, in the order of creation, truly began what he was to perfect in the order of Christ's redemption; began, that is to say, in the sense of establishing an enduring initial stage wherein what is begun *does not imply a reaching beyond itself* (a *desiderium naturale visionis, sive efficax sive inefficax*), nor (what comes to the same thing) claim to be understandable only when raised to the order of grace' (ibid., 74, emphasis mine). There is a suggestion here that a radical Maréchalian approach and a radical Barthian approach 'come to the same thing'.
70 Ibid., 77. Balthasar's understanding of the Church's holiness is exemplified in a unique way in the holiness of Mary: 'It was not in climbing the steep path to "self-perfection" that Mary became a mother, but in self-surrender to God's direct will and to the disposition intrinsic to her womanly nature and to what took flesh within it' (ibid., 78–9).
71 Ibid., 83. For further clarification of Balthasar's 'theology of history', see especially, *A Theological Anthropology*, trans. William Glen-Doepel (New York: Sheed & Ward, 1967), and *A Theology of History*, trans. not named (New York: Sheed & Ward, 1963).
72 'God Speaks as Man', in ET I, 89.
73 The following selection from Eberhard Busch, with some brief quotations from Barth, makes this clear: 'In 1951, in his book on Barth, von Balthasar made the charge that "there was a christological narrowness in my work." As Barth understood the charge, von Balthasar sought to avoid what he felt to be the narrowness by seeing holy "repetitions" of Christ's history in addition to Christ himself. Against this Barth insisted that: "The being and activity of Jesus Christ needs no repetitions. He is present and active in his own truth and power." And he asked

whether, if one saw things otherwise, "Jesus Christ would not have ceased to become the subject and origin of Christian faith"' (Busch, *Karl Barth*, 381).

74 Balthasar mentions approvingly Hans Küng's study of Barth's doctrine of justification in this context, a book which Balthasar's publishing company published, and to which Barth himself wrote the foreword.

75 KB, 289.

76 Ibid., 362.

Chapter 4: The Cosmological and Anthropological Alternatives

1 The entirety of Balthasar's short work, In the *Fullness of Faith*, should be understood in this light.

2 For a list of Balthasar's 'role models' for such a christocentric Catholicism, see, KB, 'Christocentrism', 326–63, where Balthasar mentions Michael Schmaus, Erich Przywara, Romano Guardini, Emile Mersch, and others, including Thérèse of Lisieux.

3 We are not simply interested in reiterating Balthasar's critique of Rahner in this section. In fact, it seems that many of the attempts to understand and analyze this exchange have missed the key role played in it by Barth's critique of the analogy of being. Typical of this tendency is Eamonn Conway's analysis of Balthasar's critique of Rahner, *The anonymous Christian – a relativized Christianity? An Evaluation of Hans Urs von Balthasar's Criticisms of Karl Rahner's Theory of the Anonymous Christian* (New York: Peter Lang, 1993). Because Conway does not give sufficient weight to Balthasar's continual engagement with the Protestant critique of the analogy of being, he tends to understand Balthasar almost exclusively in terms of his polemic against Rahner. This has two misleading effects: (1) It gives the impression that Rahner is the central dialogue partner for Balthasar's theological method, thereby missing the importance of Balthasar's attempt to address the legitimate questions of Barth. (2) Furthermore, isolating Balthasar's critique of Rahner from this larger concern gives the false impression that Balthasar only responds defensively/negatively to modern culture, philosophy, politics, etc. By keeping Balthasar's critique of Rahner *alongside* of his critique of Luther and Barth, we think we can show that Balthasar offers a much more positive assessment of human culture than Conway's study implies. German studies of Balthasar have been somewhat more successful in their recognition of the fact that one cannot separate Balthasar's critique of Rahner from his attempt to appropriate Barth's insights. Manfred Lochbrunner's study, *Analogia Caritatis: Darstellung und Deutung der Theologie Hans Urs von Balthasars* (Freiburg: Herder, 1981), is especially helpful in this regard. In speaking of Balthasar's critique of Rahner he notes: 'Balthasars Kritik besteht demnach darin, daß er auf einer schärferen Unterscheidung zwischen einem philosophischen und einem theologischen Begriff der potentia oboedientialis insistiert. Balthasars Position ist vom Gespräch mit Karl Barth her mitgeprägt' (118). Unfortunately, after having said this, Lochbrunner fails to give sufficient weight to this in his final evaluation of Balthasar's differences with Rahner.

4 'Disputation Against Scholastic Theology', in *Martin Luther's Basic Theological Writings*, 16.

5 HD, 32.

6 GL IV, 320. We do not wish to give the impression here that Balthasar's general view of Dionysius is a negative one. On the contrary, he is one of the few examples

of 'theological style' paid tribute to in Balthasar's volume on 'clerical styles' (GL II). In fact, it is part of Balthasar's point that these two tendencies, the cosmic and the cross-centered, must be kept together in a fully Catholic theology. Balthasar sees Maximus Confessor, for instance, as a particularly clear example of one who combines 'theologia' and 'economia' in an exemplary and balanced fashion. Cf. KL and Cyril O'Regan's provocative essay, 'Von Balthasar and Thick Retrieval: Post-Chalcedonian Symphonic Theology', *Gregorianum* 77/2 (1996), 227–60. O'Regan qualifies the above quote accordingly, 'Though Balthasar expressly denies in another text [i.e., the one quoted above] that the cross is focal for Pseudo-Dionysius, in the second volume of GL he insists that the cross is not totally ignored. There is, of course, no contradiction between the two assertions, and his proposal in the volume on clerical styles is in any case quite modest. Without in any way suggesting that Pseudo-Dionysius's fundamentally incarnational christological orientation is undermined by them, Balthasar points to the surprising presence in Pseudo-Dionysius of utterances which declare that *theosis* is explicitly dependent neither on the incarnation, nor even the resurrection, but directly in the divine humiliation of Jesus who died on the cross' (235). In reference to our assertion that Maximus remains for Balthasar the more clear example of a theologian who balances the 'cosmic' and 'christic' emphases, the same author says, 'Even the most favorable reading of Pseudo-Dionysius, then, is unable to erase the Maximan "more" which, reading between the lines, seems to involve (1) a judgment about Maximus's keener grasp of how fundamental Christian assumptions regulate and transform Neoplatonic modes of thought, and (2) a perception of the dogmatic thrust at the heart of Maximus's theology' (237). Strangely enough, this essay, although ostensibly a presentation of Balthasar's interpretation of Maximus, would be a good place to begin in an effort to understand Balthasar's particular approach to theology vis-à-vis the Barthian and Rahnerian alternatives.

7 KB, 383.

8 KB, 384.

9 In a section of the Barth book which is extremely important to the current discussion, Balthasar states: '[W]e should not fail to notice that we have traced the same movement from Maréchal to de Lubac that has led us from Schleiermacher to Karl Barth: that is, from philosophical and natural thinking to theological and historical thought. In other words, we have moved from a "natural desire" to that answer to grace that must bear the name of grace. At this point a dialogue on the theme of nature and grace is feasible without either side of the dialogue having to give up its own most deeply held position' (KB, 297). This is an immediate precursor to Balthasar's comments on Rahner where he states, 'The philosopher, even the Christian philosopher, will always have the tendency to extend the capacity of nature all the way to a vision of God. Theology, on the other hand, will follow the opposite inclination and see in the striving of nature the latent presupposition of grace, limiting the part played by nature to a passively understood *potentia oboedientialis*. But because the theological a priori in nature can never be neatly bracketed out, the battle can never be settled one way or the other. We are stuck with the tension that comes from asserting that nature has on its own no access to the world of grace, even though it has finally been created only because of grace and for grace and cannot be understood apart from grace' (KB, 301). See also Balthasar's, 'Current Trends in Catholic Theology and the Responsibility of the Christian', *Communio* 5 (Spring 1978): 'It is true that Karl Rahner is inclined to

filter all questions through the prism of his own method but, on the other hand, his pastoral concern enables him to see all problems – theological and secular – in their realistic complexity, and to accept other than his own attempts of solution … *The transcendental school of thought will be criticized only if the historical facts of revelation are not given sufficient expression* …' (85, emphasis mine).

10 Balthasar can even become somewhat defensive when people refer to his 'aesthetics' as his 'chief work', as the following interview response makes clear: 'Nur ganz kurz zum, "Hauptwerk": Ich bin nicht sicher, daß dieses die Ästhetik ist. Die Ästhetik ist ein Fragment unter anderen Fragmenten. Wie lernt man das Christliche überhaupt sehen? Es ist ein Präludium, der erste Flügel eines Triptychons. Vielleicht ist in den kleinen Werken mehr Ganzheitliches enthalten, als in diesem Bandwurm. Aber es kann auch in Büchern stecken, in denen ich andere reden lasse, z.B. Origenes oder Bernanos.' From, 'Geist und Feuer: Ein Gespräch mit Hans Urs von Balthasar', *Herder-Korrespondenz* 2/30 (February 1976), 74. Balthasar is insistent that the three transcendental attributes of being, the true, the good, and the beautiful, must always interpenetrate each other. If one were only to read GL, in other words, one could – although I am not sure how – get the impression that Balthasar is not interested in the truth of the Christian faith, only in its splendor. But really, even in the individual parts of the 'triptych' all three attributes are present. To pursue truth, for instance, apart from beauty is to make the same mistake that was made in the Enlightenment.

11 TL I, 19: 'Es ist eine Frucht des modernen Rationalismus, der das Feld der Wahrheit auf ein vermeintlich isolierbares rein Theoretisches einzeugen trachtete, daß das Gebiet des Guten und des Schönen dadurch außerhalb des erkenntnismäßig Nachprüfbaren geriet und einer wie immer gearteten subjektiven Willkür oder doch privaten Glaubens- und Geschmackswelt über die Wahrheit verunmöglicht. Gesprochen wird fürderhin nur noch über allgemein zugängliche, im letzten belanglose Inhalte, während die tiefsten Wahrheitsfragen, die ohne Entscheidung und Geschmack nicht berührt werden können, in falscher Scham dem Schweigen überantworten bleiben. Wenn die Wahrheit entscheidungslos ist, dann ist die persönliche, weltanschauliche Entscheidung wahrheitlos. Eine solche Unterbindung des Gesprächs über die Wahrheit kommt – wie sich später zeigen wird – einer Vernichtung der Wahrheit selbst gleich.'

12 GL I, 155.

13 Dionysius the Areopagite, *The Divine Names*, IV, 13, trans. C. E. Rolt (London: SPCK, 1940), pp. 105–6. Cited in GL I, 122.

14 This is a weakness of the otherwise excellent dissertation by David Yeago: 'The Drama of Nature and Grace: A Study in the Theology of Hans Urs von Balthasar' (Yale University, 1992). Because Yeago understands Balthasar's theology primarily in terms borrowed from George Lindbeck and Hans Frei, he is unable to distinguish sufficiently Balthasar's and Barth's 'types' of theology. The appropriation of Wittgenstein's language-games in order to articulate the fact that Christianity is a religion which always proceeds from the concrete story of Christ is not fully consistent with Balthasar's concern. Balthasar begins, not with the 'Word' of Protestant theology, but with the 'Epiphany' of Catholic theology. The objective appearance of the glory of God in the person of Jesus Christ can be recognized as such with the eyes of faith. In the light of faith, the disciple can see that Christ really is the 'recapitulation' and fulfillment of all things. So, the Christian is not locked in a cultural-linguistic community, but is given a new understanding of the whole *in* this concrete. In Lindbeck's view it would seem that the Christian's

connection to his or her narrative is basically the same as the Muslim's connection to his or hers. Balthasar is more inclined to speak of Christianity as the only religion in which the universal has become concrete.

15 By 'postmodern' I mean that philosophical movement, already nascent in Kierkegaard and Nietzsche, and most fully developed in the later writings of Heidegger, which insists on highlighting the hermeneutical aspect of all knowing, and on exposing the Enlightenment claim to 'universality' as merely another example of a narrative interpretation of the world. As Lyotard has succinctly stated it: 'I define *postmodern* as incredulity toward metanarratives ... Thus the society of the future falls less within the province of a Newtonian anthropology (such as structuralism or systems theory) than a pragmatics of language particles. There are many different language games – a heterogeneity of elements. They only give rise to institutions in patches – local determinism' ('The Postmodern Condition', in Kenneth Baynes, James Bohman and Thomas McCarthy, eds, *After Philosophy: End or Transformation?* (Cambridge, Mass.: MIT Press, 1987), 74). However, in what follows, our use of postmodern in conjunction with Balthasar will bear more closely the stamp of the late Heidegger–Gadamer trajectory than the direction taken by Derrida, Foucault, Lyotard and others, who seem to have blended Heidegger's philosophy of language all too easily with Wittgenstein's 'language games', as the above quote makes clear. While Balthasar is aware of the 'hermeneutical circle', and its essential correctness, he shows no influence of Wittgenstein in his writings. The difference between Gadamer's and Wittgenstein's philosophies of language is carefully summarized in David E. Linge's introduction to Gadamer's *Philosophical Hermeneutics*, trans. and ed. David E. Linge (Berkeley, Calif.: University of California Press, 1976). According to Linge, the essential difference lies in Gadamer's understanding of the universality of the hermeneutical problem, which is rooted in the universal capacity for language. This universal capacity to interpret grounds the dialogue and possible 'horizon-fusion' of various 'languages games'. While it is language that is primal for Gadamer, then, it is 'language games' which are primal for Wittgenstein, or at least for his progeny. Far from being 'trapped' within a language game – and this may be a questionable interpretation of Wittgenstein but is surely found in many of his self-proclaimed disciples – the 'game', for Gadamer, is larger than any one player's horizon. In other words, for Gadamer, language is important precisely in its disclosive function and it is precisely 'by reference to the disclosive function of language that hermeneutics dispels the linguistic relativism that has accompanied the investigation of language from Humboldt to Wittgenstein' (xxx). Again, I am not endorsing Linge's interpretation of Wittgenstein here, but I am distinguishing Gadamer's more 'sacramental' understanding of language from some postmodernists who uncritically blend Heidegger and Wittgenstein in the manner of Lyotard. Elsewhere Linge puts this accordingly, 'Understanding is essentially linguistic, but this statement does not mean – as every form of relativism assumes – that understanding is frozen into one static language in such a fashion that translation from one language to another is impossible' (xxxi). And then, quoting Gadamer, 'The task of understanding and interpreting ... always remains meaningful. In this is demonstrated the superior universality with which reason is elevated above the limits of every given system of language. The hermeneutical experience is the corrective through which thinking reason escapes the power of the linguistic even while it is itself linguistically constituted' (xxxi). Balthasar is like Heidegger and Gadamer in his insistence upon the crucial role

of the particular and linguistic in all of our experience of what is transcendental, universal, and this provides him with the philosophical foundation for understanding Christ as the concrete-universal.

16 Rowan Williams, 'Balthasar and Rahner', in *The Analogy of Beauty* (Edinburgh: T&T Clark, 1986), 29–30. It would seem that Rahner was more intent upon completing Maréchal's engagement with Idealism than in engaging more recent philosophies. In an interesting essay, written by Balthasar in 1946(!), Balthasar is already pointing out the need for Catholic philosophy to engage post-Idealist philosophy: 'But the period of Idealism is past; it was followed by the period of the philosophy of life. At first glance, one can see in this period a striking impoverishment of speculative power – something of which the philosophy of life is indeed proud – and one can feel tempted to judge it a product of the decline of the Western spirit ... But one cannot overlook the fact that even the philosophy of life defends genuine Christian concerns over against the formalism which it overcomes in epistemology and ontology ... The concern of the philosophy of life is that thinking always contains an element that in every case lies beyond the concept, cannot be captured in the concept and yet gives the concept its foundation and justification.' This is taken from, 'On the Tasks of Catholic Philosophy in Our Time', *Communio* 20 (Spring 1993), 179. I do not mean to insinuate that Rahner's theology does not contain a sustained critique of Idealism. One need only recall the heavy influence of Ignatius and the *Spiritual Exercises* on Rahner's theology. In contrast to the formalism and obsession with epistemology which marks Idealism, Rahner, following Ignatius, places great emphasis upon the concrete encounter between the individual believer and Christ. This 'existential encounter' precedes theology's more speculative aspect. For a helpful and concise treatment of this aspect of Rahner's theology, see Paulette Skiba, 'The Transcendental Christology of Karl Rahner: A Resource for Catholic Social Teaching?' (unpublished dissertation, Marquette University, 1997), especially, 43–73. As Skiba puts it: 'What Rahner calls "existentiell christology," or the actual living in a relationship of faith, hope and love with Jesus of Nazareth, precedes theology. The starting point for christology is, according to Rahner, an "encounter with the historical Jesus"' (55). My point is only that even Rahner's critique of Idealism is undertaken within the context of an engagement with it, and while making use of many of its terms and categories. Balthasar's philosophical point of departure, conversely, is the more recent dialogical and personalist philosophies which were undertaken as self-conscious critiques of Idealist subjectivism.

17 Hans Urs von Balthasar, *Love Alone*, trans. Arthur V. Littledale and Alexander Dru (New York: Herder & Herder, 1969), 4.

18 In speaking of the relationship between philosophy and theology in the context of this reversal, Balthasar says: 'Weil aller Sinn der Welt in Jesus Christus an ihn gezogen worden ist: "Niemand kommt zum Vater, außer durch mich." In ihm ist die Fülle der Gottheit leibhaftig da. Er hat gleichsam Religion und natürlich Theologie in sich erfüllt und absorbiert. D.h. *der suchende Mensch ist gefunden worden von Gott*' ('Geist und Feuer', 75, emphasis mine).

19 *Love Alone*, 44: 'The second approach is that of aesthetics. This forms a third area, apart from that of thought or action, and is independent of these. When one experiences startling beauty (in nature or in art) then phenomena normally veiled are perceived in their uniqueness. What confronts us is overpowering, like a miracle, and only as a miracle can it be understood; it can never be tied down by the person having the experience. The appearance of its inner unfathomable

necessity is both binding and freeing, for it is seen clearly to be the appearance of freedom itself ... If there *is* a finale to the "Jupiter" symphony – and I cannot guess this, deduce it or explain it from anything in me – then it can only be as it is; its present form is necessary, every note is irrevocable – unless possibly Mozart would change it.' See also, George Steiner, 'Real Presences', in *No Passion Spent* (New Haven, Conn.: Yale University Press, 1996), 35.

20 *Love Alone*, 9.

21 In a very illuminating study of Thomas Aquinas, one which quite consciously incorporates Balthasar's reading of Thomas, Francis J. Klauder articulates this aspect of 'givenness' very nicely: 'Hence a philosophy of contingent beings cannot avoid being a philosophy of "the given." "Given" by what or by whom? "Given" by intelligence? Yes, but "given" also by love. This is so, because being, as we find it, is not merely intelligible or true, but also good. Consequently the philosophy of being becomes the philosophy of the good, the philosophy of those who love whatever exists. Christian philosophy thus becomes the counterpart of a Christian theology, which seeks not only to know but to love whatever God has revealed. Speaking along this line of thought, during the centennial celebration of the publication of Pope Leo's encyclical on Christian philosophy, Pope John Paul II commended the openness of Thomistic philosophy "to the whole of reality in all its parts and dimensions." It is in virtue of this fact, he goes on to say, that "the philosophy of St. Thomas is able to, and indeed, must go beyond all that presents itself directly in knowledge as an existing thing (given through experience) in order to reach 'that which subsists as sheer Existing and also as creative Love"' (Francis J. Klauder, *A Philosophy Rooted in Love: The Dominant Themes in the Perennial Philosophy of St. Thomas Aquinas* (New York: University Press of America, 1994), xvii).

22 *Love Alone*, 11–14.

23 See especially, 'Fathers, Scholastics, and Ourselves', trans. Edward T. Oakes, SJ, *Communio* 24 (1997), 370–2.

24 Ibid., 373–7.

25 Ibid., 372.

26 Ibid., 374.

27 *Love Alone*, 14.

28 Ibid., 15.

29 Ibid., 19–20.

30 Ibid., 21.

31 *Presence and Thought*, 13.

32 'Fathers, Scholastics, and Ourselves', 373.

33 Carabine, 'The Fathers: The Church's Intimate, Youthful Diary', 77.

34 Balthasar, 'Fathers, Scholastics, and Ourselves', 374.

35 Ibid., 375.

36 Carabine, 'The Fathers: The Church's Intimate, Youthful Diary', 82.

37 GL I, 327–8 (emphasis in original).

38 Deirdre Carabine summarizes Balthasar's difficulties with Greek *theosis* accordingly, 'It is also the concept of kenosis which determines his understanding of the return of the soul. Man wants to soar up to God, just as the Word wants to descend to man; the result will be a crossing of swords and a clashing of purposes. Therefore, instead of endorsing the Patristic concept of the ascent of the soul to deification as *anabasis*, instead of going past God's word in its descent and pursuing a rash ascent to the Father ... we are admonished to turn around

and go back down with the Word, to find God on the road to the world. It is here that Balthasar finds humanity's likeness to God; it is not something which can be discovered in the depth's of one's soul in private, polished up and used to see the reflection of God's glory, a theme which is given majestic expression in Gregory of Nyssa. It is rather, a likeness which is constituted in action: being like the Son in his descent from the Father, being sent out (*Sendung*) by the Father with the Son' (Carabine, 'The Fathers: The Church's Intimate, Youthful Diary', 83). The difference between Balthasar's religious order, the Society of St John, and that of previous religious orders can be located in this basic difference.

39 Ibid., 79.

40 This is part of Balthasar's manner of 'retrieving' the theology of the Fathers: he focuses on the distinctively Christian elements within their thought and uses this to correct the overly Platonic elements. This is quite clear throughout GL I: 'The beauty and glory which are proper to God may be inferred and "read" off from God's epiphany and its incomprehensible glory which is worthy of God himself. But in trying to perceive God's own beauty and glory from the beauty of his manner of appearing, we must neither simply *equate* the two – since we are to be transported *per hunc (Deum visibilem) in invisibilium amorem* – nor ought we to attempt to discover God's own beauty by a mere causal inference from the beauty of God's epiphany, for such an inference would *leave this epiphany behind.* We must, rather, make good our *excessus* to God himself with a *theologia negativa* which never detaches itself from its basis in a *theologia positiva* ... When later on we analyze the Areopagite and John of the Cross – the two theologians who relied most consistently on the apophatic method – we will see that they never divorced it from the cataphatic approach ... For this reason they can be considered the two most decidedly aesthetic theologians of Christian history' (GL I, 124–5). Or, addressing the same issues later, 'But, while for the more radical Origenists this "condensation" (Incarnation) of the Logos is only an occasion for man to join him on the way to spiritualisation, for Macarius this event whereby God participates in the realm of the senses in Christ is the positive expression of his love: through the sensual we are to come to know God's spiritual love' (GL I, 270).

41 'Maximus', in *The von Balthasar Reader*, trans. Robert J. Daly and Fred Lawrence, ed. Medard Kehl and Werner Löser (New York: Crossroad, 1982), 390 (hereafter, VBR).

42 Ibid., 391.

43 GL IV, 323.

44 We need point out here only two occasions in which Balthasar makes this clear: (1) In an afterword to an essay in *New Elucidations*, trans. Sister Mary Theresilde Skerry (San Francisco: Ignatius Press, 1979) entitled 'Human Religion and the Religion of Jesus Christ', in which Balthasar strings together a number of quotations from Rahner in order to illustrate a tendency towards an Enlightenment-style 'transcendental unity of religion', Balthasar has the following to say: 'The quotations in italics come for the most part from the article "Dogmen- und Theologiegeschichte – gestern und morgen" ...; a few words were taken from his *Grundkurs des Glaubens* as well as from *Schriften* ... I do not by any means claim to have presented (or "exposed") Rahner's central intention here; it is evident that as a Catholic theologian his thought is more subtle and differentiated. But despite all the retardant insertions, formal basic structures still emerge. Thus it seemed beneficial to single out certain statements – after digging them out of their thick protective packing – in order to show that by their own dynamics they "lead where

you do not want to go", namely, towards a "transcendent unity of religions" …' (*New Elucidations*, 86). (2) In the important afterword to *The Moment of Christian Witness* Balthasar states: 'In addition, there is the fact that Karl Rahner, in his bold but often one-sided proposals, which are not always coordinated among themselves (there are many Karl Rahners!), often had to suffer the fate of the sorcerer's apprentice who was no longer able to exorcise from his disciples the spirits he had conjured up. Many of the more recent directions in his thinking are inspired by apostolic motives and, in Rahner himself, are still surrounded by a protective screen of theology (for example, the whole theory of the "anonymous Christian" based on the supernatural existential) but they immediately excite careless interpretations, which have also just as quickly made their appearance among disciples of a radical bent. Who does not appeal to Rahner today more or less in this fashion when it is a question of some liberal broadening of dogma, of some transformation of its content into a "non-objective" reality, into something expressed only indirectly, or, in any case, something eminently capable of alteration?' (MCW, 148). Two things: (1) Balthasar acknowledges that Rahner is a careful and subtle thinker who always tries to place what may sound like a liberal reduction into a solid, theological context. (2) Given the modern tendency toward the transcendental and away from the categorial – that is toward the subsumption of the distinctively Christian into a vague, universal religiosity – even the use of such Idealist categories can be misleading for one's disciples. Thus, in spite of the fact that Rahner is motivated by a properly theological concern, he is unable to control the 'spirits' which he has unleashed, and is also often unable to keep complete control of his own categories. We will return to this line of thought later, but it can be said now that this is hardly the same as a wholesale rejection of Rahner's thought. Nor does it seem, as some have insisted, terribly unfair.

45 See, *Test Everything: Hold Fast to What is Good* (an interview with Hans Urs von Balthasar, by Angelo Scola), trans. Maria Shrady (San Francisco: Ignatius Press, 1989): 'I openly admit that I have never understood what place Rahner's categorical and transcendental categories, which he borrowed from Kant, can occupy in a Christian theology. Apparently Erich Przywara could not understand it either, for – according to Msgr. Strobl – he asked Rahner at a meeting in Vienna: "What on earth are they for?" – That Rahner wished to open the door to salvation for the countless persons lacking explicit faith in Christ is certain; his theological inquiries were predominantly motivated by pastoral concern. But were the old notions of *Fides Implicita, Baptismus in Voto* and so forth not sufficient?' (38–9).

46 This is the strategy taken in the very thoughtful and helpful apologetic for Rahner's work presented by Thomas F. O'Meara in the more 'Balthasarian' journal, *Communio*: 'Drawing upon Kant's analysis of the dynamic and world-creating aspects of the human mind (which Aristotle and Aquinas admitted) or fashioning a theology which accepts as thought-forms but not ideologies the centrality of subject, freedom, and history (Friedrich Schlegel's three characteristics of modernity) – these are not capitulations to the systems of Schelling and Hegel (already criticized by German Catholics in the 1820s) or an imitation of the increasingly contentless and relativist Protestant liberal theologies which appeared after 1840. And yet, theology must be done out of the culture and period in which people live. Because of a positive view of the human being even after the fall and of that collective personality which is culture, Aquinas and Roman Catholicism agree that there can be no major historical-cultural periods which are intrinsically

evil.' Taken from, 'Karl Rahner: Some Audiences and Sources for His Theology', *Communio* 18 (1991), 244–5.

47 *Truth is Symphonic*, 47 (emphasis mine).

48 TL I, 19: 'Christliche Philosophie wird sich daher hüten müssen, auch nur unbewußt und ungewollt einem solchen Rationalismus Vorschub zu leisten' (translation mine).

49 TL I, 20: 'Erstlich gilt, daß die Welt, so wie sie konkret existiert, eine Welt ist, die je schon positiv oder negativ in einem Verhältnis zum Gott der Gnade und der übernatürlichen Offenbarung steht, und daß es in diesem Verhältnis keine neutralen Punkte und Flächen gibt. Die Welt, als Gegenstand der Erkenntnis, ist immer schon in diese übernatürliche Sphäre eingebettet, und so steht auch entsprechend das Erkenntnisvermögen des Menschen immer schon unter dem positiven Vorzeichen des Glaubens oder dem negativen des Unglaubens' (translation mine).

50 Lochbrunner, *Analogia Caritatis*, 115.

51 Ibid., 118: 'Balthasars Kritik besteht demnach darin, daß er auf einer schärferen Unterscheidung zwischen einem philosophischen und theologischen Begriff der potentia oboedientialis insistiert. Balthasars Position ist vom Gespräch mit Karl Barth her mitgeprägt.' Although the Barth book was written after the early review of Rahner, Balthasar had already written articles which addressed Barth's critique of the analogy of being. Among the more important of these is Balthasar's essay, 'Analogie und Natur. Zur Klärung der theologischen Prinzipienlehre Karl Barths', *Divus Thomas* 23 (1945), 3–56, where he explicitly critiques Rahner's *Hearers of the Word* in the context of Barth's thought. The discussion of Rahner takes place on pages 38–49.

52 From the early date of Balthasar's review of Rahner's *Geist in Welt*, Balthasar was concerned that Rahner's understanding of *Vorgriff*, intended as it was to retrieve the Thomistic tradition, threatened to obscure Thomas's teaching on the real distinction between *esse* and *essentia*. Thus Lochbrunner, in referring to this early review, puts it: 'Balthasar würdigt zunächst Karl Rahners Interpretation der Erkenntnislehre von Thomas als "vielleicht die tiefsinnigste der neueren Scholastik …". Er rückt die Deutung Rahners nahe an das Ethos Fichtes heran: "radikale Bindung des Geistes an die (als Material der Selbstverwirklichung, als die Ebene des Nicht-Ich, des anderen als solchen, der 'materia' erfahrene) Sinnlichkeit …". Den Ansatz seiner Problematik wählt Rahner in der absoluten Bindung der Erkenntis an die Sinnlichkeit als einziger Quelle inhaltlichen Wissens. "So ist die Frage die, wie auf der bleibenden Ebene der Sinnlichkeit dennoch eine Metaphysik, d.h. eine Erschlossenheit von Sein überhaupt, möglich sei …". Die Antwort auf diese Frage geschiet durch den Verweis auf intellectus agens, "der (hier folgt Rahner Maréchal) der leere, d.h. unanschauliche Vorgriff (excessus) auf das Sein im Ganzen ist, der in einem in der affirmatio eines Partikulär-Existierenden den Existenzcharakter des Sein im Ganzen (Gottes) implizit affirmiert und damit vom Partikulären als solchem sich distanziert (es objiziert) …". *Nun referiert Balthasar die Realdistinktion zwischen esse und essentia*' (Lochbrunner, *Analogia Caritatis*, 114–15, emphasis mine). The quotes from Balthasar throughout are from, 'Karl Rahner, *Geist in Welt. Zur Metaphysik der endlichen Erkenntnis bei Thomas von Aquin*', review *Zeitschrift für katholische Theologie* 63 (1939), 371–9. As we will see, without a proper emphasis on this real distinction, the 'Vorgriff' of being in every individual act of knowing threatens to extend to an 'object' which is properly theological. Balthasar's alternative is presented in

terms of a 'fourfold distinction', and will be discussed in the next chapter under the heading, 'Christian philosophy?'

53 Balthasar, 'Karl Rahner, *Geist in Welt*', 377; Lochbrunner, *Analogia Caritatis*, 115.

54 In 'Current Trends in Catholic Theology', *Communio* 5 (1978), 79, Balthasar states Rahner's program accordingly: 'Because it was God's intention from the beginning to surrender himself totally to his creatures, man – the final product of natural evolution – is from the outset projected beyond himself toward union of God and man, a union that came into existence in the person of Christ. Anthropology thus becomes inchoate or deficient Christology. And because all the truths of revelation have their center and their foundation in Christ, there is in man a potential that corresponds to every dogma, if not in his objective categorical, finite world of objects, at any rate in the transcending impulsions of his knowledge and his freedom which must be kept expectantly open to God's gratuitous coming into finiteness.'

55 All of these questions are implicit in Balthasar's review of *Geist in Welt* mentioned above, and become even clearer in the article, also cited above, 'Analogie und Natur'.

56 MCW, 147. We will deal with this in more detail below.

57 Balthasar, 'Karl Rahner, *Geist in Welt*', 377–9.

58 'Analogie und Natur', 43: 'Der qualitative Abstand zwischen der Offenbarkeit des "principium et finis" und der Offenbarung des nun wirklich personal *redenden* Gottes ist hier nicht genügend beachtet. Der Inhalt dieser Religionsphilosopie kann nur von der je schon ergangenen Rede Gottes selber geschöpft sein, er ist somit unbewußte Theologie. Und wenn zuletzt wirklich durch die sittliche Selbstentscheidung des Menschen die so bestimmte potentia oboedientialis in die Hand des Menschen gelegt wird, wenn er also dem Wort Gottes "die Möglichkeit nehmen kann", gehört zu werden, er ihm diese Möglichkeit also auch *geben* kann, so droht der "Vorgriff" nun wirklich zum Übergriff in die Theologie zu werden' (translation mine).

59 'Analogie und Natur', 44: 'Ein Schweigen Gottes "hört" das Geschöpf nicht, außer mit den "übernaturalichen" Ohren des Glaubens (oder Unglaubens) dem gnädigen (oder zürnenden) Gott gegenüber. Hält man diese Schranken nicht ein, so bekommt Barths Kritik des "Anknüpfungspunktes" ihr Recht' (translation mine).

60 Joseph Maréchal, 'Jugement "scholastique" concernant la racine de l'agnosticisme kantien', *Mélanges* (1914), 278. Cited in KB, 293.

61 KB, 294.

62 KB, 295.

63 KB, 296.

64 After raising the question as to whether de Lubac is guilty of collapsing the realms of nature and grace, Balthasar responds in the negative, 'for although creation in its own way is completely undeserved (*ungeschuldet*) and so is a grace, its elevation to being adopted by God is a second and loftier work that should not be explained in terms of the first level but from its own intrinsic character' (KB, 296).

65 Balthasar distinguishes de Lubac's view from Maréchal's and Rahner's accordingly: 'This "*capacitas*" excludes, on the one hand, any inner-worldly (and thus "natural") final goal. … But neither can it be satisfied by an "eternal striving" after the vision of God, an eternal asymptotic approach to this vision. (Here de Lubac parts company with Maréchal and his disciples.) Such a striving would not be "natural beatitude" but the torture of Tantalus. On the other hand, there is, in

the "*capacitas*" that constitutes the innermost being of the created spiritual nature, no trace yet of supernatural grace or even such an orientation. For this reason, de Lubac is not interested in hearing about Karl Rahner's supernatural existential. Insofar as this were to signify a "mediation" for the order of grace, "the problem would not be solved but only displaced". This is in no way a denial of the fact that the concrete ("elicited") act of concrete man as a movement toward his final goal is, of course, borne by grace. It is first a question only of the signature inscribed in the created spiritual nature, unknown to this nature itself as created, purely "habitual", lying, as a "lack", at the basis of all consciousness' (*The Theology of Henri de Lubac: An Overview*, trans. Susan Clements (San Francisco: Ignatius Press, 1991), 70–1). The difference here is a subtle one, but, at least in Balthasar's view, not without significance. The key issue centers around de Lubac's 'natural' capacity as a 'lack' and Rahner's 'supernatural existential' as the 'self-communication' of God. Rahner, too, as the following quote should make clear, wants to preserve the gratuity of grace without thereby making God's self-offer something extrinsic to the human person *qua* human person. 'In order to understand this thesis we must first of all consider that the thesis proposed here about the innermost and ultimate characteristic of our basic statement that man is the event of God's absolute self-communication does not refer to a statement which is valid only for this or that group of people as distinguished from pagans or sinners. Without prejudice to the fact that it speaks of a free and unmerited grace, of a miracle of God's free love for spiritual creatures, the statement that man as subject is the event of God's self-communication is a statement which refers to absolutely all men, and which expresses an existential of every person. Such an existential does not become merited and in this sense "natural" by the fact that it is present in *all* men as an existential of their concrete existence, and is present prior to their freedom, their self-understanding and their experience. The gratuity of a reality has nothing to do with the question whether it is present in many or only a few people' (*Foundations of the Christian Faith: An Introduction to the Idea of Christianity*, trans. William V. Dych (New York: Crossroad, 1984), 127).

66 KB, 296.

67 Balthasar is quoting a summary of de Lubac's thought contained in 'P. Delaye's essay in *Orientierung* (Zurich, June 30, 1950): 138–41', cited in KB, 295. (Balthasar does not tell us who puts the emphasis on 'from the goal to nature'.)

68 KB, 298. The critique to which Balthasar is referring is reprinted in *Theological Investigations*, vol. I: *God, Christ, Mary and Grace*, trans. Cornelius Ernst, OP (Baltimore, Md.: Helicon Press, 1961), 297–317, although he never makes this clear. He refers neither to the title of the article nor to the specific page numbers.

69 Cited in KB, 298.

70 Cited in KB, 298–9.

71 KB, 299.

72 In 'Current Trends in Catholic Theology', Balthasar says, 'The act of God's incarnation in Christ, though it did take place historically at a given time and place, is seen so much as the transcending fulfillment of all that is human, that Rahner has difficulty in proving the necessity for an explicit, historical Christianity. If a man follows the guidance of his own conscience and does what he believes is right, he is caught up in the grace of God and may be called an "anonymous Christian," no matter what religion or atheistic worldview he may adhere to ... But when God sends his own living Word to his creatures, he does so, not to instruct them

about the mysteries of the world, nor primarily to fulfill their deepest needs and yearnings. Rather he communicates and actively demonstrates such unheard-of things that man feels not satisfied but awestruck by a love which he never could have hoped to experience. For who would have dared describe God as love, without having first received the revelation of the Trinity in the acceptance of the cross by the Son?' (79–80).

73 KB, 299–300.

74 KB, 300–1.

75 KB, 301.

76 KB, 297.

77 Even as sympathetic a reader as Russell Reno admits that while Rahner is technically right to insist on the concept of 'pure reason' as a *Restbegriff*, 'Rahner is not always at his best.' Reno goes on to give an example from Rahner's Christology: 'In *A New Christology* ... [Rahner] tries to provide a "searching Christology" which will show the "fit" between human transcendence and "Jesus and his self-understanding." The goal of this apologetic strategy is to reject a false dichotomy between unbelief and "mythological credulity." For Rahner, there must be a middle way. Our beliefs about Christ must be, in some decisive sense, integral to our beliefs about life as a whole (and in that respect, "credulous" without being "mythological"), otherwise faith cannot save *us*. However, in pursuit of this admirable goal – a goal implied by the notion of amphibious existence – Rahner begins to transform the "fit" into an equation of human transcendence with the "essential" content of Jesus' life, death, and resurrection. He winds up saying that the mystery of God *is* the mystery of human existence. In a dogmatic context, the line of implication clearly runs from the mystery of God in Christ to humanity, and the identity statement is the *terminus ad quem* of both theological reflection (*reductio in mysterium*) and human destiny (*theosis*). However, coming as it does in the context of an apologetical exercise, the line of implication is inevitably reversed. The identity statement comes to function as the *terminus a quo* of the theological project. Humanity defines God in Christ. Not surprisingly, then, Rahner is led towards a strikingly reductive definition of faith: "Whoever accepts his humanity completely (and this is inexpressibly difficult to do; it is doubtful whether any of us really ever does it) has at the same time accepted the Son of Man" (p. 17). The platitudes about how "difficult" the mystery of humanity is to accept do not hide the logic of the definition. The reversal is obvious: the mystery of man *is* the mystery of God' (Reno, *The Ordinary Transformed*, 88). This type of questioning is directly in the line of Balthasar's, i.e., that even if in theory Rahner's construal of the relationship between nature and grace is technically correct, and even serves as a corrective to his own more 'christocentric' approach, in practice it often degenerates into a reduction of Christology to anthropology.

78 KB, 302.

79 Sokolowski, *God of Faith and Reason*, 39.

80 MCW, 146–7.

81 In a very helpful article Marc Ouellet has discussed the importance of Balthasar's understanding of Aquinas for an understanding of his differences with Rahner. He describes Balthasar's understanding in terms of 'paradox', versus Rahner's 'supernatural existential'. 'For Balthasar, the Thomist *esse* is not in the first place the "condition of possibility of finite, categorical knowledge," but the *mystery* of the openness of finite freedom to infinite freedom. This mysterious openness belongs to the very essence of freedom as a *given* autonomy which points back to

an infinite freedom whose (possible) openness constitutes the a priori horizon of the finite spirit. According to Balthasar, at the root of the subjective dynamism of the human consciousness towards *esse* as the object of its desire, lies the finitude of the consciousness and of its act of being (*distincto realis*). This finitude points the consciousness to the polarity and passivity of having been given to itself with an awareness oscillating between its own nothingness and transcendental plenitude. With this, the ultimate horizon of given freedom appears to be the openness of divine freedom, before which the created subject finds it always already in a condition of receptivity (of letting be), even before the condition of desire. And here we see the paradoxical nobility of the human person – of the being created in Jesus Christ as a partner of God, as a possible interlocutor of a Word which he or she desires without being able to demand, anticipate, or postulate from its transcendental openness. The human person is freedom in quest of Freedom. According to Balthasar, the Thomist paradox of *esse* and the corresponding interpretation of finite freedom as the *desiderium naturale visionis* does not imply that there is a supernatural element in the finite spirit's natural aspiration to the openness of divine freedom …' (Marc Ouellet, 'Paradox and/or Supernatural Existential', *Communio* 18 (1991), 263–4). Ouellet goes on to point out that such a construal does not rule out the possibility of a supernatural existential, it only insists on the priority of the natural paradox of human freedom.

82 '… I would at least like to ask the reader to take the not-at-all exegetical but theological manifesto *Glaubhaft ist nür Liebe* (1963; Eng. ed. *Love Alone*) into consideration as the background of *The Moment of Christian Witness*' (MCW, 'Afterword', 146).

83 *Love Alone*, 43–4.

84 Ibid., 45.

85 'Such a basic starting point [i.e., the transcendental] can still emphasize, after the fact and to its heart's content, that the transcendence of the spirit can be realized only by turning back to a historical categorial. But it still cannot justify the incomparable nature of *this* definite categorial that is foundational for Christian catholicity' ('The Claim to Catholicity', in ET IV, 74–5). This goes back to Balthasar's concern to emphasize, against Barth, that the analogy of being is there in order to highlight the 'ever greater dissimilarity' (here, 'incomparable nature') between God and what is not God.

86 Reno, *The Ordinary Transformed*, 88–9. In my view, few people have understood the basic differences between Balthasar and Rahner better than Reno has. First, he recognizes that Balthasar's criticism of Rahner does not imply a wholesale rejection of Rahner's intentions. He does not, that is, reject the need for a point of contact between modern thought and the historic faith. As Reno puts it, '[f]or Balthasar, Rahner's "idea of Christianity" – Rahner's strategy for infusing epistemic significance into faith – is not mistaken as a theological aspiration' (218). Second, Reno makes the crucial distinction, which Balthasar insists upon consistently, between Rahner's theoretical score and the actual performance (application) of that score. In a passage which could serve as a concise summary of what we have been trying to say, Reno states, 'Rahner's fulfillment of this aspiration suffers from insufficient attention to the limitations of the characteristic "languages" of modernity. For Balthasar, these limitations are essentially two-fold. On the one hand, modern concerns about subjectivity and self-consciousness alienate us from the world and make the ordinary uninhabitable for those who take existence "seriously." In other words, modernity tempts us toward a stance of radical transcendence. On

the other hand, with all the gestures toward the "abyss," the "absolute mystery of existence," the "pre-thematic" which characterize radical transcendence, a dismissive attitude develops toward the written and preached, present and quite thematized *Ernstfall* of Christ's death and resurrection. Modernity translates the particular shape and structure of God's extraordinary grace into an appendage of subjectivity and self-consciousness. In other words, what begins as radical transcendence with respect to "spirit" becomes pure immanence with respect to Christ. In short, Balthasar finds typically Rahnerian formulations inadequate to the amphibious Christian vision, even as the architecture of Rahner's thought gives that vision striking centrality (the key to Balthasar's deep respect for Rahner's project). Here, then, we might agree with Balthasar and set aside Rahner's use of the distinctively modern language of transcendence, while at the same time commending the amphibious vision of transcendence, the very vision with which Rahner seeks to bend, perhaps unsuccessfully, modernity's preoccupations' (218–19).

87 Balthasar addresses Karl Löwith's thesis – that the concept of history contained in Hegel, Marx and the Enlightenment in general is in fact just a secularized version of the Judaeo-Christian conception – in his essay, 'The Word and History', ET I, 31–55.

Chapter 5: Applications and Conclusion

1 By 'correlationist' I intend any approach which attempts to relate, in a positive manner, the philosophical, religious, or cultural viewpoints of humanity to the Christian religion. In itself such an approach is legitimate, and it should be clear by now that both Balthasar and Rahner intended to undertake such a correlation. The approach only becomes 'extreme' to the degree that it allows a 'cultural viewpoint' to become the criterion by which the distinctively Christian solution is measured.

2 For a brief description of this divide, see our introduction above, especially the reference to David Tracy's introduction to *God Without Being* (Chicago, 1991).

3 TD IV, 290.

4 TD IV, 321–2.

5 TD IV, 322.

6 'If I wanted to launch a counterattack, I would say that there is a modern tendency ... to develop a theology of the death of God that, in the last analysis, seems to me to be gnostic. One can find this in Hans Urs von Balthasar and in Adrienne von Speyr, although naturally much more marked in her than in him. It also appears in an independent form in Moltmann. To put it crudely, it does not help me to escape from my mess and mix-up and despair if God is in the same predicament ... It is to me a source of consolation to realize that God, when and insofar as he entered into this history as into his own, did it in a different way than I did. From the beginning I am locked into this horribleness while God – if this word continues to have any meaning at all – is in a true and authentic sense the God who does not suffer, the immutable God, and so on. In Moltmann and others I sense a theology of absolute paradox, of Patripassianism, perhaps even of a Schelling-esque projection into God of divide, conflict, godlessness, and death.' Cited in Oakes, *Pattern of Redemption*, 281–2.

7 See the helpful discussion of this in John Saward, *The Mysteries of March: Hans Urs*

von Balthasar on the Incarnation and Easter (London: Collins Religious Publishing, 1990), 7–9.

8 Karl Rahner, *Foundations of Christian Faith* (New York: Crossroad, 1984), 265–6. (Hereafter, *Foundations*).

9 *Foundations*, 282–3.

10 TD IV, 279–80. See also, Ralph Del Colle, 'The Triune God', in *The Cambridge Companion to Christian Doctrine*, ed. Colin E. Gunton (Cambridge: Cambridge University Press, 1997), 136–9.

11 See note 6.

12 See MP: 'We have already referred to the limitations of a theology of the Cross, which would set up the "Absolute Paradox" in a static and absolutized fashion ... More fateful is something different: the interpretation of the Pauline *pro me* (Galatians 2.20) in an at any rate tendentially anthropocentric sense ("how can *I* find a gracious God") – which has exerted a baleful influence in Protestant theology down to our present day. The entire existential seriousness of the *pro me* is only maintained undiminished if the opening up of the Trinitarian love for sinners which there becomes visible is responded to by an integral *pro te*, and if, furthermore, one understands that, in the *pro me* of Christ's self surrender, one is oneself already taken over by that love and yielded up, so that faith is not one's own "work" but the ratification of what God has done in finished form and, in that, one's transferral to the sphere of the triune Love. The anthropocentric tendency will never be able to keep within view the Trinitarian background of the Cross ... [T]he Son's Cross is the revelation of the Father's love (Romans 8.32; John 3.16), and the bloody outpouring of that love comes to its inner fulfilment in the shedding abroad of their common Spirit into the hearts of men (Romans 5.5)' (139–40).

13 Thus Fergus Kerr in his article, 'The Doctrine of Atonement: Recent Roman Catholic Theology', *Epworth Review* 22 (January 1995), 19–26: 'God as Trinity has to be understood as a drama of self-giving – which is why the history of salvation is also a drama of such self-giving. Like his great compatriot Karl Barth, Balthasar centres his understanding of the Redemption on the doctrine of God as Trinity. With an emphasis on self-emptying (*kenosis*) that comes more from Adrienne von Speyr, Balthasar sees history as a progressive story of divine self-emptying: Creation, Incarnation, and finally the Cross. But this story reflects or prolongs God's own internal "story": the drama of reciprocal self-emptying which is the life of the Trinity. If Calvary is the supreme moment of "God-lessness", that is because it continues the God-lessness of the inner-Trinitarian life itself. None of the divine persons ever retains the divinity for himself but is always giving it away. Divinity is always an economy of gift, we might say. What seems to us in history the terrible dereliction of Calvary is in the eternal mystery of the life of God just one more (though final) sign of the Son's kenotic response to the Father' (22).

14 Saward, *Mysteries of March*, 47–8.

15 Hans Urs von Balthasar, *Herrlichkeit: Eine theologische Ästhetik*, vol. III/2/2: *Neuer Bund* (Einsiedeln: Johannes Verlag, 1969), 193. Cited in Saward, *Mysteries of March*, 49–50.

16 Del Colle, 'Triune God', 137–8.

17 For an excellent treatment of the relationship between word and silence in Balthasar's theology see, Raymond Gawronski, *Word and Silence: Hans Urs von Balthasar and the Spiritual Encounter between East and West* (Edinburgh: T&T Clark, 1995).

[18] TD III, 188.

[19] Saward, *Mysteries of March*, 6.

[20] For a helpful summary of de Lubac's influence, see Kevin Mongrain, *The Systematic Thought of Hans Urs von Balthasar: An Irenaean Retrieval* (New York: Crossroad, 2002), 1–12.

[21] This is obviously not to say that Luther's and Augustine's theology do not begin and end with Christ. It is simply to say that, while the soteriology of, say, Maximus the Confessor is clearly a part of his Christology, one gets the impression that Luther's Christology is a phase of his soteriology. Again, this has everything to do with the semi-Pelagianism which Luther had to combat, but it does place certain limitations on the value of his treatment of the question of election.

[22] For a discussion of the controversy, see Timothy George, 'What God Knows,' *First Things* 134 (June/July 2003), 7–9.

[23] Luigi Giussani, *The Religious Sense*, trans. John Zucchi (Montreal: McGill-Queen's University Press, 1997). For a discussion of Giussani's paradoxical understanding of nature and grace, see Rodney Howsare, 'Against the Theological Prejudices of the Age', in Elisa Buzzi, ed., *A Generative Thought: An Introduction to the Works of Luigi Giussani* (Montreal: McGill-Queen's University Press, 2003), 133–42.

[24] TD II, 189–242.

[25] This is, in fact, exactly how Balthasar frames the question. While 'defining the theme', Balthasar quotes C. S. Lewis accordingly, 'The man who does not regard God as other than himself cannot be said to have any religion at all. On the other hand, if I think God other than myself in the same way in which my fellow-men, and objects in general, are other than myself, I am beginning to make Him an idol. I am daring to treat His existence as somehow *parallel* to my own. But He is the ground of our being. He is always both within us and over against us. Our reality is so much from His reality as He, moment by moment, projects into us. The deeper the level within ourselves from which our prayer, or any act, wells up, the more it is His, but not at all less ours. Rather, most ours when most His' (TD II, 193–4).

[26] TD II, 247–8.

[27] TD II, 250.

[28] TD II, 250.

[29] For a typically brilliant treatment of predestination, see Herbert McCabe's essay of that name in, Herbert McCabe, *God Still Matters*, ed. Brian Davies (New York: Continuum, 2002), 182–6. As McCabe, in very Balthasarian fashion, puts it, 'Our predestination means that our Christian lives are part of the pattern of God's revelation of himself in Christ. We are playing a part in the divine drama … It is a question of being part of the divine drama which is the death and resurrection of Christ, of arriving into heaven with Christ and in Christ, taking part in the Ascension. So that in seeing and welcoming us, God is seeing and welcoming his beloved Son … Does this mean that we have lost our freedom, that we cannot choose for ourselves? Well of course it doesn't. The predestined one, remember, is primarily Jesus Christ; he is the one fulfilling the plan of God, enacting the divine drama. Does he strike you as unfree? As obsessive? As incapable of spontaneity, imprisoned by neurotic fears and guilt? Of course not: he is obviously the free human being. Not only because he is human and not a machine, but because he is not hampered by all those anxieties and illusions which are the way that sin seeks to enslave us: the shackles of the kingdom of darkness. In the plan of God, Jesus is precisely predestined to be free, to be uniquely himself, and our predestination is nothing but our sharing in this predestined freedom that Christ has' (183–4).

[30] TD III, 159.

[31] 'On the Tasks of Catholic Philosophy in Our Time', *Communio* 20 (Spring 1993), 147–8.

[32] I am borrowing this term from Étienne Gilson. For a discussion of its use in this context, see Josef Pieper, *Guide to Thomas Aquinas*, trans. Richard and Clara Winston (Notre Dame, Ind.: University of Notre Dame Press, 1987), 125–33.

[33] GL IV, 404. The entire discussion of Aquinas as 'kairos', and the 'real distinction' is found in this same section, 393–412.

[34] GL IV, 406 (emphasis mine).

[35] See the helpful article by Martin Bieler, 'Meta-anthropology and Christology: On the Philosophy of Hans Urs von Balthasar', *Communio* 20 (1993), 129–45.

[36] John Kevern makes this clear in his previously mentioned article, 'Form in Tragedy'.

[37] GL V, 613–24.

[38] GL V, 636.

[39] See Jean-Luc Marion, 'Christian Philosophy and Charity', *Communio* 19 (Fall 1992), 465–73.

[40] GL V, 637.

[41] GL V, 646–7.

[42] Carabine, 'The Fathers: The Church's Intimate, Youthful Diary', 79.

[43] It should be mentioned at this point that a recent and likely standard study to Luther's theology for years to come has some reservations concerning this Finnish interpretation of Luther. See, Bernhard Lohse, *Martin Luther's Theology: Its Historical and Systematic Development*, trans. Roy A. Harrisville (Minneapolis: Augsburg Fortress Press, 1999), where Lohse says, '[W]e should not adopt the thesis recently defended by a few Finnish scholars that Luther gave a great weight to the ancient church's idea of "deification." Though one cannot dispute a "deification" motif among others, we must be cautioned against overestimating this line of tradition' (220–1).

[44] Hans Urs von Balthasar, 'Peace in Theology', trans. Stephen Wentworth Arndt, *Communio* 12 (Winter 1985), 401.

[45] Ibid., 398.

Bibliography

Von Balthasar

Von Balthasar, *Absolutheit des Christentums* [herausgegeben von Walter Kasper, *et al.*]. Freiburg: Herder, 1977.

Von Balthasar, 'Analogie und Dialektik', *Divus Thomas* 22 (1944): 171–216.

Von Balthasar, 'Analogie und Natur', *Divus Thomas* 23 (1945): 3–56.

Von Balthasar, *Bernanos: An Ecclesial Existence*, trans. Erasmo Leiva-Merikakis. San Francisco: Communio Books/Ignatius Press, 1996.

Von Balthasar, *The Christian State of Life*, trans. Mary Francis McCarthy. San Francisco: Ignatius Press, 1983.

Von Balthasar, *Convergences: To the Source of the Christian Mystery*, trans. E. A. Nelson. San Francisco: Ignatius Press, 1984.

Von Balthasar, 'Current Trends in Catholic Theology and the Responsibility of the Christian', *Communio* 5 (Spring 1978): 77–85.

Von Balthasar, 'Die Eine Kirche und die vielen Kirchen', *Civitas. Monatsschrift der Schweiz* 7 (1952): 633–55.

Von Balthasar, *Einfaltungen*. Munich: Koesel, 1969. Trans. E. A. Nelson, *Convergences: To the Source of the Christian Mystery*. San Francisco: Ignatius Press, 1983.

Von Balthasar, *Elucidations*, trans. John Riches. London: SPCK, 1975.

Von Balthasar, *Epilog*. Einsiedeln: Johannes Verlag, 1987.

Von Balthasar, *Explorations in Theology*, vol. I: *The Word Made Flesh*, trans. Arthur V. Littledale and Alexander Dru. San Francisco: Ignatius Press, 1989.

Von Balthasar, *Explorations in Theology*, vol. II, *Spouse of the Word*, trans. A. V. Littledale and Alexander Dru. San Francisco: Ignatius Press, 1991.

Von Balthasar, *Explorations in Theology*, vol. III: *Creator Spirit*, trans. Brian McNeil. San Francisco: Ignatius Press, 1993.

Von Balthasar, *Explorations in Theology*, vol. IV: *Spirit and Institution*, trans. Edward T. Oakes, SJ. San Francisco: Ignatius Press, 1995.

Von Balthasar, 'The Fathers, Scholastics, and Ourselves', trans. Edward T. Oakes, *Communio* 24 (1997): 347–96.

Von Balthasar, 'Geist und Feuer: Ein Gespräch mit Hans Urs von Balthasar', *Herder-Korrespondenz* 30 (1976): 72–82.

Von Balthasar, *The Glory of the Lord: A Theological Aesthetics*, vol. I: *Seeing the Form*, trans. Erasmo Leiva-Merikakis. San Francisco: Ignatius Press, 1979.

Von Balthasar, *The Glory of the Lord: A Theological Aesthetics*, vol. II: *Studies in Clerical Style*; vol. III: *Studies in Lay Style*, trans. Andrew Louth, John Saward, Martin Simon, Rowan Williams, Francis McDonagh and Brian McNeil. San Francisco: Ignatius Press, 1982.

Von Balthasar, *The Glory of the Lord*, vol. IV: *The Realm of Metaphysics in Antiquity*, trans. Brian McNeil, CRV, Andrew Louth, John Saward, Rowan Williams and Oliver Davies. San Francisco: Ignatius Press, 1989.

Von Balthasar, *The Glory of the Lord*, vol. V: *The Realm of Metaphysics in Modernity*, trans. Brian McNeil CRV, Andrew Louth, John Saward, Rowan Williams and Oliver Davies. San Francisco: Ignatius Press, 1991.

Von Balthasar, *The Glory of the Lord*, vol. VI: *The Old Covenant*, trans. Brian McNeil, CRV and Erasmo Leiva-Merikakis. San Francisco: Ignatius Press, 1991.

Von Balthasar, *The Glory of the Lord*, vol. VII: *The New Covenant*, trans. Brian McNeil, CRV, San Francisco: Ignatius Press, 1989.

Von Balthasar, *In the Fullness of Faith: On the Centrality of the Distinctively Catholic*, trans. Graham Harrison. San Francisco: Ignatius Press, 1988.

Von Balthasar, 'Karl Rahner, *Geist in Welt. Zur Metaphysik der endlichen Erkenntnis bei Thomas von Aquin*', review, *Zeitschrift für katholische Theologie* 63 (1939): 371–9.

Von Balthasar, *Love Alone*, trans. Arthur V. Littledale and Alexander Dru. New York: Herder & Herder, 1969.

Von Balthasar, 'The Meaning of Christ's Saying, "I am the Truth"', *Communio* 14 (1987): 158–60.

Von Balthasar, *The Moment of Christian Witness*, trans. Richard Beckley. San Francisco: Ignatius Press, 1994.

Von Balthasar, *My Work in Retrospect*, trans. Cornelia Capol. San Francisco: Ignatius Press, 1993.

Von Balthasar, *Mysterium Paschale: The Mystery of Easter*, trans. Aidan Nichols. Grand Rapids, Mich.: William B. Eerdmans, 1993.

Von Balthasar, *New Elucidations*, trans. Mary Theresilde Skerry. San Francisco: Ignatius Press, 1986.

Von Balthasar, 'On the Tasks of Catholic Philosophy in Our Time', *Communio* 20 (1993): 147–87.

Von Balthasar, 'Peace in Theology', *Communio* 12 (1985): 398–407.

Von Balthasar, *Presence and Thought: Essay on the Religious Philosophy of Gregory of Nyssa*, trans. Mark Sebanc. San Francisco: Ignatius Press, 1995.

Von Balthasar, *Razing the Bastions: On the Church in this Age*, trans. Brian McNeil, CRV. San Francisco: Ignatius Press, 1993.

Von Balthasar, *A Short Primer for Unsettled Laymen*, trans. Michael Waldstein. San Francisco: Ignatius Press, 1985.

Von Balthasar, *Test Everything: Hold Fast to What is Good* (an interview with Hans Urs von Balthasar, by Angelo Scola), trans. Maria Shrady. San Francisco: Ignatius Press, 1989.

Von Balthasar, *Theo-Drama*, vol. I: *Prolegomena*, trans. Graham Harrison. San Francisco: Ignatius Press, 1988.

Von Balthasar, *Theo-Drama*, vol. II: *The Dramatis Personae: Man in God*, trans. Graham Harrison. San Francisco: Ignatius Press, 1990.

Von Balthasar, *Theo-Drama*. vol. III, *Dramatis Personae: Persons in Christ*, trans. Graham Harrison. San Francisco: Ignatius Press, 1991.

Von Balthasar, *Theo-Drama*, vol. IV: *The Action*, trans. Graham Harrison. San Francisco: Ignatius Press, 1995.

Von Balthasar, *A Theological Anthropology*, trans. William Glen-Doepel. New York: Sheed & Ward, 1967.

Von Balthasar, *Theologik*, vol. I: *Wahrheit der Welt*. Einsiedeln: Johannes Verlag, 1985. Trans. Adrian J. Walker, *Theo-Logic*, vol. I: *Truth of the World*. San Francisco: Ignatius Press, 2000.

Von Balthasar, *Theologik*, vol. II: *Die Wahrheit Gottes*. Einsiedeln: Johannes Verlag, 1985. Trans. Adrian J. Walker, *Theo-Logic*, vol. II: *Truth of God*. San Francisco: Ignatius Press, 2004.

Von Balthasar, *Theologik*, vol. III: *Der Geist der Wahrheit*. Einsiedeln: Johannes Verlag, 1987.

Von Balthasar, *The Theology of Henri de Lubac: An Overview*, trans. Joseph Fessio and Michael Waldstein. San Francisco: Ignatius Press, 1991.

Von Balthasar, *A Theology of History*, trans. not given. New York: Sheed & Ward, 1963.

Von Balthasar, *The Theology of Karl Barth: Exposition and Interpretation*, trans. Edward T. Oakes. SJ. San Francisco: Ignatius Press, 1992.

Von Balthasar, *Truth is Symphonic: Aspects of Christian Pluralism*, trans. Graham Harrison. San Francisco: Ignatius Press, 1987.

Von Balthasar, *The von Balthasar Reader*, trans. Robert J. Daly and Fred Lawrence, ed. Medard Kehl and Werner Löser. New York: Crossroad, 1982.

Von Balthasar, *Who is a Christian?* trans. John Reedy. New York: Newman Press, 1968.

Other Authors

Althaus, Paul. *The Theology of Martin Luther,* trans. Robert C. Schultz. Philadelphia: Fortress Press, 1966.

Aquinas, Thomas. *Aquinas on Nature and Grace*, trans. and ed. A. M. Fairweather. Philadelphia: Westminster Press, 1954.

Balás, David L. 'Response to Prof. O'Meara', *Communio* 18 (1991): 252–8.

Barth, Karl. *Anselm: Fides quaerens intellectum*, trans. Ian W. Robertson. London: SCM Press, 1960.

—— *The Humanity of God*, trans. Thomas Wieser and John Newton Thomas. Richmond, Va.: John Knox Press, 1960.

—— *Karl Barth: Letters, 1961–1968*, ed. Jürgen Fangmeier and Heinrich Stoevesandt, trans. Geoffrey Bromiley. Grand Rapids, Mich.: William B. Eerdmans, 1981.

—— *Church Dogmatics*, trans. and ed. Geoffrey Bromiley and Thomas F. Torrance. Edinburgh: T&T Clark, 1956–69, 1975.

—— *Die Theologie und die Kirche*. Munich: Chr. Kaiser Verlag, 1938.

—— *The Word of God and the Word of Man*, trans. Douglas Horton. New York: Harper & Row, 1956.

Baynes, Kenneth, James Bohman and Thomas McCarthy, eds. *After Philosophy: End or Transformation?* Cambridge, Mass.: MIT Press, 1987.

Beeck, Franz Josef van, SJ. *God Encountered: A Contemporary Catholic Systematic Theology,* vol. I: *Understanding the Christian Faith*. San Francisco: Harper & Row, 1989.

Beer, Theobald. *Der fröliche Wechsel und Streit: Grundzüge der Theologie Martin Luthers*. Einsiedeln: Johannes Verlag, 1980.

Beker, J. Christian. *The Triumph of God: The Essence of Paul's Thought,* trans. Loren T. Stuckenbruck. Minneapolis, Minn.: Fortress Press, 1990.

Bieler, M. 'Meta-anthropology and Christology: On the Philosophy of Hans Urs von Balthasar', *Communio* 20 (Spring 1993): 129–46.

Bornkamm, Heinrich. *Luther, Gestalt und Wirkungen*. Gütersloh: Gütersloher Verlagshaus Gerd Mohn, 1975.

Braaten, Carl E. 'The Finnish Breakthrough in Luther Research', *Pro Ecclesia* 5 (Spring 1996): 141–3.

Busch, Eberhard. *Karl Barth: His Life from Letters and Autobiographical Texts*, trans. John Bowden. Philadelphia: Fortress Press, 1976.

Capol, Cornelia. *Hans Urs von Balthasar: Bibliography, 1925–1990*. Einsiedeln: Johannes Verlag, 1990.

Carabine, Deirdre. 'The Fathers: The Church's Intimate, Youthful Diary', in *The Beauty of Christ: A [sic] Introduction to the Theology of Hans Urs von Balthasar*, 73–91, eds. Bede McGregor, OP, and Thomas Norris. Edinburgh: T&T Clark, 1994.

Casarella, Peter. 'The Expression and Form of the Word: Trinitarian Hermeneutics and the Sacramentality of Language in Hans Urs von Balthasar's Theology', *Renascence* 48 (Winter 1996): 111–35.

Chantraine, Georges, SJ. 'Exegesis and Contemplation in the Work of Hans Urs von Balthasar', in *Hans Urs von Balthasar: His Life and Work*, 133–48, ed. David L. Schindler. San Francisco: Ignatius Press, 1991.

Congar, Yves. *Dialogue Between Christians*, trans. Peter Loretz. Westminster: Newman Press, 1966.

Conway, Eamonn. *The Anonymous Christian – a Relativised Christianity? An Evaluation of Hans Urs von Balthasar's Criticisms of Karl Rahner's Theory of the Anonymous Christian*. New York: P. Lang, 1993.

de Lubac, Henri. *Letters of Étienne Gilson to Henri de Lubac*, trans. Mary Emily Hamilton. San Francisco: Ignatius Press, 1988.

—— *The Mystery of the Supernatural*, trans. Rosemary Sheed. New York: Herder & Herder, 1967.

—— 'A Witness of Christ in the Church: Hans Urs von Balthasar', in *Hans Urs von Balthasar: His Life and Work*, 271–88, ed. David L. Schindler. San Francisco: Ignatius Press, 1991.

Del Colle, Ralph. 'The Triune God', in *The Cambridge Companion to Christian Doctrine*, 121–40, ed. Colin E. Gunton. Cambridge: Cambridge University Press, 1997.

Doran, Robert M., SJ. 'Lonergan and Balthasar: Methodological Considerations', *Theological Studies* 58 (March 1997): 61–84.

Dupré, Louis. 'The Glory of the Lord: Hans Urs von Balthasar's Theological Aesthetic', in *Hans Urs von Balthasar: His Life and Work*, 183–206, ed. David L. Schindler. San Francisco: Ignatius Press, 1991.

—— *Passage to Modernity: An Essay in the Hermeneutics of Nature and Culture*. New Haven: Yale University Press, 1993.

Forde, Gerhard. *On Being a Theologian of the Cross: Reflections on Luther's Heidelberg Disputation, 1518*. Grand Rapids, Mich.: William B. Eerdmans, 1997.

Gadamer, Hans-Georg. *Philosophical Hermeneutics*, trans. and ed. David E. Linge. Berkeley, Calif.: University of California Press, 1976.

—— *Truth and Method*, trans. Joel Weinsheimer and Donald G. Marshall. New York: Crossroad, 1991.

Gawronski, Raymond. *Word and Silence: Hans Urs von Balthasar and the Spiritual Encounter between East and West.* Edinburgh: T&T Clark, 1995.

Gilson, Étienne. *Being and Some Philosophers.* Toronto, Canada: Pontifical Institute of Mediaeval Studies, 1949.

—— *The Unity of the Philosophical Experience.* New York: Charles Scribner's Sons, 1937.

Hacker, Paul. *Das Ich im Glauben bei Martin Luther.* Cologne: Styria, 1966.

Hoffman, Bengt. *Luther and the Mystics: A Re-examination of Luther's Spiritual Experience and His Relationship to the Mystics.* Minneapolis, Minn.: Augsburg, 1976.

Jüngel, Eberhard. *God as the Mystery of the World.* Grand Rapids, Mich.: William. B. Eerdmans, 1983.

Kant, Immanuel. *Religion Within the Bounds of Reason Alone*, trans. Theodore M. Greene and Hoyt H. Hudson. New York: Harper Torchbooks, 1960.

—— 'The Strife of the Faculties', in *German Essays on Religion*, 4–13, ed. Edward T. Oakes, SJ. New York: Continuum, 1994.

Kay, Jeffrey Ames. 'Balthasar: A Post-Critical Theologian?', in *Neo-conservatism: Social and Religious Phenomenon*, 84–9, ed. Gregory Baum and Marcus LeFebure. Edinburgh: T&T Clark, 1981.

—— *Theological Aesthetics: The Role of Aesthetics in the Theological Method of Hans Urs von Balthasar.* Bern: Herbert Lang, 1975.

Kelly, Anthony. 'Is Lonergan's *Method* Adequate to Christian Mystery?' *The Thomist* 39 (1975): 437–70.

Kerr, Fergus. 'The Doctrine of Atonement: Recent Roman Catholic Theology', *Epworth Review* 22 (January 1995): 19–26

—— *Immortal Longings: Versions of Transcending Humanity.* Notre Dame, Ind.: University of Notre Dame Press, 1997.

Kevern, John R. 'Form in Tragedy: Balthasar as Correlational Theologian', *Communio* 21 (Summer 1994): 311–30.

Klaghofer-Treitler, Wolfgang. *Gotteswort im Menschenwort: Inhalt und Form von Theologie nach Hans Urs von Balthasar.* Innsbruck: Tyrolia, 1992.

Klauder, Francis J. *A Philosophy Rooted in Love: The Dominant Themes in the Perennial Philosophy of St. Thomas Aquinas.* New York: University Press of America, 1994.

Lindbeck, George. *The Nature of Doctrine: Religion and Theology in a Postliberal Age.* Philadelphia: Westminster Press, 1984.

Lochbrunner, Manfred. *Analogia caritatis: Darstellung und Deutung der Theologie Hans Urs von Balthasars.* Freiburg: Herder, 1981.

Louth, Andrew. *Discerning the Mystery: An Essay on the Nature of Theology.* Oxford: Oxford University Press, 1983.

Luther, Martin. *D. Martin Luthers Werke. Kritische Gesamtausgabe* (Weimar Ausgabe). Weimar: Hermann Böhlau, 1883–.

—— *Luther's Works*, eds. Jaroslav Pelikan and Helmut T. Lehmann. Philadelphia: Fortress Press, 1958–72.

—— *Martin Luther's Basic Theological Writings*, ed. Timothy Lull. Minneapolis, Minn.: Augsburg Fortress Press, 1989.

Manns, Peter. 'Absolute and Incarnate Faith–Luther on Justification in the Galatians' Commentary of 1531–1535', in *Catholic Scholars Dialogue with Luther*, 121–56, ed. Joseph Lortz. Chicago: Loyola University Press, 1970.

Marion, Jean-Luc. 'Christian Philosophy and Charity', *Communio* 19 (Fall 1992): 465–73.

—— *God Without Being*, trans. Thomas A. Carson. Chicago: University of Chicago Press, 1991.

McCormack, Bruce L. *Karl Barth's Critically Realistic Dialectical Theology: Its Genesis and Development 1909–1936.* Oxford: Clarendon Press, 1995.

McSorely, Harry, SJ. *Luther, Right or Wrong?* London: Newman Press, 1969.

Milbank, John. *Theology and Social Theory: Beyond Secular Reason.* Cambridge, Mass.: Blackwell, 1990.

—— *The Word Made Strange: Theology, Language and Culture.* Cambridge, Mass: Blackwell, 1997.

O'Donnell, John J. *Hans Urs von Balthasar.* London: Geoffrey Chapman, 1992.

O'Hanlon, Gerard F. *The Immutability of God in the Theology of Hans Urs von Balthasar.* New York: Cambridge University Press, 1990.

O'Meara, Thomas F. 'Karl Rahner: Some Audiences and Sources for His Theology', *Communio* 18 (1991): 237–51.

O'Reagan, Cyril. 'Von Balthasar and Thick Retrieval: Post-Chalcedonian Symphonic Theology', *Gregorianum* 77 (1996): 227–60.

—— 'Von Balthasar's Valorization and Critique of Heidegger's Genealogy of Modernity', in *Christian Spirituality and the Culture of Modernity: The Thought of Louis Dupré*, 123–58, eds. Peter Casarella and George P. Schner, SJ. Grand Rapids, Mich.: William B. Eerdmans, 1998.

Oakes, Edward. *Pattern of Redemption: The Theology of Hans Urs von Balthasar.* New York: Continuum, 1994.

Oberman, Heiko. '*Facientibus Quod in se est Deus non Denegat Gratiam*: Robert Holcot O.P. and the Beginnings of Luther's Theology', *Harvard Theological Review* 55 (1962): 317–42.

—— *The Harvest of Medieval Theology*. Cambridge, Mass.: Harvard University Press, 1963.

—— *Luther: Man Between God and the Devil*, trans. Eileen Walliser-Schwarzbart. New York: Doubleday/Image Books, 1992.

—— *The Masters of the Reformation: The Emergence of a New Intellectual Climate*, trans. D. Martin. New York: Cambridge University Press, 1981.

—— 'Simul Gemitus et Raptus: Luther and Mysticism', in *The Reformation in Medieval Perspective*, 219–51, ed. Steven Ozment. Chicago: Quadrangle Books, 1971.

Ouellet, Marc. 'Paradox and/or Supernatural Existential', *Communio* 18 (Summer 1991): 259–80.

Pelikan, Jaroslav. *The Christian Tradition: A History of the Development of Doctrine*, vol. VI: *Reformation of Church and Dogma (1300–1700)*. Chicago: University of Chicago Press, 1984.

Pieper, Joseph. *Guide to Thomas Aquinas*, trans. Richard and Clara Winston. Notre Dame, Ind.: University of Notre Dame Press, 1987.

Placher, William C. *Unapologetic Theology: A Christian Voice in a Pluralistic Conversation*. Louisville, Ky.: Westminster/John Knox Press, 1989.

Rahner, Karl. *Foundations of the Christian Faith: An Introduction to the Idea of Christianity*, trans. William V. Dych. New York: Crossroad, 1984.

—— *Spirit in the World*, trans. William Dych, SJ. New York: Continuum, 1994.

—— *Theological Investigations*, vol. I: *God, Christ, Mary and Grace*, trans. Cornelius Ernst, OP. Baltimore, Md.: Helicon Press, 1961.

Ratzinger, Joseph Cardinal. 'Luther and the Unity of the Churches: An Interview with Joseph Cardinal Ratzinger', *Communio* 11 (Fall 1984): 210–26.

Reno, Russell R. *The Ordinary Transformed: Karl Rahner and the Christian Vision of Transcendence*. Grand Rapids, Mich.: William B. Eerdmans, 1995.

Reumann, John, Joseph Fitzmyer and Jerome Quinn. *'Righteousness' in the New Testament*. Philadelphia: Fortress Press, 1982.

Riches, John. 'The Biblical Basis of Glory', in *The Beauty of Christ: An Introduction to the Theology of Hans Urs von Balthasar*, eds. Bede McGregor, OP, and Thomas Norris. Edinburgh: T&T Clark, 1994.

Roberts, Louis. *The Theological Aesthetics of Hans Urs von Balthasar*. Washington, DC: Catholic University of America Press, 1987.

Rumscheidt, H. Martin, ed. *The Way of Theology in Karl Barth: Essays and Comments*, trans. George Hunsinger. Allison Park, Pa.: Pickwick, 1986.

Rupp, Gordon. *The Righteousness of God: Luther Studies*. London: Hodder & Stoughton, 1953.

Saarinen, Risto. 'Salvation in the Lutheran–Orthodox Dialogue', *Pro Ecclesia* 5 (Spring 1996): 202–13.

Sanders, E. P. *Paul and Palestinian Judaism.* Philadelphia: Fortress Press, 1977.

—— *Paul, the Law, and the Jewish People.* Philadelphia: Fortress Press, 1983.

Saward, John. 'Mary and Peter in Christological Constellation: Balthasar's Ecclesiology', in *The Analogy of Beauty: The Theology of Hans Urs von Balthasar*, 105–33, ed. John Riches. Edinburgh: T&T Clark, 1986.

—— *The Mysteries of March: Hans Urs von Balthasar on the Incarnation and Easter.* London: Collins Religious Publishing, 1990.

Schindler, David. 'Christology and the *Imago Dei*: Interpreting *Gaudium et Spes*', *Communio* 23 (Spring 1996): 156–84.

—— *Heart of the World, Center of the Church: Communio Ecclesiology, Liberalism, and Liberation.* Grand Rapids, Mich.: William B. Eerdmans, 1996.

—— 'On the Catholic Common Ground Project: The Christological Foundations of Dialogue', *Communio* 23 (Winter 1996): 823–51.

—— ed. *Hans Urs von Balthasar: His Life and Work.* San Francisco: Ignatius Press, 1991.

Schönborn, Christoph, OP, 'Hans Urs von Balthasar's Contribution to Ecumenism', in *Hans Urs von Balthasar: His Life and Work*, 251–63, ed. David L. Schindler. San Francisco: Ignatius Press, 1991.

Scola, Angelo. *Hans Urs von Balthasar: A Theological Style.* Grand Rapids, Mich.: William B. Eerdmans, 1995.

Sokolowski, Robert. *Eucharistic Presence: A Study in the Theology of Disclosure.* Washington, DC: Catholic University of America Press, 1994.

—— *The God of Faith and Reason: Foundations of Christian Theology.* Notre Dame, Ind.: University of Notre Dame Press, 1982.

Steinmetz, David. *Luther in Context.* Bloomington, Ind.: Indiana University Press, 1986.

Tavard, George. *Justification: An Ecumenical Study.* New York: Paulist Press, 1983.

Thompson, John. 'Barth and Balthasar: An Ecumenical Dialogue', in *The Beauty of Christ: A [sic] Introduction to the Theology of Hans Urs von Balthasar*, 171–92, eds. Bede McGregor, OP, and Thomas Norris. Edinburgh: T&T Clark, 1994.

Vignaux, Paul. 'On Luther and Ockham', trans. James Coleman, in *Reformation in Medieval Perspective*, 107–18, ed. Steven Ozment. Chicago: Quadrangle Books, 1971.

von Loewenich, Walter. *Luther's Theology of the Cross*, trans. Herbert J. A. Bouman. Minneapolis, Minn.: Augsburg, 1976.

von Speyr, Adrienne. *Erde und Himmel. Ein Tagebuch. Zweiter Teil II: Die Zeit der großen Diktate*, ed. with an introduction by Hans Urs von Balthasar. Einsiedeln: Johannes Verlag, 1975.

Wicks, Jared. Review of *Der fröhliche Wechsel und Streit. Grundzüge der Theologie Martin Luthers*, *Gregorianum* 63 (1982): 163.

Williams, Rowan. 'Balthasar and Rahner', in *The Analogy of Beauty: The Theology of Hans Urs von Balthasar*, 11–34, ed. John Riches. Edinburgh: T&T Clark, 1986.

Yeago, David Stuart. 'The Drama of Nature and Grace: A Study in the Theology of Hans Urs von Balthasar.' Dissertation, Yale University, 1992.

Index